WHY KIDS KILL

Other Works by the Author

Nonfiction

Jewish Issues in Multiculturalism
"Assessment Issues with Jewish Clients," in *Handbook of Cross-Cultural and Multicultural Personality Assessment* (edited by Richard H. Dana)

Poetry

The Last Days of John Keats and Other Poems

Theatre

Two monologues ("Anorexia" and "Obesity Talks Back") in *Young Women's Monologues from Contemporary Plays #2* (edited by Gerald Lee Ratliff)

WHY KIDS KILL

INSIDE THE MINDS OF SCHOOL SHOOTERS

PETER LANGMAN, PH.D.

palgrave
macmillan

First published in hardcover in 2009 by
PALGRAVE MACMILLAN®
in the United States—a division of St. Martin's Press LLC,
175 Fifth Avenue, New York, NY 10010.

Where this book is distributed in the UK, Europe and the rest of the world,
this is by Palgrave Macmillan, a division of Macmillan Publishers Limited,
registered in England, company number 785998, of Houndmills,
Basingstoke, Hampshire RG21 6XS.

Palgrave Macmillan is the global academic imprint of the above companies
and has companies and representatives throughout the world.

Palgrave® and Macmillan® are registered trademarks in the United States,
the United Kingdom, Europe and other countries.

ISBN: 978–0–230–10148–7

Library of Congress Cataloging-in-Publication Data

Langman, Peter F.
    Why kids kill : inside the minds of school shooters / by Peter Langman.
        p. cm.
    Includes bibliographical references and index.
    ISBN 0–230–60802–7 (hardcover)
    ISBN 978–0–230–10148–7 (paperback)
        1. Youth and violence—United States. 2. School violence—United States.
    3. Violence in adolescence—United States. 4. Violence—United States.
    5. School shootings—United States. I. Title.

HQ799.2.V56L365 2009
371.7′82—dc22   2008032597

A catalogue record of the book is available from the British Library.

Design by Newgen Imaging Systems (P) Ltd., Chennai, India

First PALGRAVE MACMILLAN paperback edition: August 2010

10 9 8 7 6 5 4 3 2 1

Printed in the United States of America.

To all young lives cut short by force;
To all hearts hurt by sudden loss

Contents

Acknowledgments

I AM GRATEFUL TO ALL those whose work laid the foundation of my research, including numerous people at the FBI, the Secret Service, the Department of Education, the National Research Council Institute of Medicine, as well as Dr. Katherine Newman and her team of researchers.

I would like to thank Brooks and Randy Brown, for their input and feedback regarding Columbine; Doug Harper and Richard Langman, for their editorial expertise; Nancy Marple, for her efforts in tracking down elusive bits of information; Dennis Peters, for providing guidance in obtaining criminal records; Stuart Rosselet, for his research efforts into Jeffrey Weise's family; Mary Ann Swiatek, Ph.D., for reviewing the text and providing editorial feedback and suggestions regarding content; and Thomas Wasser, Ph.D., for his reading of drafts of several chapters.

Special thanks are due to my agent, John Ware, for his interest in my book and his unfailing support and guidance; and to Luba Ostashevsky, my editor at Palgrave Macmillan, who believed in the project, provided feedback, and guided the book from its beginning as a proposal to the final product you hold in your hand.

Finally, I offer my deepest gratitude to my wife and fellow psychologist, Madeleine Langman, Ph.D., for support, encouragement, feedback, guidance, and putting up with late-night conversations about mass murderers when she would have preferred to be counting sheep; my son, Joshua Langman, for his precocious editorial talent; and my daughter, Anna Langman, for having nothing to do with this project and for providing me with daily reminders of the joys of life that should belong to everyone.

Preface

I DID NOT WANT TO write this book. I deliberately resisted the thought that this book needed to be written. I wanted to believe that the rash of school shootings in the late 1990s was over. It was a naive hope. The ghosts of Columbine continue to haunt the hallways of our schools, and every year there are students who seek to follow in the footsteps of Eric Harris and Dylan Klebold. In fact, it is a result of what these two boys did that led to my involvement in the issue of school shootings.

On April 20, 1999, Eric and Dylan attacked Columbine High School. They killed 13 people, wounded 23, and then killed themselves. On the day of the attack, I was working as a doctoral intern in psychology at a children's psychiatric hospital. Like the rest of the nation, I was shocked and saddened by the massacre, and I knew the attack constituted a major event in the country. I did not anticipate, however, the impact the attack would have on my life.

On April 30, 1999, just 10 days after the attack at Columbine, a teenager was admitted to the psychiatric hospital where I worked due to concerns that he might "go Columbine." He had a hit list on his Web site and had engaged in other disturbing and threatening behavior. A student became aware of his Web site and notified her father, who contacted the school. Thus began a sequence of events that brought the boy to me. I was asked to assess the risk that he might commit a school shooting—a daunting task. I needed to determine if a 16-year-old might be a potential mass murderer. People's lives could be hanging in the balance. To make the task even more challenging, at the time virtually nothing was published that provided insight into the minds of school shooters.

Since then I have evaluated one or two potential school shooters a year. As a psychologist, I felt an ethical obligation to know as much as possible about the subject. I read whatever I could find that might increase my understanding of school shooters. The more I read, however, the more I sensed that major issues were being missed.

Although I recognized these gaps, I was not sure I wanted to be the one to fill them. I was not pleased at the prospect of devoting years of my life to the study of mass murder. Many people love violent films, horror stories, and books about serial killers. I am not one of them. Nonetheless, as I studied the shooters and read the available literature, I became fascinated by the topic and the multitude of questions it raises. How could someone do such a thing? Why that particular boy, and not his brother? Why those two boys, when there were kids who suffered worse harassment? What forces drove them to such an extreme act?

Over the last nine years I have been trying to answer these questions. My perspective is that of a psychologist. I focus on people as individuals and on what goes on in their minds—their personalities, thoughts, feelings, perspectives: all the things that make up their identities. This does not mean that I ignore external influences. Family interactions, social environments, and peer relationships have a profound impact on people's identities and experiences. What I sought to understand, however, was what it was like inside the minds of the school shooters. How did they see the world? How did they understand their homicidal urges?

Although I am offering my insights, conclusions, and speculation, there is no simple explanation of school shooters or a formula for predicting who will become a mass murderer. The end of the book will not present anything like: A + B + C = School Shooter. The subject is too complicated for that, and there is much that we do not know. Nonetheless, I believe this book will shed light on a phenomenon that, despite massive media coverage, has remained mysterious. My hope is that by increasing our understanding of school shooters, we will be better able to recognize the warning signs, to intervene effectively, and to thereby save people's lives.

Note Regarding the Text

I HAVE TRIED TO BE as accurate as possible in presenting the information in this book. Nonetheless, although we live in the age of information, many details were either difficult to obtain or contradicted by other sources. In order to avoid verbal clutter, I do not encumber every sentence with phrases such as "it has been reported" or "according to" or "it is alleged that." In most cases I present the information as facts, although I expect that there are errors. Please forgive any inaccuracies this book may contain.

The sections on Eric Harris and Dylan Klebold draw heavily on the records of the Jefferson County Sheriff's Office. This is a collection of approximately 27,000 pages of materials, including interview reports, school papers by Eric and Dylan, yearbook inscriptions, the boys' journals, and miscellaneous documents. Most of these pages have been released to the public, but approximately 5,000 pages have not been. In the documents that are available, sometimes the names of students other than Eric and Dylan are blacked out to protect their identities. This forces researchers to speculate about the people involved in particular events.

Also, when quoting from the shooters' writings, I have generally corrected the spelling and punctuation so that it is easier to read.

Finally, in Chapter 7, when I write about potential shooters I have worked with, I have changed their names and other identifying details.

WHY KIDS KILL

1

SCHOOL SHOOTERS:
BEYOND THE SOUND BITE

If we have figured out the art of time bombs before hand, we will set hundreds of them around houses, roads, bridges, buildings and gas stations, anything that will cause damage and chaos. . . . It'll be like the LA riots, the Oklahoma bombing, WWII, Vietnam . . . all mixed together. Maybe we will even start a little rebellion or revolution to fuck things up as much as we can. . . . If by some weird as shit luck me and V survive and escape we will move to some island somewhere or maybe Mexico, New Zealand or some exotic place where Americans can't get us. If there isn't such a place, then we will hijack a hell of a lot of bombs and crash a plane into NYC with us inside firing away as we go down. Just something to cause more devastation.

—An 11th grader

THIS QUOTE WAS NOT written by a member of Al Qaeda or any other terrorist group. It was written by a junior in Columbine High School—a boy who came from a stable family, got good grades, and wanted to destroy the world. His name was Eric Harris.

This is a book about school shooters: Who are they? What makes them tick? Why would they even consider carrying out such horrendous acts? Facts about the attacks are easy to learn—what guns were used, how they were obtained, who was shot, and so on. What is almost impossible to find amid the media reports is an understanding of the minds of the shooters and why they committed murder. In the aftermath of school shootings—whether Columbine, Virginia Tech, or any other such attack—the same question is asked over and over from news shows to dinner-table conversations: Why do people do this? This book attempts to answer that question by looking at the psychology of the perpetrators of rampage school shootings.

What exactly is a rampage school shooting? Rampage school shootings occur when students or former students attack their own schools. The attacks are public acts, committed in full view of others. In addition, although some people might be shot because the shooters held grudges against them, others are shot randomly or as symbols of the school (such as a principal).

Rampage school shootings do not include two people having a fight that results in one shooting the other. Targeted gun violence that is related to gangs, drug deals, or boyfriend/girlfriend issues are not rampage attacks. As disturbing as these events are, they are not included in this book even if they happened on school grounds.

This book also does not focus on shootings in which an adult invades a school and kills children. For example, in 2006, a 32-year-old man named Carl Charles Roberts held a group of girls hostage in an Amish schoolhouse in Pennsylvania. He shot 10 of them, killing 5. Roberts was an adult who had no connection to the school; he picked it as the site of his attack for an unknown reason. Although he committed mass murder at a school, his actions are not considered a rampage school shooting as defined in this book because he was not a student attacking his own school.

It is important to distinguish between the type of rampage attacks discussed in this book and other types of school-related homicides. Some studies of school violence look at all gun-related murders at schools. It is problematic to assume, however, that the different kinds of attacks are perpetrated by similar people or driven by the same factors. The inclusion of both rampage and targeted attacks in the same study muddies the waters, making it difficult to draw meaningful conclusions about what type of person perpetrates a rampage school shooting. The focus in this book on rampage attacks alone has made it easier to identify patterns among the shooters.

Rampage school shootings became part of the American cultural landscape in the 1990s. They are like terrorist attacks: statistically rare events committed by a handful of people who send shock waves through the nation. The 10 shooters presented in this book killed a total of 74 people (including themselves) and wounded 92. The damage, of course, extends far beyond these numbers. The families and friends of the victims have been stricken with grief and horror. Entire schools and communities have been devastated. Around the country, students, parents, and school personnel wonder if their schools are safe. And in response to rampage attacks, schools across the nation have implemented procedures and policies in attempts to maintain safety.

Large-scale attacks at schools and college campuses may seem to be a recent phenomenon, but this is not the case. Some of these next examples do not fit the definition of rampage school shootings, but they do demonstrate that mass violence in schools is not new. In fact, the deadliest school attack in the United States occurred in 1927, when a 55-year-old man named Andrew Kehoe murdered his wife and then used dynamite to blow up a school in Bath, Michigan. In all, Kehoe killed 45 people and wounded 58; most of these were children. The total number of casualties was more than double those of Virginia Tech in 2007.

Nearly 40 years later, in 1966, Charles Whitman, a 25-year-old student at the University of Texas, went on a rampage. First he first killed his wife and mother, then he set up a sniper position in a tower on campus and gunned down 45 people, killing 14. Here too, the casualties exceeded those in the attack at Columbine High School in 1999.

The 1970s and 1980s were not devoid of school attacks. In 1979, a teenage girl named Brenda Spencer opened fire on an elementary school across the street from her home in San Diego, California. She killed 2 adults and wounded 8 children and a police officer. Ten years later, in 1989, a 26-year-old named Patrick Purdy opened fire on an elementary school playground in Stockton, California. He killed 5 children and wounded 29 children and a teacher.

Despite this history of multiple homicides at schools, "school shootings" did not become a common term until the late 1990s. The academic year of 1997–1998 saw a flurry of rampage school attacks that followed in close succession:

October 1, 1997	Luke Woodham shoots 9 people in Pearl, Mississippi.
December 1, 1997	Michael Carneal shoots 8 people in West Paducah, Kentucky.
December 15, 1997	Joseph Colt Todd shoots 2 people in Stamps, Arkansas.
March 24, 1998	Andrew Golden and Mitchell Johnson shoot 15 people in Jonesboro, Arkansas.
April 24, 1998	Andrew Wurst shoots 4 people in Edinboro, Pennsylvania.
May 21, 1998	Kip Kinkel shoots 27 people in Springfield, Oregon.

What made the attacks in the late 1990s different from the earlier ones? These attacks were committed by young students who carried out assaults at their own schools. Andrew Kehoe was 55 years old. Charles Whitman was 25. Patrick Purdy was 26. In contrast, Michael Carneal was 14, Mitchell Johnson was 13, and Andrew Golden was 11. These were children who became killers. Not only were they young, but they were gunning down their peers—their own classmates. These were sometimes the kids they had grown up with since kindergarten, the kids they played with at recess, and in some cases, the girls for whom they had tender feelings. These were not cases of killing the enemy in war or gunning down members of a rival gang. These were cases of children killing children for no apparent reason. In response, people are left wondering "Why?"

Grasping for Answers

Many explanations of why school shootings occur have been offered. Some are based on research; some are the sound bites of newscasters and journalists in the wake of shootings. Common explanations focus on such issues as the influence of violent video games and movies, peer rejection, depression and suicidal thoughts, the easy accessibility of guns, side effects from psychiatric medications, the impact of bullying, and the consequences of being a loner who is uninvolved at school and has inadequate social connections.

In the wake of a school shooting, a brief period of massive media coverage often follows. Much of the initial information that gets reported is not accurate, and by the time more accurate information has been obtained, the media has moved on to other stories. Thus, reliable versions of the events often do not reach the public. For this reason, we need to go beyond the sound bite to a more nuanced look at the factors that are often cited as contributing to school shootings.

Rampage attacks are too complex to be attributed to any one cause. Thus, any meaningful approach needs to recognize multiple influences. Some of the explanations that have been offered are based on faulty information and therefore contribute little to our understanding of school shootings. Others, however, are what I call "factors that do not explain." In other words, these factors may contribute to, but by themselves they do not explain, why school shootings happen.

For example, an oft-cited factor in school shootings is the availability of guns or what is sometimes referred to as the American "gun culture." Numerous writers have looked at the geography of where school shootings have occurred and attempted to connect the extent of gun ownership or the attitudes toward gun control in a region and the occurrence of school shootings. Obviously, if guns were impossible to obtain, there would be no shootings. The availability of guns, however, does not explain school shootings. In fact, when shootings occur in areas where gun ownership is common, the misuse of firearms should be seen as particularly unusual. If every teenager owns or has easy access to guns, and virtually none of them commits murder, school shooters are clearly aberrations. Their acts cannot be blamed on the culture, because the acts themselves are contrary to the prevalent social norm of law-abiding use of firearms.

School shootings have also been blamed on psychiatric medications. Some people have claimed that medications have such powerful side effects that they drive kids to murder. Although all medications have side effects, the case against psychiatric medications often is exaggerated beyond the available evidence. For example, people have blamed Michael Carneal's rampage on psychiatric medication; I have found no evidence, however, that Michael was taking any medications at the time of the attack. Similarly, people have claimed that both Andrew Golden and Mitchell Johnson were taking psychiatric medications. Yet according to a team of researchers led by Dr. Katherine Newman, who conducted a comprehensive investigation of the Jonesboro shooting, "There is no evidence that either boy was on any form of medication."[1]

Similarly, Kip Kinkel's rampage has been blamed on Prozac, which he supposedly was taking at the time of the attack. This is wrong. Kip had taken Prozac for a brief period but stopped using the medication approximately eight months before his rampage. In addition, he described the summer he was on Prozac as the best one he ever had. He was happier, less prone to anger, and the voices in his head were significantly diminished. Unfortunately, his parents stopped the medication after only three months. Perhaps because Kip was doing so well, they thought that he did not need the Prozac anymore. If so, they failed to realize that Prozac was making the difference for him. The irony is that if he had stayed on his medication, he might never have killed.

Nonetheless, it is true that Eric Harris was taking an antidepressant medication called Luvox at the time of the attack at Columbine High School. If you read Eric's journal, however, it is clear that he had the idea for the attack before he even started taking Luvox. And if you read the journal of Dylan Klebold, Eric's partner in the attack, you will find references to the attack months before Eric was on any medication.

Some people have argued that even though Eric may have had homicidal thoughts prior to being on Luvox, the medication pushed him over the edge. I disagree. Murder has occurred throughout human history without any psychiatric medications to push people over the edge. Medication is not necessary for murder; rage will suffice. And Eric was full of rage.

Eric was not a typical teenager who became a grandiose, raging, homicidal monster after taking Luvox. He did not need medication side effects to be grandiose and homicidal; he was grandiose and homicidal without it. The more we learn about Eric's history, the more we can see the attack not as an aberration created by Luvox but as an outcome of his personality.

Similarly, people have claimed that Jeffrey Weise, who went on a rampage in Red Lake, Minnesota, in 2005, was driven to murder by Prozac. Jeffrey had been prescribed Prozac, but it is not clear that he was still taking the medication at the time of the attack. Even if he were still taking the drug, however, this would not mean that Prozac caused his rampage. Jeffrey struggled with suicidal urges and had made at least one attempt to kill himself before he was given any medication. He described his life as "sixteen years of accumulated rage." Because he was at risk for suicide, he was given Prozac, an antidepressant. As with Eric Harris, we could take the view that the side effects of Prozac were so powerful that they pushed Jeffrey to murder. Another view, however, is that Prozac was so weak it did not make a dent in Jeffrey's rage or depression. Although it is possible that side effects played some part in Jeffrey's rampage, we have no way of determining that, and given the young man's history, there is no reason to assume he could not have committed murder without Prozac.

Most of the school shooters we will be investigating in this book were not on psychiatric medications. Psychiatric medications certainly can have serious side effects, but there is no reason to think that Eric Harris and Jeffrey Weise could not have committed murder without medication's side effects. Their violence can be understood as a result of their personalities and life histories. The focus on medication is interesting in that only 2 of the 10 shooters examined in this book were on medication, whereas at least 8 of the 10 used alcohol, marijuana, and possibly other drugs. Although psychiatric drugs have been blamed for rampage shootings, little attention has been paid to the possible influence of street drugs, even though they were used far more commonly by school shooters than prescription medications.

Another factor cited as contributing to school shootings is the extent to which the shooters are detached from their schools. Shooters often are thought to be uninvolved students lurking on the fringe of school culture. This picture is misleading. Academically, the shooters typically were average to above-average students. They were not the kids who were flunking out of school. Eric Harris, for example, was a dedicated student who maintained good grades, even as he was planning to destroy his school. Eric's teachers appreciated his interest and motivation. Several noted his "positive attitude and good cooperation."[2] On a progress report, one teacher wrote "Eric is doing awesome!"[3] Rather than hating school, Eric wrote on his Web site that he loved school (but hated homework). Why would Eric love school? One reason is that he had many friends there as well as fun classes, such as bowling and video production. Beyond this, however, Eric prided himself on being bright, and school was a forum in which he achieved recognition for his intelligence.

Many of the shooters were athletic and involved in extracurricular activities. Kip Kinkel was on his school's football team, Mitchell Johnson played football, baseball, and basketball at his school, and Eric Harris played on Columbine's soccer team and was involved with intramural soccer and volleyball. Both Andrew Golden and Michael Carneal played in their school bands. Dylan Klebold and Eric Harris were both part of the Rebel News Network at Columbine and served as assistants in the computer lab. Dylan was involved in the theater department, where he handled technical aspects of the productions. He also helped maintain the school's web server.

In short, the image of school shooters as alienated students who had no connection to, or involvement with, their schools is not accurate. Many were engaged in the classroom and participated in a variety of extracurricular activities.

Violence in television, film, video games, computer games, and books often is cited as a cause of rampage school attacks. This is a complex issue. On one hand, millions of kids are exposed to violence in the media without becoming mass murderers. Media violence cannot explain school shootings because the vast majority of people exposed to media violence do not become murderers.

On the other hand, the kids who commit rampage attacks often do have a fascination or preoccupation with violent media. They do not just play violent video games; they become obsessed with them. They do not just watch violent films; the films become their desired reality. Eric Harris and Dylan Klebold were said to have memorized nearly the entire dialogue from the movie *Natural Born Killers*. In fact, NBK, the initials of the movie, became the code name for their attack on the school. Kip Kinkel's parents were so concerned about his obsession with violent movies that they discontinued their cable service. A couple of weeks before Jeffrey Weise's rampage, he had watched the movie *Elephant* with some friends. *Elephant* is about a school shooting, and Jeffrey fast-forwarded to his favorite part—the scenes of the rampage.

What impact does media violence have on school shooters? It legitimizes violence, giving them role models for murder. It can even provide guidelines or scripts for killers to follow. When Barry Loukaitis walked into his algebra class in Moses Lake, Washington, in 1996, he shot his teacher and three classmates and then held the class hostage. He said: "This sure beats algebra, doesn't it?"[4] This was inspired by a book called *Rage* written by Stephen King (under a pseudonym), in which a student commits a school shooting in his algebra class and comments, "sure beats panty raids." It was a case of life imitating art. Of course, reading the book did not make Barry a murderer; there was a long history of mental illness and dysfunction in his family. Nonetheless, the particular action Barry took was derived from what he had read. It is perhaps worth noting that a copy of *Rage* was found in Michael Carneal's locker after his attack.[5]

Media violence can also desensitize people. Blood, gore, murder, and mutilation become entertainment. Not only that, but many television and movies imply that violence is a way to gain status. The ones who are admired, the ones who have the most prestige, are those who kill the most people. For boys who feel inadequate, this is a powerful message.

Finally, murdering people in video games or vicariously through movies like *Natural Born Killers* can serve as a rehearsal to the real thing. Having killed people thousands of times in video games or in their imagination may have desensitized the school shooters to violence and made it easier for them to pull the trigger for real.

Thus, there is no simple connection between media violence and murder. If there were, then the millions of people who play violent video games or watch violent films would all become killers. Nonetheless, violent images and content can be a powerful influence on young people who are already unstable and desperate.

Is social rejection a factor in school shootings? Perhaps, but rejection alone does not explain why the shooters gunned down innocent people. Millions of kids experience rejection and failure and do not become violent. Furthermore, when we take a closer look at school shooters, typically no single event triggered their rampages. Eric Harris and Dylan Klebold had been planning the attack at Columbine for over a year. There is no evidence that a particular incident of rejection or failure was behind their plans to blow up the school. Similarly, Andrew Golden first mentioned his idea for a shooting to Mitchell Johnson three months before they carried out the attack. No immediate event in Andrew's life has been identified as a trigger that drove him to murder.

This does not mean that experiences of rejection, failure, or other situational stresses play no part in school shootings. For example, in the weeks prior to Evan Ramsey's attack in Bethel, Alaska, in 1997, many stressful events occurred. His girlfriend broke up with him and moved away. His father, who had been in jail for 10 years after going on an armed rampage of his own, called Evan and announced that he was now a free man. Evan had a conflict with school personnel that made him angry. In addition, just five days before the attack, Evan's older brother was arrested for armed robbery. All of these events were simply the final stresses in Evan's long history of trauma and abuse. Thus, although it would be true to say that Evan experienced rejection shortly before he committed his shooting, it would be highly misleading to draw a simple connection between being rejected by a girlfriend and going on a rampage. Many other factors were involved.

A clearer connection can be made between school shootings and depression. Of the 10 shooters presented in this book, 9 suffered from depression and suicidal thoughts. Many of them felt like failures and envied their peers who seemed to be happier and more successful. This envy often turned to hatred, rage, and homicidal thoughts. The combination of suicidal and homicidal impulses is particularly dangerous because it is hard to prevent murder when killers do not care if they live or die. It is like trying to stop a suicide bomber.

Despite the prevalence of depression among school shooters, however, depression alone does not explain the shootings. Depression and suicidal thoughts are rampant among adolescents, yet the vast majority of depressed adolescents do not commit murder. Most manage to deal with their difficulties without killing themselves or anyone else. Depression is a common factor among school shooters, but it does not distinguish shooters from other depressed teenagers. Again, there are many other influences to be considered.

A popular sound-bite view of school shooters is that they are loners, a status seen as a contributing factor in their rampages. This is inaccurate. Whereas 9 out of 10 of the shooters we discuss were depressed, only 1 out of 10 was a loner. The others all had friends and acquaintances with whom they engaged in a variety of social activities. They hung out together, talked on the telephone, played video games, carried out acts of mischief, were on sports teams with their friends, and so on. They may not have experienced the social success they desired, especially with girls, but they were not loners.

An excellent example of how misleading the sound bite can be is seen in the cases of Eric Harris and Dylan Klebold, who often have been labeled loners despite all evidence to the contrary. First of all, they could not have been loners since they were best friends. Even if they had no one else, they had each other. But they did have other friends—many of them. Their social activities included bowling, paintball, a fantasy baseball league, Dungeons and Dragons, video games, a community soccer team, working at a pizza parlor with their closest friends, making movies with classmates, playing pool, going to movies, attending parties, and more. They got drunk with their friends, went shooting in the mountains with them, and engaged in criminal mischief together.

Although the view that school shooters typically are loners is inaccurate, many of the shooters did feel profoundly lonely. Even Dylan, who was involved with many peers, felt isolated. He had relationships, but they did not provide him with the emotional sustenance he needed. He believed that nobody really knew him and that, if they ever did get to know him, they would reject him. He felt unloved and unlovable. Kip Kinkel, Michael Carneal, Jeffrey Weise, and others had similar feelings of devastating loneliness. They looked with envy on their peers who seemed to be living the lives they wished they could live. Thus, although they were not loners, they felt desperately alone.

The issue that has received the most attention as a factor in school shootings is bullying. According to this sound bite, school shooters are victims of bullying who seek revenge for their mistreatment. It is understandable that this idea would take hold in the minds of many people. We can easily grasp and relate to the concept of being hurt and wanting to retaliate. If a student attacks his peers, it seems logical to think that he must have been driven to such an act. In reality, however, this sound bite is not accurate. The situation is much more complex.

Before we get into a detailed analysis of bullying in relation to school shootings, a couple of general points can be made. First, the geography of rampage attacks poses a challenge to the idea that bullying causes school shootings. Shootings have occurred in Red Lake, Minnesota; Bethel, Alaska; Edinboro, Pennsylvania; West Paducah, Kentucky; and Jonesboro, Arkansas. Why not New York City? Chicago? Los Angeles? Detroit? If bullying were to blame, what are we to make of the geography of school shootings? Certainly bullies exist in urban schools. Yet nearly all the rampage school shootings have occurred in small towns, suburbs, or rural areas. The lack of rampage school shootings in major cities suggests that shootings are not simply responses to bullying.

Second, it is hard to accept that rampage attacks are committed in retaliation for being bullied because the perpetrators rarely shot anyone who harassed them. When specific victims have been targeted, more often they are girls who rejected the shooters rather than bullies who beat them up. Most often, however, the shooters opened fire on crowds of people with no attempt to kill anyone in particular. How can the attacks be revenge for bullying when the shooters typically gunned down random people?

Beyond these two issues, let us consider the alleged connection between bullying and school shootings from several angles. For the sake of this discussion, we need to define "bullying." When people talk about bullying, they may be referring to many different kinds of behavior: physical assault, threats and intimidation, verbal hostility, spreading rumors, or ostracizing peers. Although all of these behaviors can be hurtful, I want to differentiate teasing from acts of physical aggression and intimidation. Bullying, as I use the term here, is defined by three elements.

1. The bully has more power than the victim. This could be through larger size, greater strength, superior confidence, or force of numbers (i.e., many kids ganging up on a victim).
2. Bullying involves physical abuse or intimidation through threats. The victims are made to fear for their safety. This means that being teased about one's clothes is not bullying.
3. Bullying involves a pattern of behavior. Being pushed one time does not constitute a pattern of physical harassment.

One problem with blaming school shootings on bullying is that some shooters were not bullied at all. In some cases, in fact, the shooters were the bullies. For instance, Kip Kinkel and Andrew Golden harassed their peers. They were the perpetrators, not the victims, of threats and insults. They were seen as scary and intimidating kids whom it was best to avoid.

Yet sometimes the shooters, including those who harassed others, were on the receiving end of insults or teasing. This may have contributed to their depression and rage. Teasing alone, however, cannot be said to cause school shootings. If it did, there would be murders every day at every school in the nation.

Furthermore, the fact that some shooters were teased does not mean that they were innocent victims. Some triggered their own harassment by behaving in provocative or antagonistic ways. They were arrogant, obnoxious, or insulting. When other kids told them to "knock it off" or threw insults back at them, they ended up feeling like victims. For example, Mitchell Johnson liked to intimidate his peers and throw his weight around by acting tough. He bragged that he was in a gang and flashed gang signals at school. When his classmates did not buy his stories and teased him about being a "wannabe" gangster, he felt like a victim. Nonetheless, he was the one who was known for his threatening and intimidating behavior.

Similarly, Michael Carneal felt like a victim because he was taunted and harassed by his peers. Other people, however, saw things differently. Both students and teachers reported that Michael was more of an instigator than a victim. They said that his own behavior was often so annoying and obnoxious that he alienated his peers and caused his own mistreatment.

This same dynamic occurred with Eric Harris and Dylan Klebold at Columbine High School, where they were teased in response to their own provocative behavior. In contrast, the sound bite coverage of Columbine focused on them as innocent victims of a toxic peer culture in which they were persistently harassed. This one-sided view has become fixed in many people's minds, often leading to an assumption that bullying is the primary cause of school shootings. Because this sound bite has assumed the proportion of a myth, it is necessary to take an in-depth look at what really happened. Based on the available evidence, the extent that Eric and Dylan were bullied has been exaggerated, and their harassment and intimidation of other students has been overlooked or minimized.

Eric and Dylan had many friends, but they often generated intensely negative reactions from other peers. For example, when Eric and Dylan got strikes in their bowling class, they gave Nazi salutes and yelled "Heil Hitler!" As a result, their peers harangued them.[6] This is hardly surprising, as public displays of Nazi behavior can be expected to draw hostile reactions.

In addition, they both had bad tempers, with Eric frequently erupting with anger, punching walls, and picking fights, and Dylan cursing at teachers, throwing things across the classroom, and slamming the door as he stormed out.[7] They threatened and intimidated classmates and developed reputations for violence that drove some friends away and caused others to give them a wide berth.[8] They vandalized students' homes, and built and detonated explosives. They alienated their peers with their admiration of Hitler and the Nazis, their talk of killing blacks and Jews, their preoccupation with guns and explosives, and their belligerent, hostile behavior. The fact that Eric and Dylan were teased or harassed needs to be seen within the context of who they were, what they did at school and in their neighborhoods, and the reputations they established for themselves.

This does not mean that Eric and Dylan were never the innocent victims of teasing. When they were juniors (the year preceding the attack), there was a group of athletes who had significant behavior problems and who made life miserable for many students. Although, like many other people in the school, Eric and Dylan may have been picked on by these jocks, there is no indication that they were singled out for mistreatment. In fact, many students reported that they never witnessed Eric or Dylan being harassed at all.[9] Thus, whatever teasing occurred, it could not have been as pervasive as the media has reported.

Hypothetically, however, even if school shooters were innocent victims of bullying, this could not explain why they committed their attacks. To say the shooters went on rampages because they were bullied ignores the fact that millions of students are bullied every day without committing murder. The experience of being bullied does not distinguish the child who becomes a killer from the millions of bullied children who do not. It has been said that bullying was so rampant at Columbine High School that the school had a toxic culture. Even if it did, that does not tell us why, out of the thousands of students who passed through that toxic culture, it was Eric Harris and Dylan Klebold who went on a murderous rampage.

Finally, attending a school with a toxic culture does not lead to murder. There were students who were not happy at Columbine High School because they were picked on; some got their parents to intervene, some transferred to other schools, and some quit. Trying to blow up the school and kill everyone in it was not the only option.

These arguments are not meant to deny the impact that teasing and bullying can have on someone. Rather, the point is that there is no simple relationship between harassment and school shootings. If any connection exists, it is a complex relationship that varies from one case to another. What we need is an understanding of why some kids are so fragile and vulnerable that harassment—among other factors—might contribute to their decision to commit a school shooting.

Finally, the focus on bullying misses so many other issues. The shooters described in this book were not always angry about being teased. Sometimes they were angry with teachers or administrators for being disciplined. Sometimes they were angry with girls who rejected them. And often they were angry with the peers they envied. Beyond these dynamics, the shooters were affected by their family histories, their personal histories, their mental health problems, and their personalities.

What is often missing from the commentary on school shooters is an in-depth study of the perpetrators themselves. What kind of people are they? What kind of problems do they have? What goes on inside their minds? Furthermore, if the attacks are not retaliation for bullying, then how can we understand youths who commit mass murder? What makes them tick?

This point may seem obvious, but it needs to be said: School shooters are disturbed individuals. These are not ordinary kids who were bullied into retaliation. These are not ordinary kids who played too many video games. These are not ordinary kids who just wanted to be famous. These are simply *not ordinary kids*. These are kids with serious psychological problems. This fact has often been missed or minimized in reports on school shooters.

Why, then, if school shooters are a complex phenomenon, has there been such a focus on simplistic explanations like bullying? One reason is that in the immediate aftermath of an attack, detailed information about the perpetrator is not available. It may take months or years for relevant details to be made public, and by that point, the story is no longer front-page news. As a result, the more in-depth information does not reach as large an audience as the initial reports.

Another issue is that most people are not mental health professionals and therefore cannot be expected to understand personality disorders, depression, trauma, and psychotic disorders. In addition, there is sometimes a suspicion regarding reports of psychosis. People often believe that criminals invent reports of hallucinations or delusions in order to avoid being found guilty.

There is yet another reason for the triumph of the sound bite. Put simply, we can all understand the concept of revenge. Retaliation for being victimized seems like a plausible explanation for a school shooting. After all, why else would someone shoot people at school? Superficially, such an explanation makes sense. Of course, it does not tell us why millions of other students do not commit murder in response to being teased or bullied. Nevertheless, everyone can relate to a desire for revenge.

Apart from the concept of revenge, how do we comprehend mass murder by an 11-year-old boy who simply was tired of putting up with his teachers? Or a college student who thinks he is following in the footsteps of Moses and Jesus by committing mass slaughter? How do we wrap our minds around the idea of a high school student who seeks to kick-start natural selection by eliminating unfit people from the planet? Surely he must have been picked on. Surely he must have been a victim of horrible harassment.

And when questions are asked about teasing, the answer is often "Yes, he was teased." So we focus on that, because it gives meaning to an act that otherwise seems meaningless. Revenge makes sense. A teenage boy from a good home who idolizes Hitler and fantasizes about killing off humanity does not make sense. But even though revenge seems plausible, teasing does not cause murder. Not by itself. Something was wrong within the minds of the school shooters.

The Shooters

The 10 rampage school shooters who will be presented in this book were chosen because there was enough information available to analyze them and their actions. In the cases of school shooters who are not presented in detail, either there was too little information available or the information was too inconsistent to draw meaningful conclusions. These are the 10 shooters discussed:

- **Evan Ramsey, age 16, from Bethel, Alaska**. Evan was suicidal. When he told friends that he wanted to kill himself, they encouraged him to kill other people at school. With their encouragement, he developed a hit list. On February 19, 1997, Evan went to school and shot a student and the principal. Both died. He also wounded two other students. Evan put a gun under his chin to kill himself but could not bring himself to pull the trigger. Evan remains in prison.
- **Michael Carneal, age 14, West Paducah, Kentucky**. Michael talked about "something big" that was going to happen on the Monday after Thanksgiving. On December 1, 1997, Michael went to school with five firearms: a pistol, two rifles, and two shotguns. He killed three girls and wounded five other students.

Michael yelled for someone to kill him but made no attempt to kill himself. He remains in prison, where he has attempted suicide at least twice.

- **Andrew Golden, age 11, and Mitchell Johnson, age 13, Jonesboro, Arkansas.** On March 24, 1998, the two boys carried out a sniper attack from outside the school as students and teachers exited the building after Andrew pulled a fire alarm. They killed four girls and a teacher and wounded nine other students and one other teacher. Andrew and Mitchell were too young to be tried as adults in Arkansas but were convicted as juveniles. They served their time until they turned 21. Both have been released and are free men.

- **Andrew Wurst, age 14, Edinboro, Pennsylvania.** On April 24, 1998, Andrew went to a school dinner-dance. Before leaving, he left a suicide note at home and picked up a pistol. At the dance, he shot and killed a teacher and wounded another teacher and two students. Andrew remains in prison.

- **Kip Kinkel, age 15, Springfield, Oregon.** On May 20, 1998, Kip was suspended for having a gun at school. Later that day he killed his parents. The next day he went to school and killed 2 students and wounded 25. Kip had planned to kill himself but was tackled by students before he had the chance. He yelled for someone to kill him. Kip will be in prison for the rest of his life.

- **Eric Harris, age 18, and Dylan Klebold, age 17, Jefferson County, Colorado.** On April 20, 1999, Eric and Dylan carried out a complex attack involving a sequence of bombs and shooting that they had planned for over a year. Because most of the bombs did not detonate, Eric and Dylan were forced to improvise. They began shooting outside the school, then entered the building and continued shooting. They killed 12 students and 1 teacher and wounded 23 students. Eric and Dylan committed suicide in Columbine High School.

- **Jeffrey Weise, age 16, Red Lake, Minnesota.** On March 21, 2005, Jeffrey killed his grandfather, who was a police officer. He also killed his grandfather's girlfriend. Jeffrey then drove his grandfather's police cruiser to school, where he killed the security guard, a teacher, and five students. He wounded seven other students, then committed suicide at the school.

- **Seung Hui Cho, age 23, Virginia Polytechnic Institute and State University,** Blacksburg, Virginia. Early on the morning of April 16, 2007, Seung killed 2 students in a dormitory. He then mailed a package containing a "multimedia manifesto" to NBC News. Following this, Seung went to a classroom building where he killed 30 people, including students and professors, and wounded 17 others. Seung then committed suicide.

They are a remarkably diverse group. Their ages range from 11 to 23. Most are Caucasian, but Jeffrey Weise was Native American, Evan Ramsey was at least half Native American, and Seung Hui Cho was Korean. Most came from solid, intact, middle-class families, but three did not. Most killed exclusively at school, but Kip Kinkel and Jeffrey Weise also killed family members. Most were suicidal, even if they surrendered or were stopped before they could kill themselves. In contrast, Andrew Golden and Mitchell Johnson had planned to escape in a van they had stocked with food and clothes. Some, as we will see, suffered from schizophrenia; others were completely sane.

As I studied these shooters one by one, I realized that certain shooters share characteristics with others. There are numerous parallels among their family histories, personalities, and psychological problems. Building on this insight, I began grouping the shooters into different clusters. Within each type, the shooters have many features in common. Across the different types, the shooters have little in common. Based on my research, there are three different types of school shooters: psychopathic, psychotic, and traumatized.[10] This book defines what these terms mean and illustrates the three types. There are three sections in the book corresponding to the three types, with additional chapters discussing the typology, potential school shooters who were stopped before they committed murder, and ways to prevent rampage attacks at schools.

We begin with the psychopaths.

PSYCHOPATHIC
SHOOTERS

2

"I AM THE LAW"

TWO PSYCHOPATHS

IN 1954 WILLIAM MARCH published his novel *The Bad Seed,* the story of a cute little girl who is a cold-blooded killer. She knows how to act sweet and charm the adults around her. When she finds it necessary, however, she can commit murder without any thought for the victim or guilt for her actions. This girl is a psychopath.

What is a psychopath? Psychopaths are defined by a cluster of personality traits. First, they are extremely narcissistic. Narcissism involves two related concepts: egotism and egocentrism. People who are egotistical think they are superior to other people. People who are egocentric meet their own needs with little or no concern for the needs of those around them. They are so self-centered that they have no empathy for other people. Second, psychopaths have no use for morality—no concern for traditional ideas of right and wrong—because morality interferes with the ability to meet their needs. And as a result of their lack of empathy and lack of morality, they do not experience guilt or remorse. They do what they need to do to satisfy themselves, with no concern for the consequences to others. They are essentially people without a conscience.

Several other features of psychopaths are worth noting. They tend to have problems with anger management. Because psychopaths are so preoccupied with meeting their own needs, they have extremely angry responses when their desires are thwarted. Common everyday frustrations can generate rage. And because they lack empathy and morality, their anger can be dangerous.

In spite of these traits, however, psychopaths are often quite skilled at making a good impression. They may strike people as charming, cute, or charismatic. Their narcissism allows them to present themselves as supremely confident. This ability to be appealing, which psychopaths often use to exploit others by winning their trust, is what Dr. Robert Hare calls "impression management."[1]

Finally, although all psychopaths are not sadists, the psychopathic school shooters that we discuss were sadistic. Sadists not only lack empathy but also seek out opportunities to have power over others. Sadists get a thrill and a sense of fulfillment out of making others suffer.[2]

One Plus One Equals a Million

In 1998, Jonesboro, Arkansas, was a town of 55,000 with a thriving economy and a low crime rate. People liked the town because it was a safe, close-knit community. Andrew Golden, known as Drew, grew up there, as did his father. Both parents were local postmasters. His mother, Pat Golden, after having two children from a previous marriage, had a tubal ligation. When she married Drew's father, however, the new couple was eager to have a child together, and Pat had the tubal ligation reversed. Drew was the couple's only child and the apple of their eye. A family friend said he was "the center of their world."[3]

Firearms were a significant part of Drew's family and childhood. His paternal grandfather worked for the state fish and game commission and hunted frequently. Drew's parents were leaders of the Jonesboro Practical Pistol Shooters Association. As a result of his family's affinity for firearms, Drew handled guns from a young age. "He was given a rifle for his sixth birthday and had other weapons of his own as well. Drew was fascinated, possibly obsessed, with guns; some teachers say it was his toy of choice as a young child, and the year of the shooting, he drew a picture of two rifles when asked to draw something that symbolized his family for his social studies class; he even did a skit about guns for his English class."[4]

An interest in guns was nothing unusual in his town, however. Besides, Drew was a cute boy—at least when he wanted to be. Around his parents he was said to be a sweet child. He cursed like a sailor, but his father and grandfather found it endearing and laughed. At school he was a bit of a class clown, but he was not a serious discipline problem. In the neighborhood Drew did typical things, like playing baseball and racing Go-Karts. To his family, he must have seemed like a normal boy.

When he was away from his parents and teachers, however, Drew showed a different side of himself. Neighbors described him as "a little demon," "mean-spirited," and "evil-acting." He was hostile, aggressive, and threatening toward other children. He hit girls. He cursed and yelled at his peers. He threatened to shoot them with his BB gun. He rode his bicycle with a knife strapped to his leg, intimidating other children. And then there was his behavior with cats.

Cats had a way of disappearing when Drew was around. He killed a cat by starving it in a barrel. He pushed the heads of kittens through a chain-link fence. He shot bottle rockets and BBs at cats, tied one to a clothesline and shot BBs at it, and slit the throats of others.[5]

It was no wonder that parents told their kids not to play with Drew. His own family, however, did not acknowledge this side of him. He was overindulged and not disciplined. When Drew acted up in school and was paddled, his grandfather yelled not at the boy but at the teacher. In another incident, a teacher spoke to Drew about his disruptive behavior. Drew complained about this to his parents; instead of supporting the teacher and telling Drew he needed to behave, they had him pulled out of that teacher's class. It seems his parents saw no reason to be concerned about Drew—until March 24, 1998, when Drew and his friend Mitchell Johnson committed mass murder. Mitchell was 13 years old; Drew was 11.

The attack was surprisingly well planned for children of their ages. On the morning of March 24, Mitchell told his mother that he missed the bus but would get a ride from his stepfather. Unknown to his mother, the stepfather had already left for work. Mitchell took the keys to his stepfather's van and drove off. Meanwhile, Drew's parents had left for work, and Drew deliberately missed his school bus. He hid in some bushes, waiting for Mitchell to pick him up in the van. After meeting up, the boys obtained guns from Drew's home and the home of his grandfather: an arsenal of 11 firearms and hundreds of live shells. Drew, though only 11 years old, was already an experienced shooter and an avid hunter.

Unlike most rampage attacks, the two boys did not intend to kill themselves or die in a shoot-out. Instead, they wanted to kill and make their getaway. They packed the van with food and clothes and devised a plan to kill from a distance. Just as the lunch period was ending, Drew entered the school, pulled a fire alarm, and quickly made his way to a sniper position among trees near the school. He and Mitchell waited for everyone to file out of the building, then they opened fire. When they stopped shooting, they fled toward the van but were intercepted by police. The boys were arrested, tried, and sent to jail. Because they were so young, however, they could not be tried as adults. Thus, they were held until their twenty-first birthdays and released.

Where does an 11-year-old boy get the idea to commit mass murder? Although several school shootings had occurred already, one in particular may have influenced Drew, who appears to have been the mastermind behind the attack. During his deposition, Mitchell said that Drew first talked to him about the attack sometime around Christmas 1997. Shortly before Christmas, on December 15, a boy named Joseph Todd shot two students at his school in Stamps, Arkansas. Although there is no proof that Drew knew of the shooting, there are several reasons to think this event may have influenced the boy's plan. It occurred in the same state and would have been covered in television news and in newspapers. Drew first mentioned his idea for the attack to Mitchell shortly after Todd's shooting. And all three boys carried out their shootings from hidden, protected areas. Joseph Todd did not enter the school and shoot people; he hid in a wooded area near the school and gunned people down from a distance. This is precisely what Drew and Mitchell did.

Why did two young boys shoot their classmates and teachers? What was wrong with Drew? Was he an abused child? In fact, just the opposite is true. Drew was beloved and pampered. The primary motivation Drew had for the attack was his anger at teachers. He had said to Mitchell that he was "tired of their crap."[6] But if he was angry at teachers, why did he shoot students too? Was Drew a victim of bullying? No, he was the one who threatened and intimidated other kids; he was not a victim. Was he detached from the school? No. He participated in class, generally behaved himself, and played trumpet in the school band. Was Drew ostracized or socially isolated? No; he had friends and had begun to date. Did Drew target any girls who had rejected him? Possibly. One of the wounded victims was a girl who had broken up with him.

The fact that 14 out of the 15 victims were female (12 students and 2 teachers) makes one wonder if Drew and Mitchell were targeting girls and women. The gender of the victims, however, was simply a result of their line of fire. The classes that exited the doors facing Drew and Mitchell's sniper position consisted largely of girls. There is no indication that the boys took this fact into consideration when they planned the attack.

How can we understand Drew's homicidal rage? Although some mental health professionals are reluctant to call children "psychopaths," Drew exhibited a number of traits typically associated with psychopaths. He showed skill in impression management. He behaved well in front of his parents and teachers. Even though he occasionally was reprimanded at school for clowning around, no teachers were aware of his nasty attitude or cruelty to animals.

Psychopaths also have significant difficulty managing their anger. This was evident in Drew's behavior with peers in the neighborhood, where he cursed at them, yelled at them, and threatened to shoot them with his BB gun. Another facet of psychopathy is a grandiose sense of self-worth. Drew seemed to think that school rules did not apply to him, as if he were above the ordinary guidelines of society. This was seen in his response to discipline at school, where he got himself removed from a teacher's class who expected him to follow the rules. Another possible indicator of grandiosity was the fact that one of the murdered children was a girl who had dated Drew but had broken up with him. It is possible that this was such a wound to his narcissism that he felt justified in killing her.

Drew's most disturbing trait, however, was his sadism. Sadists enjoy inflicting pain and watching people or animals suffer. Prior to the shooting, Drew's worst behavior involved his torturing and killing of cats.

Apart from his sadism, Drew's behavior during his trial raises questions about his ability to feel guilt for his actions or empathy for his victims. For example, whereas Mitchell Johnson pleaded guilty to the murder charges and offered a public apology, Drew pleaded not guilty and offered no apology. Perhaps he was acting on the advice of his lawyer in the hope of avoiding a conviction. Even after Drew had been found guilty, however, he did not apologize.

Journalists at the trial noted a disturbing lack of emotion in the boy while in court. One observer said that Drew "seemed almost insouciant in his court appearance."[7] Another said "Drew appeared to not be interested in the proceedings."[8] Still another remarked on the difference between Mitchell and Drew: "One of the boy killers sat in court yesterday looking relaxed and even smiled at his parents. Drew Golden didn't seem to have a care in the world as he listened to the charges that he committed multiple murder. In contrast his 13-year-old friend Mitchell Johnson sobbed."[9]

Drew's courtroom behavior suggests that he lacked a conscience and empathy. If so, then this is further evidence of the boy's psychopathy.

Finally, the attack itself—in the absence of other forces—seems psychopathic. It was premeditated murder by a person in full possession of his mental faculties. Drew did not hear voices telling him to shoot people. He was not paranoid or confused about reality. Nor was he full of rage because of abuse at home or bullying by peers. He was not suicidal and had no intention of dying in the attack. The only hints of motives that have come to light are his anger with teachers for setting normal limits on his behavior and possible anger at a girl because she broke up with him. It seems that in Drew's mind, one plus one equaled a million: being reprimanded by teachers and rejected by a girl justified murder.

What traits of a psychopathic shooter did Drew exhibit? Narcissism, a lack of morality, anger problems, impression management, sadism, and a lack of remorse. Though disturbing in a child of 11, these traits can be even worse in an older, more sophisticated killer. Just over a year after Drew's attack, another psychopathic shooter led a more deadly rampage. (*This section's facts were drawn from Katherine Newman's research.*[10])

Aspiring to Godhood

Eric Harris could not spell, and he knew it. How do we know this? Eric wrote about his midnight episodes of vandalism, theft, and mischief on his Web site. In one entry he said: "So we got some souvaneers (i know misspelled) and went home."[11] In another entry, he wrote: "So we got some very nice souvoneers (spelled close enuf) from that place."[12] Elsewhere, Eric referred to JonBenet Ramsey as "Jon binay however the flip you spell her spoiled name Ramsee."[13] Finally, on a page of his school planner where there were guidelines on spelling, next to the heading "Spelling Rules," Eric wrote the word "suck."[14]

He was self-conscious about his poor spelling. After all, the quotes about souvenirs and JonBenet Ramsey appeared on his Web site, where people could see them. Why did it matter to him that he could not spell? Because, although Eric tried to maintain an image of himself as a superior being, inside he felt insecure and vulnerable. It is hard to sustain the illusion of superiority when you cannot even spell the words you want to use. But Eric found a solution—he rejected the whole concept of spelling: "spelling is stupid....I say spell it how it sounds."[15]

What is the solution when there is a threat to your identity?

Eliminate the threat.

Wayne and Kathy Harris appeared to be doing well in life: intact marriage, good jobs, middle-class income. There was no parental alcoholism, domestic violence, or child abuse. Their two children, Kevin and Eric, were bright boys who did well in school.

The primary stress for Eric as a child appeared to be that due to Mr. Harris's military career, the family moved several times. Eric complained about all the times he was taken from his friends and forced to make a fresh start as the new kid in the neighborhood, and how hard that was for him.[16] Other factors, however, may also have been shaping Eric's sense of himself.

Eric was born with two physical defects. The first was a leg problem that necessitated at least a dozen visits to physicians before Eric was 19 months old.[17] A medical problem at a young age can have a significant impact on a child's identity. Perhaps Eric could not walk as early as his peers; perhaps his movements were impaired just as he was reaching the age of learning to walk. Perhaps he was teased, or felt ashamed and inadequate.

As if one birth defect were not enough, Eric had another: *pectus excavatum*, a condition that results in a sunken chest. Eric underwent surgery for this when he was 12 years old. As part of the surgical procedure, a steel strut was implanted, which was removed six months later when he was 13.[18] Thus, just as Eric was growing out of childhood and into adolescence, he had to deal with a physical defect of his chest, and the chest is a significant focus of manliness. Despite the surgery, Eric's chest apparently did not develop well. Evidence of the pectus excavatum was noted in his autopsy.[19] Thus, throughout adolescence, Eric had to deal with his flawed body.

The relationship with his body may have been complicated by the fact that he grew up in an athletic and military family, and both athletes and soldiers are required to be physically fit. As a child, Eric was small for his age and had two birth defects—it would be easy for him to feel as if he did not measure up in his family. We have a glimpse of his insecurity in a description of Eric when he was perhaps 11 or 12. At that time, he lived in Plattsburgh, New York. A former teammate recalled that Eric said he did not like baseball and played only because his father pushed him to.[20] In addition, someone recalled that when Eric was at bat, he was so timid he would not swing because he was afraid of striking out and letting down his teammates.[21] Here we see Eric's attempt to be an athlete as well as his sense of inadequacy.

Eric's flawed physique is interesting in light of his later affinity for Hitler and the Nazis. By immersing himself in Nazi ideology, Eric was embracing an ideology of biological superiority. This meant that no matter what was wrong with his body, he was still superior to others simply because of his racial identity. In fact, in a study of neo-Nazi group members, psychologist Raphael Ezekiel found that, like Eric, many of them had significant medical problems during childhood. The members were poor physical specimens who apparently sought out an ideology of superiority as a way of enhancing their inadequate identities.[22]

Beyond the ideology of superiority, the Nazis also provided Eric with a model of hypermasculinity. The macho, militaristic image of the Nazis was appealing to Eric, who was small, had a sunken chest, and felt weak and inadequate. Identifying with Nazis was a way of establishing for himself an image of hard, tough masculinity. A peer commented that Eric wore steel-toed combat boots to school and "was into combat more than anyone else I've ever seen."[23] Eric also had a preoccupation with guns, which was driven by his need to feel a sense of personal power. Without guns, he was a skinny kid with a sunken chest. With guns, he felt invincible. The day that he bought his first guns he wrote: "I feel more confident, stronger, more God-like."[24]

It is also noteworthy that Eric wrote about himself as that "weird looking Eric KID."[25] Why did he capitalize "KID"? Did he feel like a kid because of his small size? Was this an indication that despite his attempts to project a macho image, he felt he had failed to achieve manhood? Among Eric's papers there is a drawing of an imaginary humanlike creature with horns. The large horns themselves suggest extreme virility. What is striking about this figure is that he has a massive chest—the very feature that Eric did not have.[26]

We can speculate even further. Eric liked to fantasize about ripping a knife through someone's chest. Was he projecting his self-hatred onto someone else? Not long after his chest surgery, Eric bought GI Joe action figures from a friend. He liked to heat metal paper clips and insert them into the chest of the GI Joes.[27] He also liked to shoot the GI Joes with a BB gun. What was the significance of this? Was he acting out his feelings about his flawed physique? Was this a metaphorical self-mutilation?

Perhaps these acts expressed Eric's feelings of rage and hatred toward himself. A few years later he expressed his rage and hatred toward the world. On April 20, 1999, Eric Harris and Dylan Klebold carried out a rampage attack at Columbine High School in Jefferson County, Colorado. They killed 13 people, wounded 23, and then killed themselves.

There are two contradictory views of Eric Harris. One is that he was an ostracized, lonely boy who was tormented by peers into an act of retaliatory violence. The alternate view is that he was essentially an evil monster. This is a pejorative label, however, not an explanation. To understand Eric, we need to go beyond labels to the internal workings of his mind. When we do so, we find that both views—the mistreated loner and the evil monster—are inadequate.

The view of Eric as a lonely victim of harassment is not only inadequate but, to a significant extent, inaccurate. As noted in chapter 1, Eric was not a loner. He had lived in Colorado through middle school and high school, had multiple groups of friends and engaged in a wide variety of activities with his peers. He lived a highly social life and was liked by both boys and girls. On April 9, 1999, just 11 days before the attack, a group of Eric's friends took him out to dinner to celebrate his eighteenth birthday.

But he was teased, wasn't he? Yes, he was. But so were many other kids at Columbine, not to mention everywhere else. And bullying? Having read thousands of pages of interview reports from nearly every student at Columbine High School, I found only one report of an incident in which Eric was physically harassed, and this consisted of being pushed into lockers.[28]

Although Eric claimed to be retaliating against people who mistreated him, this explanation is problematic for several reasons. First, Eric planned to blow up the school, killing people regardless of whether they had victimized him or not. Second, Eric had made a hit list of students from the class of 1998 who "deserved to die." He did not, however, commit the attack in 1998. By the time he did carry out the attack, no one on that list was still at the school. Finally, as he shot students in the school's library, Eric told them that this was retaliation for everything they had done to him. The truth, however, is that he was gunning down students who had never done anything to him. The claim of vengeance was a rationalization.

To understand Eric, it is necessary to know what he planned to do to his school. The attack on Columbine High School was not intended simply as a school shooting but rather as a large-scale bombing. Eric and Dylan set bombs in the cafeteria that were timed to go off at the peak of lunch hour. If the bombs had detonated, it is estimated that they would have killed all 660 people in the cafeteria.[29] The next stage of the attack was either to shoot people as they fled the building or to enter the building and shoot whomever they found alive. Finally, Eric and Dylan had bombs in their cars that were supposed to go off after parents, the media, law enforcement officials, and rescue workers had arrived, potentially killing hundreds more.[30]

Contrary to initial reports, the attack was not targeted toward jocks, Christians, minorities, or any particular individual or group. The attack they planned would have killed a massive number of people—there were no specific targets. Even Eric and Dylan's friends would have been victims. Eric planned an indiscriminate attack against the school and everyone in it.

As horrific as the planned attack was, to focus solely on the attack itself is to ignore the extent of Eric's homicidal thoughts. His fantasies of violence ran wild, far beyond the scope of students he did not like. Sometimes he thought about destroying Denver or local neighborhoods: "God I want to torch and level everything in this whole fucking area...imagine THAT you fuckers, picture half of Denver on fire just from me and VoDkA [Dylan's nickname]. Napalm on sides of skyscrapers and car garages blowing up from exploded gas tanks...oh man that would be beautiful."[31]

A few years before 9/11, Eric dreamed about a similar attack on New York: "we will hijack a hell of a lot of bombs and crash a plane into NYC with us inside firing away as we go down. Just something to cause more devastation."[32] Eric even thought about eliminating almost everyone in the world: "Hmm, just thinking if I want all humans dead or maybe just the quote-unquote 'civilized, developed, and known-of' places on Earth, maybe leave little tribes of natives in the rain forest or something. Hmm, I'll think about that."[33]

It is difficult to read these passages and not be struck by the magnitude and intensity of Eric's desire for destruction. He was preoccupied with far more than misbehaving athletes or kids he did not like. There was little connection between being teased at school and wanting to blow up downtown Denver or crash a plane into New York City. What, then, was Eric thinking?

On the day of the attack Eric wore a shirt that read "Natural Selection." His shirt did not say "Death to Jocks," or "I Hate School," or even "Revenge." It said "Natural Selection." This was Eric's message to the world regarding the attack. He was fascinated by the Nazis' efforts to eliminate inferior people. He said in class that anyone who is not "fit" for life deserves to die. He declared, "I will kill whoever I deem unfit."[34] He wrote in his journal: "NATURAL SELECTION. Kill all retards, people with brain fuck ups...Geeeawd! People spend millions of dollars on saving the lives of retards, and why? I don't buy that shit like 'oh, he's my son, though!' so the fuck what, he ain't normal, kill him. Put him out of his misery. He is only a waste of time and money."[35]

Beyond killing "inferior" people, Eric fantasized about eliminating humanity: "the Nazis came up with a 'final solution' to the Jewish problem. Kill them all. Well, in case you haven't figured it out yet, I say 'KILL MANKIND' no one should survive."[36] In an e-mail conversation, Eric wrote of humanity: "I think I would want us to go extinct."[37] Not content with this, he added, "I just wish I could actually DO this instead of just DREAM about it all."[38]

Eric concocted a philosophy that in his mind justified his contempt for people. He rejected civilization as artificial and celebrated aggressive instinct as natural. Because he believed that morality, justice, and other values are products of civilization, he rejected them as arbitrary and therefore meaningless. He was enraged that he could not impose his convictions onto all of humanity: "Why should I have to explain myself to you survivors when half of this shit I say you shitheads won't understand and if you can then woopie-fucking-do. That just means you have something to say as my reason for killing. And the majority of the audience won't even understand my motives either! They'll say 'ah, he's crazy, he's insane, worthless!' All you fuckers should die! DIE!"[39] Eric specified in this passage that his ideology was his "reason for killing." The power of ideology to drive behavior should not be underestimated. This was exemplified in Hitler: "Leaders of Western democracies...underestimated Hitler disastrously and misunderstood him almost completely because they thought (quite rightly) that his ideas were ridiculous and beneath contempt. They failed to realize that Hitler believed in those ideas....The horror of Hitler was this: he meant what he said, he lived by his ideals, he practiced what he preached."[40]

It seems that Eric also meant what he said, lived by his ideals, and practiced what he preached. On the day of the attack, his shirt proclaimed his purpose: "Natural Selection." He was playing God and eliminating unfit people. He even went out of his way to make his intent clear: "someone's bound to say 'what were they thinking?' when we go NBK ["Natural Born Killers"—his code name for the attack] or when we were planning it, so this is what I am thinking. 'I have a goal to destroy as much as possible...I want to burn the world.'"[41] What kind of person wants to burn the world? What was wrong with Eric?

Eric had a disturbed personality consisting of several personality disorders. Many people may not be familiar with the concept of personality disorders, but to understand Eric and Dylan, it is necessary to probe their personalities. A personality disorder basically is a cluster of traits that become so extreme or so rigid that they cause significant problems. Eric's personality contained paranoid, antisocial, narcissistic, and sadistic features.

Paranoid Personality Traits

When people hear the word "paranoid," they probably think of someone who believes there is a plot to "get him." Paranoia, however, is more than thinking someone is out to get you. People with paranoid personality disorder usually are not delusional. In other words, they do not have false beliefs that someone is out to get them. Rather, the paranoid personality consists of a cluster of traits, including a preoccupation with autonomy and control as well as an extreme sensitivity to issues of status.

Eric wrote a "rant" on his Web site about things he loves and things he hates. The first thing he mentioned was his hatred for "slow people"—people who walk slowly.[42] Why? Out of all the things in the world to be bothered by, what is the significance of slow people? Slow people bothered him because when he wanted to get somewhere, they interfered with his progress. In other words, they thwarted his will.

This interpretation may seem like a stretch, but there is more. Eric complained about slow drivers. He complained about students congregating in hallways and blocking his progress, as well as people who cut in front of him in line. Why complain about such things? He fantasized about wiping humanity off the face of the earth. Why waste time on such trivialities as slow people?

Paranoid people are obsessed with independence and self-control; they are hypersensitive about being influenced by others. Dr. David Shapiro, an expert on personality patterns, has articulated the dynamics of paranoia perhaps better than anyone else. He writes: "The paranoid person is continuously occupied and concerned with the threat of being subjected to some external control or some external infringement of his will."[43] This is exactly what we see in Eric.

Eric's journal shows other evidence of his preoccupation with being controlled or influenced. He went on and on about how it is impossible for anyone to not be influenced by others. He included himself in this. No matter how hard he tried to be original, he could not be. This was highly disturbing to him:

> People say it is immoral to follow others, they say be a leader. Well here is a fucking news flash for you stupid shits, everyone is a follower! Everyone who says they aren't followers and then dresses different or acts different…they got that from something they saw on TV or in film or in life. No originality. How many do you think are original and not copied. KEINE [German for "none"]…No matter how hard I try to NOT copy someone I still AM![44]

Eric's own sense of autonomy was threatened. He desperately wanted to be his own person—to be "original"—and the fact that others influenced him disturbed his sense of self. He wrote: "I always try to be different, but I always end up copying someone else."[45] He then explained that he rebels against anyone who tells him what to do, and that is why his nickname is "Reb." He defined himself in opposition to all the external influences that sought to control him. As described by Dr. Theodore Millon, a world expert on personality disorders, paranoid people have an "intense fear of losing their identity and, more importantly, their powers of self-determination."[46] Again, this is exactly what we find in Eric's writings.

Eric also demonstrated another characteristic of the paranoid personality: a preoccupation with status. He repeatedly objected to or complained about "snobs"—people who were rich and/or "snotty" in their attitudes. Perhaps this is nothing out of the ordinary, but in Eric's case, his response to perceived snobbery was extraordinary: "I live in Denver, and god damn it I would love to kill almost all of its residents. Fucking people with their rich snobby attitude thinking they are all high and mighty."[47] He resented people who in his eyes had it easy because they were born with wealth. Keeping in mind that Eric's family was far from poor, why was he so bitter and hostile toward rich people? Sensitivity to status is related to paranoia because paranoid people tend to assume that others have achieved their success or status unfairly. Paranoid people think they have gotten a raw deal in life and that other people have manipulated the system to achieve success. To paranoid people, they are once again victims.

A related theme that appears consistently throughout Eric's rant is "coolness." He liked to think that he was cool. This is seen in his AOL user profile, where he listed one of his hobbies as "being cool."[48] He also used the term "coolios" for his friends whom he considered "cool."[49] Because he liked to think that he was cool, he could not stand others who thought they were cool. This was cutting in on his territory. He wrote about hating all kinds of people who thought they were cool: young smokers, people who think they are martial arts experts, rappers, and more.

Hating cool people is simply a variation on the theme of status. As Shapiro notes, paranoid people are "extremely aware of power and rank, relative position, superior and inferior."[50] Rich people have one kind of status, but in the world of high school social life, "coolness" carries a powerful status too. For someone who was trying to maintain his image of superiority, any perception of high status in others was a threat to his self-concept. Shapiro sums up this issue: "The paranoid person—often grandiose and arrogant though underneath feeling ashamed and small, determined to be strong and to be 'on top of things,' though underneath feeling weak—is constantly, pridefully, concerned with those who, on account of their rank or superior authority, can make him feel small and powerless."[51]

Eric's paranoid traits reveal an extraordinarily fragile identity that had to be protected at all costs, even if this meant murder. Most people with paranoid personalities, however, do not commit murder. There were other forces driving Eric toward violence.

Antisocial Personality Traits

Antisocial personality disorder is the formal diagnosis that most resembles the concept of the "psychopath." The word "antisocial" does not describe someone's social skills or refer to a person who is introverted and perhaps "unsocial" or "asocial." Someone who is "antisocial" is really "antisociety"—he or she does not operate by the rules of society. This includes laws, customs, common decency, and a consideration for the rights and feelings of others. There is a basic disregard for morality as well as a lack of empathy. Eric demonstrated several core aspects of the antisocial personality disorder.

To start with, throughout his journal, Eric dismissed traditional values as meaningless. He rejected morality and even concepts that are essential to social living. For example, he wrote "there is no such thing as an actual 'real world.' It's just another word like justice, sorry, pity, religion, faith, luck and so on."[52] In the same entry he wrote, "Just because your mumsy and dadsy told you blood and violence is bad, you think it's a fucking law of nature? Wrong."[53] Elsewhere Eric wrote: "'sorry' is just a word. It doesn't mean SHIT to me."[54] He referred to "normal" and "civilized" as "social words," as if they had no real meaning.[55] He said, "'morals' is just another word,"[56] and summed up his attitude with vehemence: "Fuck money, fuck justice, fuck morals, fuck civilized, fuck rules, fuck laws...DIE man-made words...people think they apply to everything when they don't/can't. There's no such thing as True Good or True evil."[57]

In his mind, he was above all the "false" values and morals that have been created by society. With no respect for concepts such as goodness, justice, or civilization, Eric engaged in a wide variety of illegal behaviors. His offenses included stealing from a van, stealing traffic signs, stealing computer equipment from the school, underage drinking, illegal drug use, credit card fraud, hacking into the school's computer system, using friends to illegally buy guns for him, fire-setting, vandalism, and making and detonating illegal bombs.

The lack of concern for morality and the welfare of others manifested itself not only in regard to his enemies but to his friends as well. Some of the guns used in the attack were bought by older friends of his; this was because Eric was not 18 at the time of the purchases. He knew that his friends might be arrested for this after the attack, and in fact two of them went to jail. Despite knowing this might happen, Eric callously used them to meet his own needs.

This disregard for the welfare of his friends is seen most clearly in a comment Eric made in one of several videos he made about the upcoming attack: "Morris, Nate, if you guys live I want you to have whatever you want from my room."[58] Eric was addressing two of his best friends, bequeathing to them whatever possessions of his they wanted. By saying "if you guys live," however, Eric was demonstrating his awareness that the attack very likely would kill them. Even the potential deaths of his close friends did not deter Eric from his plans.

Another core element of antisocial personalities is habitual lying. Eric described his skill at deceiving others repeatedly in his journal. He wrote, "I lie a lot. Almost constant, and to everybody."[59] Eric not only lied, but he took pride in his ability to lie: "I could convince them that I'm going to climb Mount Everest, or that I have a twin brother growing out of my back...I can make you believe anything."[60]

Beyond simply lying, however, Eric was skilled in making positive impressions when he wanted to. The father of a classmate said, "Eric was always the perfect little gentleman. He seemed more mature than other kids."[61] This ability to charm people is an example of "impression management." Perhaps the best example of Eric's impression management is the fact that he planned a massive terroristic attack for months, and no one but his coperpetrator knew about it. He went about his business, going to school, showing up for work, and hanging out with friends who most likely would have been killed if all the explosives had gone off. He hid his true intentions from his peers, family, teachers, and colleagues.

Another example of Eric's ability to manage the impression he made occurred after he and Dylan were arrested for stealing electronics equipment from an electrician's van. Both boys had to participate in a diversion program designed to keep youth from continued illegal behavior. Eric presented himself so well in his meetings with his probation officer that he received an early release from the program. A teacher who read an essay by Eric about his arrest was completely taken in by him, and even wrote a note to Eric that said "I would trust you in a heartbeat."[62] Eric also wrote a letter to the owner of the van in which he admitted his crime and apologized.[63] In his private writings, however, he presented a different face: "Isn't America supposed to be the land of the free? How come, If I'm free, I can't deprive a stupid fucking dumb-shit from his possessions if he leaves them sitting in the front seat of his fucking van out in plain sight and in the middle of fucking nowhere on a Frifuckingday night. NATURAL SELECTION. Fucker should be shot."[64] This quote not only reveals Eric's true attitude hidden behind the positive impression he made, it also shows another aspect of the antisocial personality: the tendency to not take responsibility for one's behavior and to feel like a victim. Eric committed a crime. He admitted to committing a crime. Nonetheless, he still managed to feel like he was the victim and convinced himself that the crime was the fault of the van's owner for leaving his equipment in the van.

Although many antisocial people focus on the accumulation of material possessions through various illegal activities, others are more concerned with establishing or maintaining their image or reputation. Millon describes these individuals in this way: "Antisocial acts are self-enhancing, designed to ensure that others recognize them as persons of substance—people who should 'not be trifled with.' These antisocials need to be thought of as invincible."[65]

Eric said on one of the videos he made about the attack, "isn't it fun to get the respect we're going to deserve?"[66] He also wondered if someone would write a book about him. He and Dylan discussed which director would make a film about them. Eric also said, "I want to leave a lasting impression on the world."[67] The attack was clearly a "self-enhancing" antisocial act, and during it, Eric got to experience himself as invincible. His antisocial concern with status was interwoven with his paranoid preoccupation with status. This discussion of status leads us to the next personality disorder, whose central feature is an inflated self-image.

Narcissistic Personality Traits

The word "narcissism" comes from the Greek myth of Narcissus. Narcissus was a boy who fell in love with his image in a pool of water. The wisdom of this myth is that it does not portray someone falling in love with himself but with an *image* of himself. This is what happens among people with what Millon calls "compensatory narcissism." They feel so inadequate that they create a grandiose self-image in an attempt to compensate for what is lacking in them. They present a narcissistic facade to the world in order to hide the emptiness or weakness they feel inside. Their self-image, however, is like a house of cards that is precariously balanced and threatened by anything that might bring it tumbling down. Eric experienced severe self-doubts and self-denigration along with grandiose feelings of superiority. His low self-esteem at the core, covered by a facade of superiority, indicates that Eric was a compensatory narcissist.

Perhaps the clearest statement of Eric's grandiose strivings is this comment: "I feel like God and I wish I was, having everyone being OFFICIALLY lower than me. I already know that I am higher than most anyone in the fucking welt [German for "world"] in terms of universal Intelligence."[68] He was clearly aware that he was not God, but he desperately wanted to be God. He was convinced that he was superior to "most anyone" else, but he wanted this superiority to be "official." He not only aspired to be God, but he liked to think that he had God-like power. He stated, "My belief is that if I say something, it goes. I am the law,"[69] and "No one is worthy of this planet, only me and who ever I choose."[70] He even wrote "I am God" in German in his school planner and in his inscriptions in the yearbooks of at least four classmates.[71] Thus, despite knowing that he was not really God, he liked to claim that he was.

Eric's writing clearly establishes his narcissism. As Millon observes, "These narcissists actively worship themselves; they are their own god."[72] This is a remarkably accurate description of Eric.

Did Eric's narcissism evolve into delusions of grandeur? In other words, was he out of touch with reality—that is, psychotic? Eric's fantasies of destruction, along with the comments just cited, suggest that he may have become delusional. For example, he claimed his attack would "be like the LA riots, the Oklahoma bombing, WWII, Vietnam . . . all mixed together."[73] Thinking that two teenage boys will perpetrate an attack larger than World War II and Vietnam is clearly grandiose. Eric even pondered if he would really kill all humans on the planet, or "maybe leave little tribes of natives in the rain forest or something,"[74] as if he had the power to carry out such a plan. Was this just an adolescent fantasy of power?

What are we to make of his statement that he is higher than anyone else in "universal intelligence" (whatever that is)? Was this a firm conviction? The numerous grandiose passages in his writings suggest that he believed this was true. In addition, at times he seemed to think that his attack would usher in a new era—that it was going to jump-start a "revolution" or kick-start "natural selection." For example, he said: "the human race is still indeed doomed. It just needs a few kick starts, like me."[75] Eric wrote about his activities as taking place in "the pre-war era."[76] Maybe "pre-war era" was his code name for the attack, but maybe he believed he would start a war. His comment that most people "will not see the new world"[77] sounds like a conviction, not a daydream. Did he really believe that bombing his school would lead to a transformation of society? That he was going to usher in a new world? If so, then his narcissism crossed the border into delusions.

Eric's grandiosity is clear, but what evidence do we have that Eric had a core of weakness? He revealed his vulnerability in his journal: "Everyone is always making fun of me because of how I look, how fucking weak I am . . . Then again, I have always hated how I looked, I make fun of people who look like me, sometimes without even thinking, sometimes just because I want to rip on myself. That's where a lot of my hate grows from. The fact that I have practically no self-esteem, especially concerning girls and looks and such."[78]

Another comment in his journal reveals how desperate he was for recognition: "If people would give me more compliments all of this might still be avoidable."[79] The idea that compliments might prevent mass murder suggests how utterly desperate he was for the world to acknowledge his status. Later in the entry he wrote, "maybe I just need to get laid. Maybe that'll just change some shit around."[80] What would getting laid accomplish? It would affirm his manhood.

In a list of things that he needed to do as of March 22, 1999, in preparation for the attack, Eric listed "get laid."[81] In fact, in the last entry in the journal, written on April 3, Eric wrote about his continuing effort to have sex and how baffled he was that he was not successful: "Right now I'm trying to get fucked...NBK came quick, why the fuck can't I get any [sex]. I mean, I'm nice and considerate and all that shit, but nooooo. I think I try too hard. But I kinda need to, considering NBK is closing in."[82] Here he is, planning the biggest terrorist attack in the history of the United States, and he is still preoccupied with having sex. He wanted to feel like a man, and he obviously did not. Eric's journal ends with this passage: "I hate you people for leaving me out of so many fun things. And no don't fucking say 'well that's your fault' because it isn't, you people had my phone #, and I asked and all, but no. No no no don't let the weird looking Eric KID come along, ooh fucking nooo."[83]

Regardless of whether he really was left out of things or if this was more of a paranoid or self-pitying perception, this is a remarkable passage. After all the bravado and bluster of his earlier entries, he ends his journal with a mournful whimper. Eric's writings illustrate the inadequate core of his personality as well as the grandiose facade he fabricated.

Although the question of the origin of personality is ultimately unanswerable, as it is a complex blend of genetics and environmental influences, it is interesting to speculate about the possible impact of Eric's physical defects. A medical problem does not just affect the patient; it also changes a family. A child with a disability may be treated with special care. How might this have affected Eric? On one hand, overly abundant attention and nurturing might have fed his sense of narcissism, of being special, of having the world revolve around him. On the other hand, it could have made him painfully self-conscious and ashamed that he was not like his older brother or other children he knew. Eric grew up to have a powerful blend of inadequacy and superiority in his personality: Could it have had its roots in an experience that fed both his sense of being special and of being damaged?

Regardless of the origin of these dynamics, Eric was a compensatory narcissist. Yet his narcissistic, antisocial, and paranoid traits do not capture one of his core features: the one that made him so dangerous.

Sadistic Personality Traits

A cluster of traits defines the sadistic personality. The key element of sadism, however, is experiencing excitement and satisfaction through making others suffer. Sadism is about having power over others and using that power to fill an inner emptiness with a feeling of strength.

Sadists are also prone to various forms of bigotry, intolerance, and prejudice. They are hostile toward groups that they see as lower than themselves. Eric demonstrated this in his comments about African Americans, gays, and women:

> People always say we shouldn't be racist. Why not? Blacks ARE different…We should ship yer black asses back to Afrifuckingca were you came from. We brought you here and we will take you back. America = white. Gays…well all gays, ALL gays, should be killed…Women, you will always be under men. It's been seen throughout nature, males are almost always doing the dangerous shit while the women stay back. It's your animal instincts, deal with it or commit suicide.[84]

Sadists also disdain anyone they perceive as being inferior. This is seen clearly in Eric's comments: "Kill all retards, people with brain fuck ups, drug addicts, people who can't figure out how to use a fucking lighter,"[85] and "get rid of all the fat, retarded, crippled, stupid, dumb, ignorant, worthless people of this world."[86] By seeking to dominate or eliminate those who are weaker, Eric was positioning himself as superior to them. Because he felt weak himself, attacking everyone else who was weak was a way of making the statement "I am *not* weak."

The essential hallmark of sadists, however, is the pleasure they derive from having power over others. Eric fantasized about raping girls he knew from school. He enjoyed thinking about tricking them into coming up to his room and then ripping their clothes off and raping them. Even more graphic, however, is Eric's description of his desire to mutilate people:

> I want to tear a throat out with my own teeth like a pop can. I want to gut someone with my hand, to tear a head off and rip out the heart and lungs from the neck, to stab someone in the gut, shove it up to their heart, and yank the fucking blade out of their rib cage! I want to grab some weak little freshman and just tear them apart like a wolf, show them who is god. Strangle them, squish their head, bite their temples in the skull, rip off

their jaw, rip off their collar bones, break their arms in half and twist them around, the lovely sounds of bones cracking and flesh ripping, ahhh... so much to do and so little chances.[87]

Here we see sadistic pleasure as well as the desire to show people "who is god."

During the school attack, Eric mocked people as he killed them. His pleasure in killing is the most striking example of his sadism. At one point, he looked under a table where a girl was hiding, said "Peekaboo," and then shot her. A multitude of students testified that Eric was laughing and apparently having the time of his life as he gunned down innocent people.

Violence can serve two purposes for sadists, and both are relevant to understanding Eric. Violence serves to intimidate and terrorize others, forcing their enemies to cower. This is exactly what occurred during the attack, with Eric laughing, taunting his victims, and exulting in his sense of power. Violence also provides an emotional release. Eric's frequent outbursts of temper suggest that he had rages in response to being thwarted. Eric's parents reported that he had weekly explosions of temper, often to the point of punching walls. Although the rage may be in response to a particular frustration, sadists will express their rage toward anyone, regardless of whether the person is connected to the source of their frustration or not. Millon states, "The identity of the victim is rather incidental and arbitrarily selected."[88] This explains why Eric was content to kill whoever happened to cross his path—there were no targeted victims, just long pent-up fury that had to be released.

In some cases, specific people or institutions become symbolic of all that the sadist hates. *"These symbolic figures must be obliterated... violence is a desperate, lashing out against symbols rather than reality"*[89] (my italics). In Eric's case, the symbolic figure in the macrocosm could be conceived of as the world or all humanity; in the microcosm, however, it was the school and everyone in it. The school—and the world—threatened his precarious identity.

Erich Fromm, who was both a sociologist and psychoanalyst, defined sadism as "the passion to have absolute and unrestricted control over a living being."[90] This was Eric's goal in life. In fact, he wrote, "I would love to be the ultimate judge and say if a person lives or dies."[91] During the attack, Eric got to live out this desire. But what did Eric get out of such horrific behavior? For a sadist, making others suffer is more than just exciting or rewarding—it is transformational. To a sadist, "The experience of absolute control over another being, of omnipotence...creates the illusion of transcending the limitations of human existence... *It is the transformation of impotence into the experience of omnipotence*" (italics in original).[92]

Eric sought an experience of omnipotence. He wanted to transcend "the limitations of human existence." Like the compensatory narcissist who seeks to overcome the inadequacy of his self through expansive fantasies, the sadist seeks to do the same: "He is sadistic because he feels impotent, unalive, and powerless. He tries to compensate for this lack by having power over others, by transforming the worm he feels himself to be into a god."[93] We know that Eric saw himself as a metaphorical "worm": a weird, weak, funny-looking kid. And we know that he aspired to godhood. His sadism arose to resolve the dilemma of a worm seeking to be a god.

We can make sense of Eric Harris by understanding his complex personality. He combined paranoid preoccupations with control and status, an antisocial lack of empathy and rejection of morality, a narcissistic image of himself as superior, and a sadistic need to experience power over others. The attack allowed him to release his rage at indiscriminate and/or symbolic targets and provided an opportunity to use violence to force others to cower in terror. This made him feel like a god, having the power to give life or death. Eric sought to give them death. After all, they threatened his identity.

How was Eric's identity threatened? There was no support in the world for his grandiose image of himself. He was not a high-status person at school. He could not have a steady girlfriend or even find a date for the prom. He was teased by people he despised. He was arrested and disciplined by a legal system that had power over him. Everywhere he looked there were people who had higher status or greater authority. This was unendurable. All of this was a threat to his self-image—a threat to his identity.

What is the solution when there is a threat to your identity?

Eliminate the threat.

Psychopathic Shooters

What can be said about psychopathic shooters as a group? First, the word "group" may be misleading. Of the 10 shooters presented in this book, only 2 were psychopathic. This fact is significant. People often label all school shooters psychopaths, but this is inaccurate. Most school shooters do not fit the diagnosis of psychopaths.

How alike were Drew Golden and Eric Harris? Both boys were sadistic. Eric fantasized about raping girls and mutilating people's bodies. Also, his behavior during the attack was remarkable for his taunting of his victims as well as his glee in having power over people. Drew's sadism was clearly expressed in his torturing and killing of cats.

Another common feature was their skill in impression management. Eric took great pride in his ability to con people. He so impressed his probation officer that he was given an early release. Drew also was good at keeping his dark side hidden. There is no indication that his parents or teachers had any idea that he was cruel to animals and intimidated his peers.

Both boys were also narcissistic. Eric made this abundantly clear in his writings. Although Drew left no such written record, his behavior suggests that he felt he was "above the rules." He did not accept discipline at school. In addition, to the extent that his attack was motivated by anger at teachers, this is further evidence that he felt they had no right to tell him what to do.

Eric and Drew both had anger management problems. Mr. and Mrs. Harris noted their son's explosive outbursts. Eric's rage is also evident throughout his journal and in the testimony of his classmates. Drew's anger was evident in his threatening and intimidating behavior with his peers.

Although many children think guns are cool, Eric and Drew had an unusual fascination with weapons. Drew had an affinity for guns from a young age and used guns as a topic in school assignments. Similarly, Eric was fixated on firearms. He drew pictures of soldiers and guns, he wrote numerous papers for school about guns, he made videos involving guns, he played video games full of shooting and killing, and when he finally bought his first guns, he felt more "God-like." Both Eric and Drew were obsessed with guns. John Douglas, the famous FBI profiler, calls such a preoccupation "gun fetishism."[94] For such boys, guns represent power and manhood.

Without guns, they are nothing; with guns, they have the power of life and death.

Drew and Eric were not alike in all ways, however. Perhaps the most striking difference was the ages at which they killed: Eric was 18 and Drew, 11. Drew was the youngest rampage school shooter. He engaged in sadistic behavior and murder before he reached puberty. There is no indication that Eric engaged in psychopathic behavior as a child.

The boys' rationales for the attacks also differed. Drew was angry with people at school; this seemed to be the only reason he needed to kill. Eric, however, justified his desire to eliminate inferior people and/or all of human-ity on the basis of what he believed was his great insight into the human condition and the structure of society. His philosophical rationalization made the attack resemble that of a terrorist who uses violence to make a pub-lic statement to advance his cause. The scope was different: Drew thought locally; Eric thought globally.

What is life like for psychopathic school shooters? They feel entitled to special treatment due to their perceived superiority. When they are not treated as superior, they react with fury. Ordinary frustrations gener-ate extraordinary reactions because the shooters assume that their desires should, and will, be satisfied. An insult from a peer or punishment by a teacher is like a slap in the face of a king. It is unacceptable; it is enraging; and the perpetrator deserves death.

In some cases, the narcissism is a facade that hides a weak, vulnerable identity. Anything that threatens the facade is like stripping a king naked in public, revealing him as a frail, decrepit creature. This, too, is unaccept-able. The glorious image must be maintained. Threats to the image must be eliminated. The sadistic use of force that gives the shooters the power of life and death provides a thrill of ecstasy because in that moment, they experience themselves as the superior beings they wish to be.

Drew Golden and Eric Harris came from stable homes without abuse, parental alcoholism, or other significant problems. It is striking that the two boys who perhaps had more harmonious families than any of the other shooters were the two who were most psychopathic. Whatever made them who they were, it was not psychosis, child abuse, or tragedy. The same cannot be said for the other shooters.

PSYCHOTIC SHOOTERS

3

"A GOD OF SADNESS"

A SCHIZOTYPAL YOUTH

ESPITE ALL THE MEDIA attention on school shootings, little attention has been paid to the issue of psychosis. As will be seen, however, a significant proportion of school shooters are psychotic. Before proceeding, a few words about psychosis are in order, because it is often misunderstood. Lay people may think that someone who is psychotic is completely incoherent. They may picture unkempt people on street corners babbling to themselves, completely out of touch with reality and unable to function socially. This is a misleading picture. Psychotic people can be highly functional. For example, the book (and movie) *A Beautiful Mind* tells the story of John Nash, a mathematician suffering from schizophrenia who won a Nobel Prize. He heard voices that he believed came from outer space; he also planned to become the emperor of Antarctica. Nonetheless, he was brilliant. The point to understand is that school shooters can to go to school, do their homework, play sports, and yet be psychotic.

What exactly does "psychotic" mean? The term "psychotic," in a general sense, refers to being "out of touch with reality." A person, however, can be in touch with reality in most areas but out of touch in particular ways. The two primary ways that people can be psychotic are hallucinations and delusions.

Hallucinations are sensory experiences that are not grounded in real events. Although most commonly hallucinations involve hearing voices that are not real, hallucinations can be experienced through any of the five senses.

Delusions are false beliefs. Two types of delusions are common among school shooters: delusions of grandeur and paranoid delusions. Several shooters believed they were exalted figures or godlike beings. Others believed that people, gods, demons, or monsters were intending to harm or kill them.

Psychotic symptoms are not necessarily constant or debilitating. One tragic aspect of the psychotic shooters, in fact, was their ability to cover up their psychotic symptoms so that no adults were aware of what they were going through. By hiding their psychoses, the shooters did not receive the treatment that could have allowed them to maintain safe behavior.

Although psychotic symptoms occur in a wide range of disorders, the psychotic school shooters discussed in this book had severe disorders such as schizophrenia or schizotypal personality disorder. These diagnoses are sometimes referred to as schizophrenia-spectrum disorders. Both disorders will be described more fully as we proceed, but a few introductory points are needed here.

Schizophrenia and schizotypal personality disorder both involve a range of psychotic symptoms, from bizarre thoughts and odd preoccupations to hallucinations and delusions. People with these disorders also tend to have problems establishing and maintaining relationships. They may lack emotional expression or show feelings in odd ways. This problem often results in a lack of intimacy and a sense of isolation.

An Enigmatic Killer

It is difficult to understand Dylan Klebold. Although people were shocked that Eric Harris and Dylan perpetrated the Columbine attack, they were more shaken by Dylan's participation. Eric was more arrogant, more belligerent, and more bloodthirsty. But Dylan? Dylan was often described as quiet, painfully shy, and peace-loving. How can a painfully shy, nonviolent child become a cold-blooded mass murderer?

A father whose child was killed at Columbine said of the Harrises and Klebolds: "Those parents taught those children to hate."[1] He assumed that any child who carried out such an attack must have been raised in a hate-filled home. Yet there is abundant testimony that the Klebolds were a stable, loving couple. Like Eric, Dylan came from a family with an intact marriage and no known violence or abuse of any kind. By all accounts, Dylan was a shy, insecure child, but one who was described as "the sweetest, cutest kid you'd ever meet."[2] Despite Dylan's shyness, he participated in typical activities, such as Scouts and Little League. His parents were so opposed to weapons that when Dylan was a young child, they did not even let him play with toy guns. A classmate of his in high school said, "Dylan was the least violent person I've ever known."[3]

So how do we make sense of Dylan?

In thinking of Dylan from the perspective of personality, the frequent descriptions of him as shy and socially anxious suggest an avoidant personality disorder. Avoidant personality disorder is basically an exaggerated form of shyness that is socially debilitating. It involves severe feelings of inadequacy, fears of rejection, and social anxiety. Thus, people with these traits avoid risking intimacy because they assume they will be rejected. Yet even if Dylan did have an avoidant personality, how would this account for his criminal behavior?

In reviewing all the illegal acts Dylan committed, it might make sense to think that he, like Eric, was psychopathic. After all, Dylan committed the same terroristic attack as Eric. Dylan was arrested with Eric for breaking into the van and stealing equipment. Dylan was also involved in hacking into the school's computer system to find locker combinations of students he did not like. He was suspended for this and for defacing a student's locker. Dylan stole computer equipment from school and engaged in vandalism with Eric. As discussed in the last chapter, being psychopathic involves deception and impression management. If Dylan was on the same path as Eric, but people were more surprised by Dylan's involvement in the attack, did that mean that he was better at impression management—that he was a more deceptive psychopath than Eric?

Another possibility is that Dylan was psychotic. He once wrote, "When I'm in my human form, knowing I'm going to die, everything has a touch of triviality to it."[4] "When I'm in my human form"—was he not always in a human form? What did he mean? In other quotes, he referred to himself as being godlike. Although Eric liked to write "I am God" in German, he was all too aware of the fact that he was not a godlike being. Dylan's quotes, however, sound as if he believed he had *attained* godhood. Was this just an in-joke between the two young men? A way they liked to talk? Or was Dylan delusional?

Thus, to understand Dylan, it is necessary to follow several leads: his avoidant personality traits, his psychotic symptoms, and his psychopathic behavior. Moreover, we need to make sense of the different faces he presented and shed light on the question of how a painfully shy, peace-loving child could transform himself into a cold-blooded mass murderer. To do so, we need to get inside Dylan's mind. The best way to do this is through his journal.

Dylan's journal was not released to the public until 2006. Prior to this, there had been no way to get an internal view of him. His journal opens a window to aspects of Dylan that would otherwise have remained unknown. Without access to his writing, we would have missed so much of his personality, his struggles, and his preoccupations. His journal is markedly different from Eric's in both content and style. Whereas Eric's is full of narcissistic condescension and bloodthirsty rage, Dylan's is focused on loneliness, depression, ruminations, and preoccupation with finding love. Eric drew pictures of weapons, swastikas, and soldiers; Dylan drew hearts. Eric lusted after sex and fantasized about rape; Dylan longed for true love.

Stylistically, the two journals also differ. Eric's writing is clear. Dylan's is vague, dreamy, fragmented, and strange. Eric's writing articulately expresses his rage, hatred, contempt, bigotry, and desire to destroy humanity. Dylan's writing is jumbled, disorganized, and full of tangled syntax and misused words. Eric's *thoughts* are disturbing; Dylan's *thought process* is disturbed. The difference is in *what* Eric thinks and *how* Dylan thinks.

Avoidant Personality Traits

Dylan experienced an ongoing struggle regarding friendship and female companionship. He was painfully aware of his social difficulties. He wrote about the routine of his life in this way: "Go to school, be scared and nervous, hoping that people can accept me."[5] He longed for acceptance, but he felt he never really achieved it: "nobody accepting me even though I want to be accepted...me looking weird and acting shy—BIG problem."[6] It is common for teenagers to worry about being liked, but Dylan's social anxiety was extreme. He wrote: "I see how different I am (aren't we all, you'll say) yet I'm on such a greater scale of difference than everyone else."[7] In fact, he believed that if people knew how different he was, they would abandon or persecute him: "I know that I am different, yet I am afraid to tell the society. The possible abandonment, persecution is not something I want to face."[8]

He particularly felt hopeless with women. He commented: "I don't know why I do wrong with people (mainly women)—it's like they are set out to hate and scare me, I never know what to say or do."[9] Elsewhere he wrote about girls: "I know I can never have them."[10]

Dylan's extreme insecurity is particularly striking because he was not isolated. He was liked by many kids, both males and females, and was involved in a wide range of social activities. He worked with a group of his best friends at a pizza parlor, went bowling with friends, made movies with friends, and belonged to a 12-person fantasy baseball league. His social anxiety was not a result of peer rejection.

Similarly, his fears about fitting in were not a result of being teased or bullied. Nowhere in his journal did he complain about being picked on by jocks or anyone else. In fact, when he did write about jocks, it was to express his envy of them: "I see jocks having fun, friends, women, ALIVE."[11] In another entry he wrote, "I hated the happiness that they [jocks] have."[12] In both of these passages he expressed envy of jocks because of what he perceived as their greater happiness, their greater success in living—having fun, friends, and women. They were living the life he wished he could live. This is a key point. Whatever hostility he may have felt toward jocks was driven at least partly by envy. In his journal, he never complained about being mistreated by his peers. His social struggles were a result of his lack of confidence and social skills, not rejection or harassment.

Dylan's loneliness and sense of inadequacy resulted in severe depression and suicidal thoughts, issues he discusses repeatedly in his journal. In one entry he wrote: "I am in eternal suffering, in infinite directions in infinite realities."[13] In another entry, he said: "oooh god I want to die sooo bad...such a sad desolate lonely unsalvageable I feel I am...not fair, NOT FAIR!!! Let's sum up my life...the most miserable existence in the history of time."[14]

Dylan's anguish sometimes resulted in self-mutilation, what is often referred to as "cutting." He wrote: "I was Mr. Cutter tonight—I have 11 depressioners on my right hand, and my fav[orite] contrasting symbol."[15] For

Dylan, self-injurious behavior may have been an expression of self-loathing or self-punishment, which are features of a severe depression. He wrote, "My existence is shit to me."[16] Not only was his own existence "shit," but Dylan was disturbed that he could not keep up with the lives of people around him. He wrote, "others' achievements are tormentations."[17] He was tormented by the fact that other people achieved things that he could not.

How does one cope with overwhelming anxiety, depression, and loneliness? If you cannot deal with the demands of life, one solution is to withdraw from reality into an inner world of ruminations and private meanings. Sometimes people with avoidant personalities are so inadequate to the demands of growing up that their functioning deteriorates. This appears to be what happened to Dylan. The nature of his deterioration brings us to a discussion of a more severe type of personality disorder.

Schizotypal Personality Traits

A good way to understand schizotypal personality disorder is to think of it as combining extreme social inadequacy with problems in thinking. Socially, schizotypals are severely self-conscious, anxious, and uncomfortable. They can interact with others, but they are deeply insecure and have chronic fears of rejection, often to the point of being somewhat paranoid. Schizotypals desire friendship and intimacy but lack the ability to form emotionally satisfying relationships. This is similar to avoidant personality disorder, but in a more severe form.

In addition, schizotypals have a variety of odd thought processes. These cognitive aberrations can include an idiosyncratic use of language, both in terms of misusing or inventing words, as well as having odd, or fragmented thought processes. They are also prone to having mild psychotic symptoms, such as believing strange things or having bizarre preoccupations. They often have difficulty separating reality from fantasy.

The first thing that struck me about Dylan's writing was his misuse of language. This may seem like a trivial issue, but the use of language is an important part of psychological assessment because of the light it sheds on someone's thought processes (taking into account age, education, and proficiency in language). Although psychosis generally refers to being out of touch with reality, it can also refer to disorganized thoughts.

On one of the preliminary pages to Dylan's journal, before the first entry, he wrote the word "infinency." This caught my attention because there is no such word.[18] As I read further, I found more and more examples of Dylan's use of forms of words that do not exist: depressioners, un-existable, tormentations, existor, perceivations.[19]

Dylan's odd use of words was exactly the kind of misuse of language that is seen among schizotypals. For example, a schizotypal might say, "I wasn't very talkable at work today."[20] The meaning might be clear, but "talkable" is not a word. It is not a complete invention but a modified form of an existing word. This is precisely the type of error Dylan repeatedly made.

Dylan also misused language by utilizing actual words in improper ways. This occurred most frequently with the word "halcyon," which is generally used as an adjective meaning "calm" or "peaceful." Dylan repeatedly misused the word, employing it in odd sentence structures: "We have proven to fate that we are the everything of purity & halcyon"[21] and "all the imaginative halcyons & pure existences I have with her."[22]

Dylan's third misuse of language was his odd sentence structure. Two flagrant examples occurred with his misuse of the word "me": "me is a god"[23] and "why is it that the zombies achieve something me wants?"[24] His use of "me" instead of "I" in these sentences is markedly odd. It makes him sound as if he has regressed to being a toddler.

Besides his misuse of language, Dylan demonstrated other signs of disordered thinking, such as paranoia. Dylan wrote, "I swear—like I'm an outcast and everyone is conspiring against me."[25] A few months later, he wrote, "I have always been hated, by everyone and everything."[26] Two months after that entry, he wrote, "all people I ever might have loved have abandoned me, my parents piss me off and hate me."[27] On that same day he wrote, "I get screwed and destroyed by everything."[28] These comments are contradicted not only by other people but also by Dylan himself. In an earlier entry in his journal, he listed his "nice family" among the good things in his life.[29] But in his ruminations, he became lost in feeling abandoned by everyone, hated by everyone, as if the world were against him.

A few days after he got caught for breaking into the van, Dylan wrote, "society is tightening its grip on me."[30] Assuming that this referred to his arrest, he seemed to view it not as a natural consequence for breaking the law but as part of his ongoing persecution by society. On the same day, he wrote "the zombies and their society band together and try to destroy what is superior."[31] "Zombies" was Dylan's term for all the people he looked down on, which was virtually everyone besides Eric and himself. He seemed to think that society was out to get him.

Dylan also seemed convinced that God persecuted him. After complaining that he lost two objects (which he explained he later found) and losing $45, Dylan wrote: "Why the fuck is he being such an ASSHOLE??? (God, I guess, whoever is the being who controls shit). He's fucking me over big time and it pisses me off."[32] Thus, Dylan attributed even trivial incidents to the malign intentions of some being who controlled his life.

Another unusual preoccupation for Dylan was his relationship to humanity. He felt that he was so different that he stood completely apart from everyone else: "people are alike; I am different."[33] His sense of alienation was so strong that he not only struggled with feeling like he was a normal person, he seemed to struggle with feeling that he was a person at all. He wrote that he was "made a human, without the possibility of BEING human."[34] He felt that he was such an outsider, that he was so utterly different, that he could not function as a human being. Thus, Dylan experienced himself as being detached from people in general.

Dylan was also detached from humanity in the sense of being split off from his own humanity. He wrote about himself as if a fundamental split had occurred between his human nature and his identity. This splitting of the self is one of the more bizarre aspects of his journal: "I wonder how/ when I got so fucked up with my mind, existence, problem—when Dylan Bennet Klebold got covered up by this entity containing Dylan's body."[35]

Here he wrote about himself in the third person, which suggests a detached perspective. In addition, the quote indicates a split between himself (Dylan Bennet Klebold) and some other entity that contains Dylan's body. This strange, convoluted passage suggests that in his mind, he was not really himself—whatever that might mean. Later in that entry, he wrote, "I lack the true human nature that Dylan owned."[36] He is writing as if he is not Dylan—as if he had an existence apart from Dylan. This sense of a split self—a self "cast asunder" from its own humanity—is an ongoing theme for him.

In wondering if he should call a girl he was interested in, he wrote, "calling her is a state of humanity."[37] First of all, this is an odd use of language.

Second, he seemed to be saying that to call her would be a human thing to do, as if he were not human. Two sentences later, he wrote, "my humanity has a foot fetish."[38] Again, he wrote as if it were not Dylan who had a foot fetish but rather his cast-off humanity, which was not part of his true identity. Later, in a document written shortly before the attack, he wrote: "okay, this is my will. This is a fucking human thing to do, but whatever."[39] This suggests that although he saw himself as not being human, he recognized when he was doing something that was typically human, such as writing a will. Similarly, in thinking about calling a girl he liked, Dylan wrote: "something blocks me from calling her, my human side is putting up a wall to prevent me from calling her."[40]

Dr. Theodore Millon's portrait of schizotypals describes Dylan's sense of being detached from himself: "the 'real' selves of the personalities have been devalued and demeaned, split off, cast asunder."[41] This is seen in Dylan's journal, where he split off and devalued his human self. Millon calls this a "persistent detachment or disavowal of self."[42] Dylan certainly presented himself as being detached from his own identity and disavowing his own humanity. Millon also writes that schizotypals can become "seemingly enclosed and trapped by some force that blocks them from responding to and empathizing with others."[43] This was seen in Dylan's comment about his humanity blocking him from calling a girl. Dylan's articulation of this theme is remarkably similar to Millon's description of schizotypal experiences.

Woven into the theme of not being human is the theme of being a god. This takes us back to the first quote of Dylan's that suggested a delusional quality to his thinking: "when I'm in my human form." Apparently, because Dylan could not experience success in the real world, he created a world in which he was sometimes godlike and was sometimes a god. On May 21, 1997, he was only at the level of being like a god: "I am GOD compared to some of those un-existable brainless zombies. Yet, the actions of them interest me, like a kid with a new toy."[44] He positioned himself as if he were a god looking down with amusement or curiosity on humanity. This may have been his way of coping with his extreme experience of not being a "normal" person. Dylan's defense against the anguish of being an outsider—of being abnormal—was to elevate his outsider status into a benefit, as if he were superior to ordinary humans. For example, he imagined that humanity was missing out on his superior knowledge: "Let the humans suffer without my knowledge of the everything."[45]

By September 5, 1997, however, he was writing "me is a god, a god of sadness."[46] On November 3 he was a despondent god: "some god I am…all people I ever might have loved have abandoned me."[47] On February 2, 1998, he asserted, "I am GOD."[48] Over time Dylan moved from seeing himself as being like a god, to an assertive declaration that he was God. Dylan created a substitute version of reality in which other people were viewed as zombies and he was a superior being.

In one of the videos, Dylan said "I know we're gonna have followers because we're so fucking God-like. We're not exactly human—we have human bodies but we've evolved into one step above you, fucking human shit."[49] Thus, although he recognized that he had a human form, he seemed to believe that he had evolved beyond humanity. Dylan's comments illustrate the tendency of schizotypals to withdraw from reality into fantasy worlds of their own creation.

Dylan's journal reveals other aspects of a schizotypal personality. Researchers have found that schizotypals tend to have unusual sexual preoccupations and problems with sexual adjustment.[50] Passages in his journal show that not only was Dylan unable to connect emotionally or sexually with girls, but he struggled against his sexual impulses and preoccupations, including pornography, a foot fetish, and an attraction to sexual bondage. (We see Dylan's tangled syntax in the phrase "and bondage extreme liking." The thought may be communicated, but the wording is markedly awkward. This is another example of his disorganized thinking.)

Another tendency of schizotypals, according to Millon, is an effort to protect themselves from overwhelming emotions. They often "seek to 'kill' their feelings"[51] by trying to induce a state of numbness. Similarly, Dylan tried to ease his suffering by "numbing" his emotions. In one entry, he wrote, "my emotions are gone. So much past pain at once, my senses are numbed. The beauty of being numb."[52] Here we see a retreat from being emotionally engaged in life to finding a sanctuary in numbness.

Millon also identifies a schizotypal trait he calls "undoing." "Undoing" is a process that schizotypals engage in to repent for, or nullify, behavior of theirs that causes them guilt or anxiety. Dylan clearly felt guilty about his urges and actions; he was conflicted between acting them out and suppressing them, and he tried to repent: "I do shit to supposedly 'cleanse' myself in a spiritual, moral sort of way (deleting the wads [levels of computer games] on my computer), not getting drunk for periods of time, trying not to ridicule/make fun of people."[53] He also wrote, "I'm forever sorry, infinitely, about the pornos. My humanity has a foot fetish and bondage extreme liking. I try to thwart it sometimes to no effect. Yet the masturbation has stopped."[54]

Dylan experienced guilt over ridiculing his peers. He even seemed to feel bad about his violent video games. Although he drank, he was not comfortable with this. Finally, he seemed most ashamed of his sexual impulses.

As a result of their poor social skills, emotional distress, and unusual thought processes, schizotypals are notable for seeming odd. Their oddness can be a result of their physical appearance, grooming, clothing, or mannerisms. Dylan's peers commented on his poor grooming, dirty hair, odd clothes, and odd social behavior.[55] It is interesting that although numerous people described both Eric and Dylan as "weird," no one said that Eric was "goofy." In referring to Dylan, however, several peers and the parent of a classmate described him as "goofy."[56] Even his probation officer described him as "a goofy kid" with a "bizarre sense of humor."[57] Dylan clearly struck many people as a bit strange. These are common reactions to schizotypal personalities.

Dylan entered adolescence with inadequate social skills and a deficient sense of himself. Despite his intense longing for female companionship, he hardly dated. He was too inhibited, too fearful. He simply was not able to function socially in a satisfying way. He saw himself as so different from his peers that he could never let them get to know him because he was sure he would be rejected. He was miserable in his loneliness, envying those who had fun, had friends, and lived life to the fullest, while he sat on the sidelines and felt helpless.

Under the pressures of adolescence, he withdrew into a world of his own. This, however, did not ease his suffering. If anything, it may have exacerbated his alienation from others, leaving him more lonely and depressed than before. One way of coping was to find one person who accepted him and cling to him as if his life depended on it.

Dependent Personality Traits

Many people have described Dylan as a "follower."[58] One student said that if Eric told Dylan to jump off a cliff, he would do it.[59] Another said that any ideas Eric espoused would shortly be heard coming from Dylan too.[60] In addition, Dylan used the word "abandon" or a variation of the term repeatedly in his journal. The theme of abandonment was clearly an important issue to him. What kind of person is a follower? What kind of person is preoccupied with abandonment? One who is unusually dependent on others.

Dylan's journal contains an entry that illustrates how dependent he was. The passage focused on his sense of loss when his best friend began spending time with a girl: "if anyone had any idea how sad I am . . . I mean we were the TEAM. When him & I were friends, well I finally found someone who was like me: who appreciated me & shared very common interests . . . now that he's 'moved on' I feel so lonely, without a friend."[61]

This entry reveals how desperately Dylan clung to one person. Even though the friendship was not over, Dylan was crushed by the fact that his friend spent time with someone else. He even wrote, "I wouldn't mind killing"[62] the girl because of the suffering she had caused him. It is as if Dylan's life depended on the one friend with whom he had bonded. Can this desperation to have a friend shed light on Dylan's participation in mass murder?

Let us look more closely at this friendship crisis, which occurred during the summer of 1997, between Dylan's sophomore and junior years. The friend in question does not appear to have been Eric Harris—Eric's name appears elsewhere in the journal and is not blacked out, but the police blacked out the name of the friend. (They did this to protect innocent people.) Also, there is no indication that Eric had a girlfriend that summer. If it was not Eric, then who was it?

It appears to be Dylan's longtime friend Zach. The entry in Dylan's journal mentions that the two boys engaged in vandalism and drinking. The reference to vandalism suggests the missions of mischief, theft, and vandalism that Eric and Dylan went on, and Zach was the only other person documented in the police records who also participated in these missions.[63] Zach and Dylan often drank together,[64] and Zach found a girlfriend and spent a significant amount of time with her in the summer of 1997.[65]

It thus appears that as of July 1997, Eric was not Dylan's best friend; Zach was. When Dylan felt abandoned because Zach had a girlfriend, he transferred his attachment from Zach to Eric, perhaps even intensifying the bond in a desperate attempt to prevent another abandonment. This could explain people's observations that Dylan not only dressed differently in his junior year but also seemed "darker" or "weirder."[66] He had begun to identify with Eric.

It is perhaps significant that although Dylan's journal includes suicidal statements prior to the summer of 1997, there are no homicidal comments until the fall of that year.[67] By this time, Dylan may have attached himself to Eric and adopted Eric's homicidal ideas as his own. Similarly, Dylan did not write about being a god until after the friendship crisis. Perhaps he was influenced by Eric's grandiosity. Whereas Eric knew he was not a god, however, Dylan's psychosis made him susceptible to developing delusions of godhood.

Dylan's involvement with Eric raises an important question: How could Dylan, whose family was part Jewish and who participated in Jewish holidays, affiliate with someone who embraced Nazism? Eric and Dylan gave Nazi salutes when they got strikes in bowling. They would shout either "Sieg Heil!" or "Heil Hitler!"[68] To publicly salute Hitler is simply bizarre for someone from a family where the mother identifies herself as a Jew. Although Dylan reportedly told people that Eric's neo-Nazi interests bothered him,[69] he nonetheless followed Eric's lead. This shows how much Dylan gave up his identity in order to be like Eric.

What kind of person gives up his identity to become like someone else? Millon describes people with dependent personality disorders whose identities are so inadequate that they "merge themselves totally with another such that they lose themselves in the process."[70] Can this account for Dylan's transformation? According to Millon, such dependent personalities become "so fused and entwined, that they may act at times in ways quite divergent from what has been characteristic of them."[71] This certainly describes Dylan's change from being remorseful about making fun of peers to murdering them in cold blood. It can also explain how someone from a part-Jewish family could give Nazi salutes in public. His own personality was irrelevant. The only thing that mattered was maintaining his connection to Eric.

Dylan changed his behavior in Eric's presence in multiple ways. Whereas Eric's journal contains swastikas and Nazi references, none of this appears in Dylan's writing. With Eric, however, Dylan gave Nazi salutes. Eric's journal contains racial and ethnic slurs; Dylan's does not. Yet when Dylan was at school with Eric, he made bigoted statements. Eric's writing contains homophobic comments; Dylan's does not. But when Dylan wrote in Eric's yearbook, he wrote about how they laughed at "fags." Eric identified police as the people he hated the most and wrote about killing cops. Dylan's journal says nothing about hostility toward the police, but in Eric's yearbook he made multiple references to killing cops. Eric's Web site contained mocking and condescending comments about kids at school. Dylan did not make fun of people in his journal; in fact, he wrote about the guilt he felt for making fun of people. When he wrote in Eric's yearbook, however, he made mocking comments about peers and gleefully recalled the way they picked on freshmen. Again and again, Dylan engaged in behavior with Eric that was contrary to his true self.

How did Eric and Dylan end up as a team? Why did Eric not team up with another kid who was also belligerent and aggressive? Why form a partnership with shy, quiet Dylan Klebold? The idea that "opposites attract" can be true in friendships as well as marriages. Eric was narcissistic; Dylan was insecure and dependent. Eric got to play the role of the leader, which suited his egotism. Eric compared himself to Zeus by saying that he and Zeus "like to be leaders."[72] Elsewhere Eric wrote about wanting "to be a strong leader" and the importance of leadership for someone with military aspirations.[73] Dylan, who was floundering in the social world of adolescence, got to attach himself to a figure of strength. To someone completely lacking in a sense of self, this must have seemed like salvation.

At the risk of being simplistic, it could be said that Eric had too much ego to function in society; Dylan had too little ego to function in society. Eric was full of rage because the world was not good enough for him—it did not meet his needs. Dylan was full of rage because he was not good enough for the world—he did not measure up. Thus, Eric's journal is full of homicidal thoughts, with little reference to suicide. Dylan's journal, however, is full of suicidal thoughts, with little reference to homicide. Eric's rage was directed toward inferior others; Dylan's rage was directed toward his inferior self.

Although Dylan participated in the murderous rampage, several witnesses testified that he had a subordinate position during the attack. One student reported that Eric was telling Dylan where to shoot.[74] Another student noted that not only was Eric ordering Dylan around, but Dylan was trying to "impress" Eric.[75] These observations support the idea that Dylan was essentially acting out Eric's wishes.

Despite his apparent desire to impress Eric in the attack, several fascinating events occurred. For example, as the two boys entered the school library, a girl overheard one of them say, "You with me? We are still going to do this, right?"[76] This was almost certainly Eric talking to Dylan. This suggests that either Dylan was having second thoughts about continuing the rampage, or Eric was concerned Dylan might have been having second thoughts.

Furthermore, although they left the library without shooting everyone there, Eric did not show mercy to anyone. Dylan did. He insulted a boy named Evan, but when Evan protested that he had never had a problem with Dylan or Eric, Dylan decided to let him live.[77] In another encounter in the library, Dylan came across a boy named John whom he knew. John asked if Dylan was going to kill him; Dylan said, "No dude. Run. Just get out of here."[78] In fact, one girl thought that Eric and Dylan had an argument regarding Dylan's decision to let John leave.[79] Also in the library, Dylan saw a boy named Aaron on the floor; he held a gun to Aaron's head and told him to get up. Aaron ignored Dylan's orders. Instead of shooting him, however, Dylan left him alone and went elsewhere.[80] In addition, in another part of the building, Dylan crossed paths with Timothy, a boy from the fantasy baseball league that Dylan was part of. The two were friends; Dylan had attended Timothy's birthday party the previous year; they had talked on the telephone two days before the attack. Dylan, without saying a word, withdrew and went elsewhere.[81]

Thus, despite Dylan's efforts to impress Eric during the attack, he decided to spare the lives of at least four people. These episodes suggest that something of Dylan's former self was still alive, even to the end of his life. But if part of his real self was still intact, how could he have participated in murder at all?

Dylan may have acted like a psychopath, but he was really a pseudopsychopath. Millon coined the term "spineless psychopath" to describe someone like Dylan. "Spineless psychopath" sounds like a contradiction, and in a sense, it is. Such a person is not by nature narcissistic, antisocial, or sadistic. Rather, he is weak, insecure, and inadequate. In fact, he feels so inadequate that his identity becomes intolerable. He develops psychopathic behavior as an attempt to overcome, or compensate for, his insecurity. The partnership with Eric gave Dylan a way of coping with his inadequacy, allowing him to create a strong external persona. The timid kid who did not have the courage to ask a girl on a date became an intimidating mass murderer.

Dylan's journal demonstrates that he felt bad about several areas of his behavior. Guilt, remorse, and shame are not emotions that psychopaths experience. He wrote about his efforts to "cleanse" himself in a "moral" or "spiritual" way. "Morality" does not figure in the vocabulary of a psychopath. Neither does "spirituality." These are concepts that Eric rejected, along with all other values and civilization as a whole. He celebrated only animal instincts and natural selection.

Eric and Dylan also differed in their attitudes toward their peers. Eric not only reveled in mocking condescension and vicious bigotry, but he gleefully described how he would like to mutilate and dismember someone. Dylan felt guilty for ridiculing kids; Eric fantasized about ripping them to shreds. Thus, as a spineless psychopath, Dylan engaged in psychopathic behavior, but his core personality was not psychopathic.

Dylan's Reasons for Suicide and Homicide

What reasons did Dylan articulate for carrying out the attack? To an outside observer, it made no sense. He had survived high school and was four weeks away from graduation. Dylan had been accepted into the college of his choice, had visited his future dorm room with his family, and was on the verge of moving ahead with his life. No matter how difficult high school had been, it was essentially over. He could have put it behind him. But he did not.

Instead, he threw away his own life. He planned on killing hundreds of innocent people, including hundreds he did not even know. He risked killing all the people he considered his friends. He knew that he would devastate his family. He had a few weeks to go—he could have pulled a prank on the kids who teased him. He could have vandalized their homes or just attacked the people who had been hardest on him. Or he could have waited it out.

Do his writings give any clues about his motives? Contrary to Eric, Dylan's journal expresses more suicidal thoughts than homicidal ones. One reason for Dylan's suicidal thoughts was his absolute misery. Another reason is mentioned after he was arrested: "I have been caught for the crimes I committed & I want to go to a new existence. You know what I mean (suicide). I have nothing to live for, & I won't be able to survive in this world after this legal conviction."[82] He does not, however, specify why he would not be able to live after his conviction.

Dylan also made comments about his death that are woven into his thoughts about the attack. Three journal entries mention a homicidal attack. In the first, Dylan referred to going on a killing spree "against anyone I want."[83] This gives no clue regarding motive or intended victims. On February 2, 1998, he wrote: "society is tightening its grip on me, and soon I...will snap. We will have our revenge on society, and then be free, to exist in a timeless spaceless place of pure happiness."[84] As noted earlier, this entry was written three days after he and Eric were arrested for the van break-in. Thus, "society is tightening its grip on me" likely referred to being caught and facing the consequences of the crime, although the passage seems somewhat paranoid. The reference to "revenge on society" appears to be in response to this event—there is no indication that it had anything to do with school.

What is most striking about the passage, however, is Dylan's thought that the revenge will set him free "to exist in a timeless spaceless place of pure happiness." Here we see the intersection of his fantasy world with the reality of going on a homicidal rampage. The place of pure happiness could be Heaven, but both Eric and Dylan dismissed religion as a crutch for people who cannot deal with life.[85] Thus, the meaning of this passage remains obscure.

At a later date, Dylan wrote, "I'm stuck in humanity. Maybe going 'NBK'...with Eric is the way to break free."[86] Again Dylan conceptualized the act of going NBK with some transformation in his existence—breaking free from his "humanity," presumably by his death. In another entry shortly before the attack, Dylan wrote: "Time to die, time to be free, time to love."[87] Dylan was again connecting death with freedom as well as connecting death with love. Thus, reviewing his comments in the journal, Dylan's rationale for an attack was twofold: to get back at "society" and to break free into an existence of pure happiness.

Besides the journal, what clues do we have about motive? In Eric's yearbook from their junior year, Dylan wrote "NBK!! Killing enemies, blowing up stuff, killing cops."[88] The underlining of "killing cops" suggests that this was of particular importance. The fact that Dylan did not express hostility toward police in his journal but seethed with rage toward police when writing or talking to Eric suggests that he was echoing Eric's hatred of police.

In the videos the two boys made, Dylan complained about the "stuck-up" kids who hated him, going all the way back to feeling mistreated since daycare. He named two girls whom he called "stuck up little bitches." He complained about being picked on by his older brother and the brother's friends. He also said he was put down by his entire extended family, excluding his parents.[89] In providing a rationale for the attack, nowhere does Dylan single out jocks or bullies. His hostility was directed toward his family, snobs, bitches, and cops.

Overall, Dylan's rationale for the attack remains complex and ambiguous: revenge against police (although this may have been Eric's issue, not Dylan's); rage for feeling mistreated by kids since daycare; anger for being mistreated by family members; the desire to break free from humanity; the desire to live in happiness in a spaceless, timeless place; the blending of death and love. What exactly was the point of the attack? What was he hoping to accomplish? Perhaps even he did not really know.

Perhaps the forces driving his participation in the attack were not rational but irrational. Dylan struggled with feelings of fear, anxiety, and devastating frustration for years. The deterioration of his mental health, combined with his ongoing frustration and depression regarding his inability to live a normal life, may have been the forces that drove his violence. Perhaps he never articulated clear reasons for the attack because he was unaware of them himself. Perhaps the primary reason for his participation was his surrender of himself to Eric, repressing his own personality through an identification with someone else.

Dylan and Charles Manson

On November 3, 1998, Dylan handed in a research paper called "The Mind and Motives of Charles Manson."[90] Why did Dylan write about Manson? If he wanted a gruesome topic, he could have chosen many other serial killers and mass murderers. Manson, however, was different; he transformed other people into killers. In his paper, Dylan wrote about how Manson found people from "normal" backgrounds and taught them to become cold-blooded killers. Did he see a connection between Manson's trans-formed "family" and the process of transformation that he went through as a result of his partnership with Eric? Was he aware of the parallels? Did he see that Eric was playing Manson's role in changing shy Dylan Klebold into a cold-blooded killer?

Although his paper sometimes has been seen as a straightforward account of Manson and his followers, there are several revealing and sug-gestive passages. Dylan began the paper by writing about the two killers in the film *Natural Born Killers*. He stated that the killers "got lost in their own little world."[91] This could be applied to two other killers: Eric and Dylan, who named their attack "NBK" after the initials of the movie. Did Dylan have a sense that he was getting lost in a fantasy world?

Dylan wrote that Manson trained his followers "to try to be exactly like him," commenting that they "started to live Manson's reality."[92] He quoted a former follower who said that Manson "can get people to do things for him, without them questioning his motives."[93] Robyn, one of Dylan's closest friends, said that Eric was able to convince Dylan to do things.[94] In addi-tion, Dylan appears to have adopted Eric's reality and followed him without questioning his motives.

In writing about people joining Manson's family, Dylan said that it was "a way to stray from the norm and live opposite of what one was raised to learn."[95] This was exactly what Dylan did in following Eric. In fact, Mrs. Klebold stated that Dylan did not commit murder because of how he was raised but in contradiction to how he was raised.[96]

Dylan acknowledged that Manson was labeled "insane." According to Dylan, however, "The question of whether or not he is insane is a question of opinion; which cannot have a 'true' right answer."[97] Dylan was defend-ing Manson, and possibly himself, by claiming that insanity is a matter of opinion. Similarly, Dylan wrote that Manson and his family can still "logically explain his actions."[98] Dylan, who was already planning NBK with Eric, apparently wanted to believe that murdering innocent people could be explained logically.

According to Dylan, Manson preached that "death was not bad, just another high."[99] In reading the book *Helter Skelter* (it was listed in the bibliography), Dylan would have seen other Manson comments about death. Manson told his followers that "death is only an illusion," saying that it was a releasing of the soul.[100] Manson also said "Death is beautiful."[101] These passages could explain Dylan's references to dying and achieving happiness.

What was the connection among death, happiness, and love? Perhaps the most intriguing line in Dylan's report occurs in the context of describing Manson's life with his so-called family: "'We played a lot of music, we did a lot of drugs, we loved, we were happy' replies Manson when later asked about life at the ranch. The family did these things, and more. They lost their humanity at the ranch."[102]

That last sentence sometimes has been seen as Dylan's recognition that what Manson and his followers did was "inhuman." There is another possible interpretation, however, based on Dylan's frequent use of the word "humanity" in his journal.

Dylan wrote about his humanity as an impediment. His humanity blocked him from calling a girl he liked. His humanity had a foot fetish. His human side was associated with the "zombies" he looked down on—all the normal people living their normal lives. Thus, "humanity" had a particular meaning for Dylan. In addition, he did not write that Manson's followers lost their humanity by committing murder. Rather, they lost their humanity in the midst of happiness and love. Dylan seems to be saying that Manson and his family lost their humanity by transcending to a higher realm of existence, a realm of pure love and happiness. Perhaps this is why he wrote: "I'm stuck in humanity. Maybe going 'NBK'... with Eric is the way to break free." In Dylan's mind, murder, death, freedom from humanity, love, and happiness were entwined. It seems his thinking was influenced by Manson's ideas on the beauty of death.

Apart from his paper on Manson, Dylan's behavior suggests that he was deliberately following in the footsteps of Manson and his family. Besides Eric and Dylan's well-known nicknames (VoDkA and Reb), the boys had other nicknames they apparently only used between themselves. Dylan was "Green" and Eric was "Indigo."[103] In the 1970s, Manson created the Order of the Rainbow and assigned his core followers nicknames: Squeaky Fromme was Red, Sandra Good was Blue, Susan Atkins was Violet, Leslie Van Houten was Green, Patricia Krenwinkle was Yellow, and Nancy Pitman was Gold.[104] It appears that Eric and Dylan copied the Order of the Rainbow.

Various forms of the word "pig" were favorite terms of Manson and his family. At one murder site, the followers wrote "Political Piggy." At another, they wrote the word "Pig." At a third, "Death to Pigs." Each time the words were written in a victim's blood. On the same page of Eric's yearbook where Dylan addressed Eric as Indigo and signed himself as Green, he wrote about looking forward to killing "pigs" and a "piglet."[105] Dylan also used the word "piggies" in a short story about the mass murder of students he wrote for school several weeks before the attack.[106] The most obvious imitation of Manson's followers occurred when Dylan spray-painted "Death to Pigs" on a pawnshop.[107]

Finally, Manson and his followers referred repeatedly to a coming "judgment day," which apparently was going to be a day of mass murder.[108] On the morning of April 20, 1999, Eric filmed Dylan saying, "Hey Mom, I gotta go. It's about a half hour till judgment day."[109]

Perhaps once again Dylan was following in the footsteps of Manson and his family.[110]

Dylan not only surrendered his identity to the influence of Eric Harris to become a pseudopsychopath, but was also shaped by what he read about Manson. Dylan's comments in his journal about death can be seen in a new light when read alongside his paper on Manson. In addition, his use of terminology adopted from Manson's family suggests that he used them as models.

A Schizotypal Shooter

Dylan entered adolescence with avoidant and dependent personality traits. Under the pressures of being a teenager, his personality deteriorated. What pressures resulted in his deterioration? They were the same issues that all adolescents face, but Dylan was woefully inadequate to face normal challenges. Although he participated in activities with friends, the relationships were superficial; he found no emotional sustenance in them. He was desperately in love at times but felt unable to pursue the girls he had feelings for and was convinced that he could never be loved. He had no

direction in life and found no meaning in anything he did, despite graduating from high school and being accepted to the college of his choice. He
was arrested and saw himself as a criminal; he wrote that the thought of
going to court made him want to kill himself. He was hopeless, depressed,
and full of frustration and rage. He was suicidal for a long time, and eventually became homicidal too. In response to his anxiety and misery, Dylan's
development followed two different paths. Internally, he withdrew into a
schizotypal world of strange ideas, odd preoccupations, and fantasies of
godhood. Externally, he merged his identity with that of Eric and became
a spineless psychopath.

Despite the complexity of his personality, Dylan belongs in the psychotic category. His misuse of language, paranoia, fragmented identity,
detachment from humanity, and preoccupation with being a god all indicate the disordered thinking of a schizotypal personality. His schizotypal
traits alone, however, were not sufficient to make him a killer. His desperate dependency led to an identification with Eric Harris. As a result of this
identification, Dylan took on the role of a spineless psychopath to compensate
for his inadequacy.

This is why Dylan was such an enigma. It is as if he had been living
three different lives. With Eric, Dylan was the spineless psychopath, acting
tough, engaging in vandalism and other crimes, and planning a murderous
assault. By himself, writing in his journal, he was schizotypal—lost in fantasies, confused, lonely, despondent, self-deprecating and yet elevating himself
to godhood. With his parents and others, he often seemed like a typical
high school kid—maybe a little different or "goofy," but going about the
activities that normal kids engage in. He socialized, went bowling, attended
class, and had a couple of part-time jobs—all the usual activities of teenagers.
Apparently no one had any inkling of his whole internal world.

Shortly before the attack, Dylan went with his family to see his future
dorm room at college; he seemed happy, hopeful, eager to move on with
his life. He went to the senior prom three days before the attack with his
closest female friend, a bright, attractive girl who invited him to go with her;
he interacted with people and seemed to have a good time. He even talked
about staying in touch after graduation. No one knew he fantasized about
being a godlike figure. No one knew he was suicidal. No one knew he was
homicidal. No one knew Dylan at all.

Dylan's inability to disclose his suffering and his psychotic symptoms is one of the saddest aspects of Columbine. He could have gotten help if only he had opened up about what was happening inside him. Unfortunately, he was not the only psychotic shooter who failed to communicate his dire psychological distress.

4

"NONE OF THIS IS REAL"

FOUR SCHIZOPHRENICS

S CHIZOPHRENIA IS A SEVERE psychotic disorder defined by a cluster of symptoms, including hallucinations and delusions. In addition, schizophrenics often have disorganized thoughts. What this means is that the flow from one thought to another is odd, or their thoughts are so jumbled that they become incoherent. Schizophrenics also tend to have severe impairments in their ability to relate to others. They have poor social skills and often have significant deficits in their ability to experience and express emotions.

Schizophrenia is more debilitating than schizotypal personality disorder. Schizotypals can have mild psychotic symptoms or strange thoughts and odd preoccupations. In comparison, schizophrenics often have vivid hallucinations and/or significant delusions. For example, Dylan Klebold sometimes felt that everybody hated him. This was a mild form of paranoia. In contrast, Michael Carneal believed a man with a chainsaw lived under his house and intended to cut off his legs. This was a severe paranoid delusion.

Schizophrenics are also typically more impaired in their social functioning than schizotypals. Whereas schizotypals have deficits in expressing their emotions and establishing meaningful relationships, schizophrenics can virtually lose their ability to express any emotions. In extreme cases, they can be practically nonverbal and unresponsive to people in their environment. Most of the schizophrenic shooters, however, were not impaired to this extent.

Finally, it needs to be emphasized that most schizophrenics do not commit murder. Those who do kill constitute a minuscule portion of the schizophrenic population. In fact, schizophrenics are no more violent than the general population.

As with Drew Golden, Eric Harris, and Dylan Klebold, all four schizophrenic shooters discussed came from families where there was no known abuse, neglect, parental alcoholism, or parental incarceration. Outwardly, at least, there were no significant problems.

"I Think I'm an Alien"

Michael Carneal did not have an easy time. By all appearances, however, he should have. He was a bright boy from a loving family in the small town of West Paducah, Kentucky. His father was a respected lawyer. His mother was a devoted homemaker. Both parents were sincere, generous, and actively involved in their family and their community. Michael's sister was both a social and an academic success. Michael, however, did not fit in with his family.

When Michael was approximately 14 years old he wrote something titled "The Secret," which contained this passage: "I have been led to believe that there is a secret in my family that my parents and my sister know...I am always excluded from things...I overheard my parents debating 'whether they should tell me or not.' I still don't know what they were talking about. I think I'm an alien but I'm not sure."[1]

One source referred to this as a short story written for school, but two other sources identified it as a "note."[2] It may have been a story that expressed metaphorically how much Michael felt like a misfit in his family. Alternatively, it may have articulated how much Michael was losing touch with reality. Perhaps he really thought he was an alien. If so, he was not the only school shooter to have this belief.

Michael was not only a misfit in his family. He did not fit in well with his peers either, although he tried hard to be accepted. He played saxophone in the school band but was on the periphery of the group. He tried to fit in with the Goths or "freaks" by engaging in antisocial behavior. He stole money from his father and gave it to the Goth students. He stole a fax machine and other items that he then brought to school in an effort to impress the Goths or to buy their friendship. He brought in his own CDs and claimed to have stolen them. Although the Goths tolerated him, they did not truly accept him.

Michael also engaged in odd behavior, such as drinking white correction fluid, drinking salad dressing, and setting off stink bombs. He even came to school wearing the plastic mat from the game "Twister" as a cape. Some kids laughed at his antics, but others thought he was pathetic. It is not clear whether Michael knew he was being strange. Perhaps he thought he was acting cool. The reality, however, seemed to be that other kids thought he was clueless.

Michael was not a loner, however. He had a girlfriend for a while and had several friends. He visited their homes, stayed overnight, and was invited on family outings with them. Thus, despite his social difficulties, he did experience some success with his peers.

There were mixed reports about harassment. Michael felt like a victim. He reported being harassed about his clothing and glasses, being threatened, and even being spit on. Perhaps the most devastating event was when a gossip column in the student newspaper implied that Michael was gay. As a result, he was called "gay" and "faggot" at school. He tried to act as if this did not bother him, but he was so upset that he took seven Tylenol in an apparent suicide attempt.

Despite Michael's reports of harassment, however, the picture of his social life remains unclear. One reason for this is that his reports may not be accurate. In addition, Michael had a reputation as a prankster and troublemaker at school. Whatever harassment he received may have been in response to his own problematic behavior. In fact, one teacher stated: "[Michael] was an instigator. I know that a lot of times [the] media want to make it look like kids that become shooters are picked on until they just can't take it anymore. But he was a picker, not a kid who was picked on. If [Michael] felt inferior, and I'm sure he did, that was something that was going on more in his own mind. It wasn't anything external."[3]

A classmate of Michael's also saw him as exaggerating his claims of victimization and not recognizing the extent of his misbehavior: "He was just always annoying. He's always the one who got us in trouble in classes just for pulling pranks all the time...[He was] always the one who teased everyone else. And then when he comes out and says he was picked on, it's like, wait a minute."[4]

Regardless of whether Michael's difficulties were a result of being victimized or of his own misbehavior, how do they explain his decision to commit mass murder? On December 1, 1997, when Michael was 14, he went to school with five guns. He walked into the lobby where a group of students were finishing their prayer circle. Michael fired eight shots, killing three students and wounding five others. He then put his gun on the ground and yelled for someone to kill him.

Was Michael part of a larger plot to wreak havoc at the school? When first questioned by police, Michael said that other students had conspired with him. Later, however, he said that he had just been telling the police what it seemed like they wanted to hear. He has subsequently maintained that he acted alone, and the police investigation did not find anyone guilty of conspiracy. The fact that Michael brought five firearms does not mean that other students were involved. In other shootings, perpetrators have brought large arsenals to school.

Did Michael commit murder in retaliation for being teased? This seems unlikely; there is no evidence that any of the victims had picked on him. In fact, Nicole, one of the girls he killed, had been a good friend to him. Michael may have had feelings for her that she did not return, but they talked on the telephone almost every night and she was a significant person in his life. Another girl whom he killed was someone Michael had asked out on a date a month before the attack. The deaths of these two girls suggest that Michael was getting revenge on girls he felt had rejected him. Although this is possible, Michael reportedly warned Nicole to stay away from the lobby that day. If so, then the attack was not a retaliation against her. Michael insisted that he did not mean to hurt Nicole; he said he stopped shooting when he saw her on the ground bleeding.

Why would someone from a good home walk into school one day and randomly shoot innocent people? To answer this question we have to begin with what we know of Michael's psychological functioning. To put it simply, Michael was schizophrenic.

Michael's most prominent symptom was paranoia, which manifested itself in a variety of ways. A mild aspect was his frequent fear of being assaulted. For example, three days before he went on his rampage, Michael and his father were walking across a peaceful college campus and Michael said, "Boy, you could really get mugged out here."[5] He was also afraid to go to restaurants because his family might be robbed.

There were, however, more severe symptoms. At age 14, Michael was afraid to sleep in his room alone. He thought that strangers or monsters were hiding under his bed. He was afraid they might climb through a window in his room. He believed demons would hurt him. He was so afraid to be in his room that he often slept on a couch in the living room. He even smuggled kitchen knives into his room for protection.

Michael was not only afraid in his bedroom. When going to the bathroom, he would yell, "I know you're in there!" before entering; this was to let the monsters or demons know that he was aware of their presence. When he took showers, he covered the vents in the bathroom to keep snakes from slithering in. When he finished with showering, he covered his body with up to six towels, apparently as some form of protection. At times, he would maneuver across a room from one piece of furniture to another without letting his feet touch the floor to avoid the monsters.

Perhaps his most bizarre delusion was that someone was lurking under the house with a chainsaw to cut off his legs. After Michael's arrest, his mother found metal objects under the mattress. Michael explained that he thought these would protect him from the chainsaw.

Making the situation even harder to bear, Michael believed that anyone who helped him would be targeted by the demons. Thus, he could not report his fears to someone without endangering that person. He was trapped within his own paranoid delusions.

Michael also had hallucinations—he heard voices talking to him. They threatened him, called him stupid, and told him to do things. Before opening fire at school, he believed he heard people in the prayer group talking about him.

In addition to hallucinations and delusions, Michael's writing was bizarre. In fact, a few weeks before the shooting, his teacher noticed that the assignments he was handing in had no connection to the readings he had been assigned. In addition, his handwriting had become increasingly illeg- ible, with the words running together. These facts suggest that Michael's thought processes were becoming disorganized.

The most disturbing aspect of his writing, however, was the violent content. Michael wrote a story for school called "The Halloween Surprise." It is a bizarre tale in which a boy named Michael and his younger brother murder and mutilate "preps." At one point, Michael (the narrator) wants to get his mother a birthday present, so he goes to the "Your Mom Has a Birthday Only When There's a Riot" store.[6] This may have been meant as humor, but it makes no sense. The story ends with graphic descriptions of brutal assaults on five preps, including crucifying someone on a metal cross that had been heated until it was red hot and heating a drill bit and drilling into someone's eyes. The last line of the story is: "Then he gave the bodies of the preps to his mom for a good Halloween surprise."[7] This is a disturbing piece of writing.

Michael's sexuality had a dark side. He downloaded material about the "Raping of a Dead Corpse" and a story about cartoon characters (Smurfs) that were shot, burned, microwaved, and driven into a frenzy where they raped each other. Although disturbed sexuality suggests the possibility that Michael had been molested, there is no evidence of this, and he made no such disclosure during hours of evaluation after the attack.

Michael had been suicidal for some time. When the freshmen were asked to write notes to themselves that they would open when they were seniors, Michael's included the sentence: "If you are reading this I am sur- prised your [sic] still alive."[8] In another assignment, students were asked, "If you could walk in the shoes of any celebrity, who would it be?" Michael wrote about Kurt Cobain and Vincent Van Gogh, both of whom committed suicide.

Michael has made contradictory statements about his intentions and expectations regarding the shooting. At one point, he reported that he thought he would become popular simply by bringing guns to school: "Everyone would be calling me and they would come over to my house or I would go to their house. I would be popular. I didn't think I would get into trouble. I didn't think I would get expelled or put on probation or go to jail."[9] Having said this, however, Michael then added: "People who go

He said, "I thought if I killed myself I would make the world a better place."[18] (*This section's facts were drawn from Katherine Newman's research.*[19])

"I Died Four Years Ago"

Edinboro, Pennsylvania, is a prosperous community of 7,000 people not far from Lake Erie. In 1998 the middle school planned an end-of-year celebration in the form of a dinner-dance at a local banquet hall. The eighth-grade students looked forward to the event and went through the typical ordeal of trying to find dates. It was to be a fun evening in anticipation of graduating from middle school. The theme of the celebration was "I Had the Time of My Life."

On the evening of April 24, 1998, Andrew Wurst, like his classmates, got dressed for the dinner-dance. Unlike his peers, Andrew left a suicide note in his bedroom and sneaked his father's .25-caliber pistol out of the house by hiding it under his shirt. During the evening, Andrew hinted to his friends that he had a gun. They were concerned that he might kill himself, and tried to keep a close watch on him. Nobody notified any adults.

As the evening was nearing its end, Andrew took out the gun and began randomly shooting teachers and students. He killed one teacher and wounded another teacher and two students. James Strand, the owner of the banquet hall, lived next door. He heard gunshots and came running over with a shotgun. He aimed at Andrew, who pointed his pistol at Strand. Strand yelled twice for Andrew to drop his gun. Andrew hesitated. Then someone else yelled for him to drop his weapon, and he complied. As Andrew was apprehended, he was agitated and babbling nonsense: "I died four years ago. I've already been dead and I've come back. It doesn't matter anymore. None of this is real."[20]

What did Andrew mean when he said he "died four years ago"? Why did he say "none of this is real"? What was the matter with him? Andrew was schizophrenic. Some of his paranoid symptoms were remarkably similar to Michael's, but Andrew's psychosis was even more severe. Also, as in the case of the Carneals, there was mental illness in the family background, with at least one aunt having been institutionalized.

During a psychiatric evaluation after the attack, Andrew reported that he was afraid of monsters in his closets. Each night his mother "had to make sure that there was nobody under the bed or in the closet and leave a light on in his room."[21] These bedroom fears were similar to those of Michael Carneal. Such fears are not unusual in toddlers, but in a 14-year-old they indicate a serious problem. The fear of monsters in his closet and people under his bed, however, was only the tip of the iceberg of Andrew's paranoia.

Andrew suffered from complex delusions about the nature of reality and his identity. In his world, only he was real. Everyone else was "unreal." He believed that all the unreal people were programmed by the government or mad scientists or a "psycho" to act a certain way. Unreal people were given "time tablets" that determined their intelligence and personalities. According to Andrew, unreal people could become real when they were in his presence but ceased to exist when they left his presence. He also thought that unreal people "are going to screw me over."[22] Andrew believed he was the only person who could really think his own thoughts. Given the mental world Andrew lived in, there was nothing wrong with killing the teacher because "he was already dead or unreal."[23]

Andrew had other odd beliefs, including thinking that he had returned from a future world to prevent something bad from happening, and believing that there was an archenemy who would try to foil his mission. Andrew also told his psychiatrist he had been brought to Earth at age four from his original world. Thus, his parents were not really his parents. This is an interesting parallel to Michael Carneal's writing about being an alien.

The evidence of Andrew's psychosis does not come solely from his postattack evaluation. Prior to the attack, Andrew had talked to his former girlfriend about real and unreal people. He told her: "We are all in reality in hospital beds being monitored and programmed by these mad scientists."[24]

Andrew also heard voices, although less has been reported about his hallucinations than his delusions. Prior to the attack, he mentioned the voices in a letter to a friend. Afterward, he admitted to the evaluating psychiatrist that he heard voices. What the voices said has not been made public.

Andrew reported that his unusual thoughts began when he was 8 years old and that by age 10 he was convinced that he was the only real person in a world that was not real. If this report is accurate, then Andrew experienced a very early onset of schizophrenic symptoms. The age of typical onset of schizophrenia in males is mid-20s.

Besides symptoms of schizophrenia, what other stresses might have contributed to Andrew's attack? He had friends, including boys and girls, and had gone steady with at least one girl. Andrew reportedly was talkative among his peers and fun to be with. He was disappointed that his former girlfriend would not go to the dinner-dance with him. When Andrew asked another girl to the dance, she laughed at him. Andrew reportedly told her, "Then I'll have to kill you."[25] This is the kind of comment that could have been a joke, but in retrospect seems like a threat. Yet when Andrew was at the dance, he made no attempt to carry out his threat against her.

Andrew had talked about killing people at the dance and then killing himself, but no one reported this to any adults. He told one girl he wanted to shoot people and then commit suicide. When asked why, he said it was because he hated his life. This girl also said that Andrew had talked about wanting to shoot his parents. Why did none of his friends report such comments?

One reason that his peers did not take him seriously is that Andrew was known for saying odd things. He talked about Hitler and the anti-Christ being "cool." He sometimes referred to himself as "Your God, Satan." This may have been an attempt at humor or perhaps it was a delusion. Andrew also made joking references to the school shooting in Jonesboro, Arkansas, that occurred in March, 24, 1998, one month before his attack. He thought the attack was "cool." When he said that someone should commit a similar attack at his school, and even when he said that he was going to do it himself, no one took him seriously. Given that he often said strange things, his peers brushed off his statements about killing people at the dinner-dance.

What motive did Andrew have for killing people? Objectively, none. He was rejected by two girls he wanted to take to the dance, but this does not account for murder, especially when he made no attempt to kill either one of them. He did not even know the teacher he shot, although it has been suggested that the teacher may have resembled Andrew's father.

Andrew was not a victim of bullying. Rather, during the spring semester of 1998, he seemed to be acting more cocky than usual. He made clear his dislike of "popular students" and athletes, criticizing them for being stuck up. There is no evidence that he was harassed by athletes or popular students. Why, then, would Andrew be hostile toward them? Most likely because they represented everything he was not. He was not a good athlete. He was not a good student, and his grades had recently dropped to Ds and Fs. He had friends but was not popular. His hostility toward athletes and popular students was probably a result of his envy of them.

When asked during the attack why he was doing it, Andrew "responded by putting his free hand to his head, twirling his extended finger, and yelling, 'I'm crazy, man!'"[26] If "crazy" meant psychotic, then this was an accurate statement.

Andrew twice tried to recruit a friend to join him in the attack, but the friend refused. Andrew understood his friend's choice, commenting that the boy had so much going for him, such as having a girlfriend. This suggests that part of Andrew's suicidal depression was driven by his lack of a girlfriend.

Problems with girls and sexuality are common features among school shooters. Dylan Klebold had a disturbed sexuality, including a fascination with bondage and a foot fetish. Eric Harris had fantasies of raping girls at school. Michael Carneal had documents on his computer about raping corpses and Smurfs raping each other. What do we know about Andrew's sexuality? Unlike the cases of Eric Harris and Dylan Klebold, we do not have a journal or diary of Andrew's, so we do not know about his sexual fantasies or interests. Some of his behavior, however, suggests poor sexual adjustment. There was a girl who Andrew apparently found attractive; he alternated between telling her she was beautiful and calling her a "whore." Andrew also told classmates that his mother was a prostitute. Perhaps he was angry with her at the time, but to degrade his mother in this way is striking.

The mother of a friend of Andrew's had known him a long time and generally had a good impression of him. She was shocked one time when she "overheard him speaking in a harsh, disturbing voice, making a crude and angry comment about girls."[27] Andrew also engaged in behavior that could be construed as stalking. After the attack, a girl told the police that Andrew had seemed obsessed with her, showing up to see her throughout the school day. Another report that came out after the attack was that a few weeks before the shooting, Andrew suspected his girlfriend was cheating on him. Whether she was cheating or if this were another manifestation of Andrew's paranoia remains unknown.

Apart from problems with girls, what was on Andrew's mind? We know that he was depressed. The night of the dinner-dance, he left a suicide note at home. After the attack, Andrew told his psychiatrist that he had been feeling miserable that night. When the psychiatrist asked why he was miserable, Andrew said "nuclear wars, viruses, murders, robberies, school."[28] This was a strange conglomeration of things to be concerned about. It was as if Andrew's personal problems merged with world problems in an overwhelming mix of fears and anxieties, as if there were no boundary between his internal world and external reality.

Although this tells us something about his mental state the night of the attack, it does not account for the attack. First of all, the existence of world problems does not explain murder. Second, Andrew had mentioned committing a shooting at the dinner-dance well before that night. The attack was not an impulsive act. He had been angry and depressed for a long time.

But why would he think about killing his parents? Things at home were not stable. Mr. and Mrs. Wurst had marital trouble, sometimes even getting into physical altercations in front of Andrew and his two older brothers. One source of conflict in the marriage was their different attitudes toward Andrew. Mr. Wurst expected him to be mature and hardworking, helping out in the family landscape business as his brothers did. Mrs. Wurst realized that Andrew was different, and was more lenient and supportive of him.

Andrew expressed his hostility toward his parents in a letter to his former girlfriend: "I got yelled at again by my dad. Let me think that's—4 times now give or take. He started that 4th commandment on me you know. 'Honor thy father and mother.' Gee I feel soo bad. (cry, cry). Not. Fuck them thanks to them I'm in my shit life on the edge of insanity, murder and suicide."[29]

Marital conflict and being lectured, however, do not explain contemplating the murder of one's parents. Whereas Dylan felt like he was not human, and Michael may have thought he was an alien, Andrew actually believed that he had been brought to his parents from another world. Thus, in his mind, they were not really his parents. It is easier to think about killing your mother and father if you are convinced that they are impostors.

One other family dynamic is worth noting, especially in comparison to Michael Carneal and his "star" sister. Although Andrew's older brothers do not appear to have been stars, they apparently were normal boys who met their father's expectations without difficulty. Andrew, like Michael, was the one who did not measure up.

Andrew had one foot in reality and one in a delusional world. His social problems were all too real. He might have been able to cope if it were not for his delusions. He became lost in a world of psychosis. Yet even then it was not too late for intervention, if only someone had known. (*The facts on Andrew are from DeJong, Epstein & Hart's work.*[30])

"God Damn These VOICES inside My Head!"

On May 20, 1998, less than a month after Andrew Wurst's attack, Kip Kinkel did what Andrew had only talked about doing: He killed his parents. The following day he went to school and shot 27 people, killing 2 and wounding 25. Kip was 15 years old.

Kip had struggled in his family for years, especially with his father. His father valued two things: academic excellence and athletic prowess. Kip failed in both. He was dyslexic, and as late as eighth grade misspelled his last name. Although he tried to play sports to please his father, he did not have much talent. He made the football team but sat on the bench. Like Andrew Wurst's parents, Mr. and Mrs. Kinkel disagreed on how to handle Kip, with Mr. Kinkel taking a more hard-line approach. As Kip expressed it, his mother thought he was a good kid with bad habits, while his father thought he was a bad kid with bad habits.

Kip's family structure was remarkably like that of the Carneals: two parents, an older daughter who was a star, and a younger son who (like both Michael Carneal and Andrew Wurst) was a misfit in his own family. Kristin Kinkel, Kip's sister, was an attractive, popular, athletic girl who received a cheerleading scholarship to college.

Socially, however, Kip functioned reasonably well. Students reported mixed impressions, with some seeing Kip as popular, fun, and a joker, and others seeing him as dark, scary, and threatening. He once joined 11 other kids to set the school's "toilet paper" record, sneaking out at midnight to cover the property of an elderly couple with over 400 rolls of toilet paper. Kip engaged in mischief with other friends, including theft and throwing rocks at cars from an overpass. The day Kip killed his parents, he had a conference call with two friends who called him just to chat. Some people even thought that Kip was among the "in crowd," citing the fact that he was on the football team. And although Kip was disappointed in love, he was not isolated from girls. He exchanged notes with at least one girl in his class. A surprisingly positive view of Kip came from one of the students he shot. During Kip's trial, she said: "I remember watching you in Spanish class, thinking that you were really kind of cool, and that I would like to get to know you better. You seemed to have a good sense of humor and you seemed to be a nice guy."[31] Kip was clearly not a loner; nor was he ostracized by his peers.

Was Kip bullied? Apparently not. In fact, Kip acknowledged this in an interesting quote: "I feel like everyone is against me, but no one ever makes fun of me."[32] Thus, to the extent that his thinking was based in reality, he knew that he was not made fun of. Despite this, however, he was paranoid.

He was called a "fag" once by a boy, but one incident of name-calling does not constitute a pattern of harassment. In fact, Kip frequently harassed his peers and called them "fags." As just mentioned, some students saw him as scary and threatening. A friend of his said, "Kip teased and laughed at other kids, but the one thing he hated most was being laughed at himself."[33]

Kip also had a bad temper, which was probably part of the reason some classmates found him scary. His interest in violence also might have alienated his peers. He gave a speech in class about how to make a bomb and bragged about wanting to be the next Unabomber. He also talked about torturing and killing animals, although it is not clear if he actually engaged in such behavior. Even if it were only talk, however, that kind of talk could alienate his peers.

Kip had two enemies he talked about killing: the boy who called him a "fag" and a boy named Jacob. Kip had several reasons for hating Jacob. Jacob was the star of the football team. While Kip sat on the bench, Jacob was eventually voted the team's Most Valuable Player. Perhaps even more important, Kip was interested in a girl who happened to be Jacob's girlfriend. Making the situation even worse, Kip's father held up Jacob as a model, asking Kip why he could not play football as well as Jacob. In his father's eyes, Kip fell short in his family compared to his sister, and he fell short at school compared to Jacob.

All these issues, however, are the ordinary stuff of adolescence. Kip had bigger problems: He suffered from prominent hallucinations and delusions.

The court testimony of Dr. Orin Bolstad, who conducted a psychological evaluation of Kip after the attack, provides details of Kip's psychotic symptoms. Kip reported that he began hearing voices when he was in sixth grade. The first time he heard a voice it told him, "You need to kill everyone, everyone in the world." It also told him, "You are a stupid piece of shit. You aren't worth anything."[34] Thus, from the onset of his psychosis, Kip heard voices that urged him toward both homicide and suicide.

When asked where he thought the voices came from, Kip had a couple of ideas. One idea was that he was hearing the devil. Another possibility was that the government might have put a computer chip in his head, with satellites transmitting messages to the chip.

Kip went on to describe three different voices: A, B, and C. The "A voice" was loud and authoritarian and told him what to do. The "B voice" made derogatory statements to him. The "C voice" repeated what the other two said or commented on them. Sometimes he heard the voices talking to each other about him. Kip tried a variety of things to make the voices stop, including exercise, watching television, and punching himself in the head. After he was arrested and was giving his confession, he cried out about the voices and began banging his head against the wall.

Less than a month before the attack, Kip yelled in class, "God damn this voice inside my head."[35] He was cited for misbehavior, and a disciplinary form that quoted his outburst was sent home and signed by his mother. When his teacher asked Kip if he were really hearing voices, Kip denied it. He was painfully aware that being "crazy" would lead to ostracism at school and be a major disappointment to his parents. Thus, his fear of being labeled as crazy prevented him from getting the help he desperately needed.

Kip's delusions included paranoia that China was going to invade the United States. In preparation for this, Kip had built bombs and stockpiled guns. Kip said about China: "They are so huge. They have nuclear weapons. Seemed like I would end up fighting them. I had lots of fantasies about fighting the Chinese."[36] Another of Kip's obsessions was his fear that the world was about to experience a plague. He feared the end of the world and the falling apart of society. He wanted to build a bomb shelter and accumulate food and supplies. Kip also believed that Disney was taking over the world and would replace the American dollar with the Disney dollar, featuring a picture of Mickey Mouse. In talking about Disney, Kip told Dr. Bolstad, "No one of average intelligence sees it with Disney. You have to be smarter."[37]

Kip had other delusions. He said that sex criminals had chips put in them. He seemed to think that the television show *The X Files* indicated that the government was experimenting with putting chips in people. He said that chips can produce voices, adding, "Maybe that's the way they're controlling me."[38] Here we see Kip's inability to distinguish the fiction of a television show from reality. After the attack, Kip continued to be paranoid. Dr. William Sack, a psychiatrist who worked with Kip in prison, reported that Kip thought visitors to the jail might have cameras in their eyeglasses. He also was afraid that his medication might be poisoned.

Besides auditory hallucinations, Kip may have also experienced visual ones. He told strange stories about a man who allegedly lived nearby and drove a car with bullet holes in it. Kip was so afraid of him that he said bought a stolen gun because he needed protection in case the man came after him. It is not clear if Kip was paranoid about a real man who lived nearby, or if he was having visual hallucinations.

Kip was obsessed with guns and knives. Once a couple of friends decided to play a joke on him by hiding one of his hunting knives. When Kip realized it was gone, he flew into a rage, grabbed a kitchen knife, and screamed, "Give me my knife back!"[39] The boys locked themselves in a room, and Kip tried to stab through the door with the kitchen knife. As soon as he was told where to find the missing knife, he calmed down. Kip's reaction sounds like a combination of rage and panic—as if his whole existence were threatened by the loss of his knife. When his parents threatened to take his guns away, Kip wrote: "My guns are the only things that haven't stabbed me in the back."[40] It was as if his sense of identity were completely dependent on having weapons, as if the weapons made the man.

How did Kip become so disturbed? He was a misfit in his family and was a significant disappointment to his father. In addition, though Mr. and Mrs. Kinkel were both teachers who had excellent reputations in the community, things at home were not so stable. Mr. Kinkel had a bad temper and could be verbally abusive to Kip. Mrs. Kinkel was known to be emotionally unstable. Kip said his mother once was called by the school because he had been late for class twice. He described her reaction: "She picked me up from school. Screamed at me, grabbed her hair, went nuts. Said,

'You must hate me' and stuff like that. Like I was embarrassing to her. It was just a couple of tardies."[41] Mrs. Kinkel's sister confirmed this tendency, commenting that Kip's mother "could get totally hysterical, unreasonably hysterical—it scared me."[42]

In addition to the impact his parents' emotional outbursts had on him, Kip was genetically predisposed to psychological problems. Mental illness was rampant on both sides of his family. Kip's paternal great-uncle was delusional; he thought a police officer was a Nazi soldier. He attacked the officer with a knife; the officer shot and killed him. A maternal cousin thought he was the Second Coming of Christ. In a decidedly un-Christlike action, the man built a bomb and threatened people where he worked. Another maternal cousin was schizophrenic and suicidal; she heard voices telling her what to do. At least eight relatives in Mrs. Kinkel's family, plus several on Mr. Kinkel's side, had been institutionalized.

Thus, Kip inherited a genetic predisposition to mental illness from both parents. In addition, he was exposed to his parents' emotional instability. On top of this, Kip was a misfit in his family who could not live up to his parents' expectations or his sister's example. No wonder he was full of rage and anguish. These passages from Kip's journal express his frustration, rage, and suicidal anguish:

> I don't know who I am. I want to be something I can never be. I try so hard every day. But in the end, I hate myself for what I've become...My head just doesn't work right. I know I should be happy with what I have, but I hate living...I need help. There is one person that could help, but she won't. I need to find someone else. I think I love her, but she could never love me. I don't know why I try.
>
> Oh fuck. I sound so pitiful. People would laugh at this if they read it. I hate being laughed at. But they won't laugh after they're scraping parts of their parents, sisters, brothers, and friends from the wall of my hate.
>
> Please. Someone, help me. All I want is something small. Nothing big. I just want to be happy.....Oh God, I don't want to live. Will I see it to the end? What kind of dad would I make? All humans are evil. I just want to end the world of evil.... If there was a God, he wouldn't let me feel the way I do....Love isn't real, only hate remains.[43]

These excerpts illustrate Kip's confusion and agony. He did not know who he was. He longed to be normal and could not understand why he was not. He could look at his life objectively and say, "I know I should be happy with what I have," but he was not happy—he was absolutely miserable, and he did not know why. He knew his head did not work right. He longed for love but felt that only hate was real. He wanted love and happiness but also wanted to kill and to die. In the midst of all this, he wondered what kind of father he would make. This is a jumbled, disturbing blend of thoughts and feelings.

Though Kip has been called a cold-blooded psychopath, this is wrong. He did not lack a conscience, as psychopaths do. His conscience is clearly visible in the passage he wrote after killing his parents but before the attack at the school the next day:

> I have just killed my parents! I don't know what is happening. I love my mom and dad so much…I'm so sorry. I am a horrible son. I wish I had been aborted. I destroy everything I touch. I can't eat. I can't sleep.…My head just doesn't work right. God damn these VOICES inside my head. I want to die. I want to be gone. But I have to kill people. I don't know why. I am so sorry! Why did God do this to me? I have never been happy. I wish I was happy. I wish I made my mother proud. I am nothing! I tried so hard to find happiness. But you know me I hate everything. I have no other choice. What have I become? I am so sorry.[44]

These are not the words of a psychopath. Kip knew he committed a horrible act and was devastated by guilt and remorse. He was not narcissistic like a psychopath; on the contrary, he was severely self-loathing: "I wish I had been aborted."

If he was empathic enough to feel guilty for killing his parents, why did he do it? And why did he go to school the next day and kill more innocent people? During his confession, Kip could offer no rationale for his acts. He just kept saying "I had to" and "I had no other choice." He reported that the voices told him he had to kill people.

The day before the school shooting, Kip was arrested for having a gun at school. Mr. Kinkel was very upset about this. Kip reported that his father lectured him and made numerous demeaning comments to him after picking him up at the police station. Mr. Kinkel reportedly said to Kip, "You disgust me."[45] After getting Kip home, Mr. Kinkel called a "boot camp" program in the hope that he could enroll Kip there and straighten him out. Perhaps a combination of his father's insulting comments and the thought of being sent away to a military-style program, in addition to his paranoia and hallucinations, pushed Kip beyond the limit of his self-control. He had been hearing voices for years telling him to kill people; now he finally listened. Kip went to his bedroom, picked up a gun, and walked downstairs. His father's back was to him. He shot his father in the head.

Kip offered twisted logic in an attempt to explain why he had to kill his mother. He said that because he loved her, he had to kill her. Perhaps he was thinking that because he had killed his father, his mother could not live with the loss of her husband and the knowledge that her son had killed him. Perhaps he saw the murder of his mother as an act of mercy.

Why did he go on a rampage at school? Why not just kill himself at home? After all, he intended to kill himself during the shooting at school. As Dr. Bolstad pointed out during the trial, the lack of motive—the utter senselessness of the attack—indicated just how psychotic Kip was. As Kip explained in his confession: "It didn't seem real. I hate everybody, myself especially. I hated the voices most of all. The B voice said later, 'Get guns and bullets. Go to school and kill everybody.' I argued with them. I told them to shut up. They ignored me. All night long, I didn't sleep."[46] Kip was desperate, full of rage, paranoid, and hearing voices telling him to kill. He had fought against the voices for three years. Eventually he did as he was told, only to regret it: "These events have pulled me down into a state of deterioration and self-loathing that I didn't know existed."[47]

"Thanks to You, I Die like Jesus"

The media has often described school shooters as "loners." Harris and Klebold, for example, were called loners. As I have explained, however, the reports that they were socially isolated were highly inaccurate. Michael Carneal was said to be a loner, but he had friends. He was not a loner. Neither was Andrew Golden, Andrew Wurst, or Kip Kinkel. Nor was any of the three boys discussed in the next chapter. A close inspection, therefore, reveals no connection between loners and school shooters—until Seung Hui Cho.

Seung was born in Korea. As a young child, he was sickly, very quiet, and had few friends. His severe introversion concerned his family, and his social difficulties became worse when he moved with his family to the United States when he was eight years old. Although he was a well-behaved child, he rarely spoke and became markedly anxious in the presence of strangers.

At school, Cho was made fun of as a foreigner who could not speak English. His older sister was also teased, but she was able to take it in stride. Seung was not.

At Virginia Tech, Seung was socially isolated in the midst of thousands of classmates. He had roommates but barely spoke to them. He went to class but did not interact with anyone. He had no friends and no girlfriends. He resisted efforts to get him to speak. His peers would sometimes try to get to know him, but after failing in their attempts, they eventually left him alone.

This point needs to be emphasized: Cho was not a loner at college because he was driven into solitude by harassment or ostracism. He had a lifelong history of severe social impairment. At Virginia Tech, he was a loner not because of his peers' behavior but in spite of their attempts to get to know him and help him make friends. He was virtually a silent man.

On the rare occasions when he did speak, his comments may have left his peers even more bewildered than his silence. He told his roommates that he had an imaginary girlfriend named Jelly who was a supermodel who lived in outer space. Yet he once asked a roommate to leave because Jelly was visiting him, suggesting that he thought she was real. He said that Jelly called him Spanky. Another set of odd comments involved Russian leader Vladimir Putin. Seung said he spent Thanksgiving vacation in North Carolina with Putin, and claimed that he and Putin had grown up together in Moscow.

Seung once signed his name on a class roster with a question mark. Some of his classmates began to refer to him as "the question mark" kid. He used "Question Mark" as his name on Facebook. Sometimes he called his own dorm room, identified himself as Seung's (nonexistent) twin brother Question Mark, and asked to speak to Seung. Once when Seung was attracted to a young woman, he visited her dorm and introduced himself as "Question Mark." It was a peculiar way to pursue a romantic relationship.

In fact, *peculiar* is a good word to describe Seung. His most notable aspect was his severe social impairment. Most people in college find a peer group or at least someone to talk to. They know how to hold a conversation or answer a question. Seung did not have a single friend and, through four years of college, was barely heard to utter a complete sentence.

The silent man spoke to the world on April 16, 2007. The day began with Seung killing two students in a dormitory. Then Seung left campus and mailed a "multimedia manifesto" to NBC News. He then returned to campus, entered a building of classrooms, chained the doors shut to prevent escape, and began going from room to room, executing students and professors. When police stormed the building, Seung killed himself. His attack left 32 people dead and 17 wounded. Survivors described him as having a blank expression throughout the attack—killing without emotion.

Seung exhibited two classic deficits associated with schizophrenia. First, he barely spoke. The formal term for this is "poverty of speech," referring to a significant decrease in the amount of speech that someone utters. Earlier in Seung's life, his lack of speech was diagnosed as severe social anxiety or selective mutism—the refusal to speak in situations in which speaking is expected. After his delusional thinking developed, however, it makes sense to view this symptom as part of schizophrenia.

The second deficit associated with schizophrenia is what is called "affective flattening," meaning having little or no emotional expression. Seung was described as not showing signs of happiness, anger, or any other emotion. It is as if his feelings were turned off, at least in his social interactions. This does not mean that he did not have any feelings, but the normal expression of emotions was noticeably absent. One classmate stated that he never showed any emotion. A student who witnessed the attack said, "I saw his eyes... There was nothing there, just emptiness."[48]

Besides these symptoms of schizophrenia, is there any evidence that Seung was psychotic? We do not know if he heard voices. We also do not know if his statement about his imaginary girlfriend is evidence of a delusion. By calling her imaginary, he seemed to know that she was not real. Or was this just a way to disguise his psychosis from his roommates? And if he knew she was not real, why did he tell a roommate that she was in the dorm? What about his claim to have spent his vacation with Vladimir Putin: Was that an attempt at humor? Or a delusion?

The clearest evidence of psychosis is in Seung's statements indicating delusions of grandeur and paranoia. In his manifesto, he compared himself to Jesus and Moses, indicating that he had delusions of grandeur. He said: "Thanks to you, I die like Jesus Christ, to inspire generations of the weak and defenseless people."[49] He also said: "Like Moses, I split the sea and lead my people."[50] He ended his manifesto with the words, "Let the revolution begin!"[51] Like Eric Harris, who made numerous comments about "kick-starting" a revolution, Seung apparently believed his attack would begin a social revolution. Although Seung does not claim actually to be Jesus or Moses, his view of himself as a leader of a revolution who will inspire generations to come is clearly grandiose and out of touch with the reality of who he was.

Even clearer, however, was his paranoia. He was a mass murderer who killed innocent people, yet he felt like he was the victim of some grand conspiracy: "You had a hundred billion chances and ways to have avoided today.... But you decided to spill my blood. You forced me into a corner and gave me only one option. The decision was yours. Now you have blood on your hands that will never wash off."[52] Whom was he addressing? What did he mean, "You decided to spill my blood"? Nobody was shooting him. He was the killer, but he thought he was the victim. This is typical of people with paranoid delusions. Elsewhere he wrote: "Don't you just wish you finished me off when you had the chance?"[53] What was he talking about? Nobody was trying to finish him off. This can refer only to something going on inside his mind.

A year before the actual attack, Seung wrote a short story about a student named Bud who planned a school shooting but did not go through with it. Bud was both depressed and full of rage. He told another student, "I'm nothing. I'm a loser. I can't do anything.... Damn it I hate myself." Bud is described as categorically different from everyone else. In the story, all the students are seen as "smiling and laughing as if they're in heaven-on-earth." There was "something magical and enchanting about all the people's intrinsic nature that Bud will never experience."[54] Like Dylan, Kip, Michael, and Andrew Wurst, Seung apparently felt that he was completely shut out from normal human experience, as if he had an alien, nonhuman identity.

Although we cannot answer this question, it is worth asking: Who did Seung think he was? Did he even know? There are reasons to think that he may have been confused, if not deluded, about his own identity. The comparisons to Jesus and Moses show how out of touch he could be regarding who he was and how he would be remembered.

Why did he identify himself as "Question Mark"? Not only is this strange, but the fact that he chose a question mark as his "name" suggests that he did not know who he was. Just to add to the complexity, sometimes he was Question Mark and sometimes his nonexistent brother was Question Mark. Was this all a game? If so, it was a strange one.

And what are we to make of his use of the name Ishmael? The words "Ismail's ax" were written in red ink on his arm. When he sent his multimedia manifesto to NBC, he wrote a false return address, giving his name as "A. Ishmael." He even used the name to sign some of his email messages. Besides viewing himself as akin to Jesus and Moses, did he think he had some connection to the biblical character of Ishmael? Or perhaps this was not a biblical reference but a reference to the character from *Moby-Dick*. After all, Seung was an English major. Did he think he was Ishmael? Was "A. Ishmael" an alter ego? Was Seung delusional about his own identity?

A potential clue about Seung's identity comes from a female student he had anonymously pestered online. When she asked in an e-mail for the sender to confirm that he was Seung, she received a message stating: "I do not know who I am."[55] This could have been a game he was playing, but it could have been an accurate statement. Perhaps he really did not know who he was.

There is yet another nagging question that cannot be answered: Was Seung the victim of sexual abuse? This question is worth asking because in two plays he wrote, sexual abuse is a theme. In addition, he made references to John Mark Karrs and Debra LaFaves, two people in the media as a result of their sexual involvement with children. The theme of sexual victimization, however, needs to be viewed within the context of both Seung's paranoia and his preoccupation with victimization in general.

For example, in his play *Richard McBeef*, a 13-year-old boy named John accuses Richard, his stepfather, of being a child molester. Why does John make this accusation? Because in the midst of a heart-to-heart conversation, the stepfather touched John's leg. There is nothing in the play to indicate that Richard was a molester. John then accuses Richard of murdering his father. Again, there is nothing in the play to suggest the accusation was true. Finally, John accuses Richard of having conducted a cover-up of the murder: "You committed a conspiracy. Just like what the government has done to John Lennon and Marilyn Monroe."[56] Not content with this, John points out that Richard once worked as a janitor for the government, as if this connected him to conspiracies and cover-ups. It appears that John, like Seung, was paranoid.

Seung's comments in his manifesto made numerous references to victimization. There is religious imagery, where he compared himself to Jesus and asked, "Do you know what it feels like to be humiliated and impaled on a cross?"[57] Elsewhere, he used political references to express his sense of victimization. For example, "Now that you have gone on a 9/11 on my life like [fucking] Osama."[58] Seung also expressed his sense of victimization in graphic descriptions: "Do you know what it feels like to dig your own grave?... Do you know what it feels like to be torched alive?"[59] Thus, Seung's references to sexual victimization are part of a larger preoccupation with an overwhelming sense of being victimized.

Where did this preoccupation come from? Reportedly Seung had been teased in middle school and high school, but there is no evidence that anyone at college had picked on him. Rather, many people have reported that they tried to befriend him and draw him out of his shell, only to be rebuffed. Nonetheless, the teasing he had experienced earlier may have left deep scars.

There were other influences at work as well. Like other psychotic shooters, Seung had an older sister who was a "star." When she applied to colleges, both Harvard and Princeton accepted her. She chose Princeton. After graduation, she was hired by the State Department. For Korean immigrants in general, and Seung's family in particular, success is highly valued, especially for males. Seung's mother once said she wished her son had attended Princeton instead of her daughter. A Korean professor commented, "The sister epitomized the immigrant success story, while the brother represented its failure."[60]

Besides being a failure in his family, Seung was a failure with women. He was attracted to them but failed utterly in his approaches. He also engaged in disturbing behavior, including harassing and stalking women and taking photographs of their legs in class. These behaviors are particularly interesting in light of the theme of sexual victimization. We have no way of knowing Seung's sexual fantasies, but it would not be surprising if he had fantasies of molestation or rape. If so, it would be in keeping with paranoia to project these fantasies onto others and become fearful that "they" will victimize him. This could explain his preoccupation with molestation. He may have feared the very acts that he thought about perpetrating on others.

This would also make sense of his ranting about the "debaucheries" and "hedonistic needs" of people around him. It is odd for someone about to commit mass murder to be concerned with perceived hedonism. Murder is far more heinous than hedonism. Perhaps he concerned himself with such things because he wanted to be hedonistic, but either lacked the social skills or felt prohibited by his morality. Seung envied people who enjoyed life and clearly expressed his longing to be like them: "Oh the happiness I could have had mingling among you hedonists, being counted as one of you."[61] He raged against people who were doing the things he wished to do himself. This is reminiscent of Dylan Klebold's envy of jocks, whom he perceived as having fun, friends, and women, as well as Michael Carneal's criticism (perhaps driven by envy) of kids in the prayer group who were sexually active.

Similarly, Seung's ranting about rich people is reminiscent of Eric Harris's preoccupation with "snobs." For example, Seung stated, "Your Mercedes wasn't enough, you brats. Your golden necklaces weren't enough, you snobs."[62] As discussed in chapter 2, paranoid people are often highly sensitive to issues of status. People with higher status pose a threat to their identity.

What was wrong with Seung Hui Cho? He was both depressed and angry about his life: his failure to measure up in his family, his failure to function socially, his failure with women, and the harassment he endured when younger. He both envied and hated people who lived richer, fuller lives than he did. To compensate for feeling like a failure, he developed grandiose ideas that he was like Moses and Jesus and would lead a revolution and inspire others by his example.

What example did he set? In his mind, he represented the uprising of the downtrodden. He felt like a victim, so he lashed out against the world that he believed was destroying him. All his life he was different. All his life he was a misfit. With the onset of psychosis, he lost touch with the real world, but his paranoia magnified the internal reality of his pain. In a bizarre twist, he thought he was dying like Jesus, a victim of persecution, when in reality he was slaughtering innocents.

Psychotic Shooters

The five psychotic shooters present a wide range of symptoms with significant similarities as well as differences. This is not surprising. Every person is unique, and each manifestation of a schizophrenia-spectrum disorder is unique. Nonetheless, the psychotic shooters share several common features.

The only psychotic symptom they all shared was paranoia. The level of paranoia varied significantly across the shooters, but they all were paranoid. At the milder end of the spectrum, Dylan Klebold felt that everyone he knew hated him. At the more extreme end of the spectrum, Kip Kinkel had a delusion that China was going to invade the United States and he would need to defend himself against the onslaught; he also thought that maybe the government planted a computer chip in his brain. Michael Carneal had multiple paranoid delusions about monsters, demons, and a man with a chainsaw whom he believed lived under his house. Andrew Wurst believed that humans were controlled by the government and were all lying in hospital beds with their brains programmed by scientists. Seung Hui Cho believed that people were trying to kill him and that he had to defend himself by murder.

Apart from paranoid delusions, the psychotic shooters had a mix of other symptoms. Some had delusions of grandeur. For example, Dylan believed he was a godlike being, and Seung thought he was a great leader like Moses and Jesus. Other shooters experienced hallucinations. Kip had the most prominent hallucinations, with three distinct voices that spoke to, and about, him. Andrew Wurst and Michael Carneal, however, also heard voices.

Finally, all five psychotic shooters had varying levels of social impairment. In some cases, this was not obvious. Dylan and Kip, for example, had friends and acquaintances and were involved in activities at school. Their journals, however, make clear that they felt desperately alone, isolated, and miserable. They were suffering profoundly even though they were able to present reasonably well in public. Seung Hui Cho was different. Everyone knew he had profound social impairments. He barely spoke, hardly answered a direct question, and typically showed no emotion. He was by far the most socially impaired of the psychotic shooters.

The social detachment they experienced, exacerbated at times by their paranoid delusions, caused a profound sense of alienation. Dylan Klebold, for example, felt that he could never be human, and wrote about his human nature as if it were a foreign element in his being. Michael Carneal wrote "I think I'm an alien." Was this a figurative expression of how utterly different he seemed to be from everyone else, or was this something Michael really believed? Andrew Wurst clearly believed he was an alien; he thought he had been brought to Earth from another world. Kip Kinkel knew he was human but was convinced he could never be a normal human being. And Seung Hui Cho? His alienation seemed to go to the core of his identity, with evidence suggesting that he did not even know who he was.

What we see among the psychotic shooters is a varying mix of paranoid delusions, delusions of grandeur, auditory hallucinations (voices), and severe social impairment. The combination of these factors created a sense of profound alienation and desperation.

What was life like for the psychotic school shooters? They did not measure up in their families. They did not measure up at school. They were a disappointment to their parents. They felt socially awkward. Even if they had friends, they felt hopelessly alone. They felt unloved and unlovable. And they did not understand why. Why them? Why was there nothing wrong with their brothers and sisters? Why was everyone else normal?

The psychotic shooters were suicidally depressed and full of rage at the inexplicable unfairness of life. They hated themselves, they hated the world, and in particular they hated people who appeared to have everything going for them—which was just about everybody else. On top of their anguish and rage, their coping skills were woefully inadequate. They lacked resilience, supportive relationships, and other assets that might compensate for their deficits.

In addition, they were not living in reality. They all believed that people or monsters conspired to do them harm. A few heard voices talking to them; sometimes the voices told them to kill. The world seemed to be a dangerous and threatening place. They were confused and desperate and lost in the mazes of their minds.

They sometimes knew they were losing touch with reality, but they were so afraid or embarrassed about what was happening that they hid their symptoms. To admit to hearing voices or to thinking that the government put a computer chip in their brain would be a shock and disappointment to their parents. To let their peers know would be to invite ostracism for being "crazy," which would put an end to any chance for friends or girlfriends. It would mean the end of their hopes for happiness. Ironically, admitting their problems and getting help would have been their best hope for happiness.

Thus, psychosis among school shooters, although rarely discussed in the media, is a significant factor in many rampage attacks. Yet not all school shooters are psychotic. In the next chapter we explore three who were not in the least bit psychotic. They had other kinds of problems.

TRAUMATIZED
SHOOTERS

5

"EVERY MAN'S NIGHTMARE"

THREE TRAUMATIZED CHILDREN

CHILDREN ARE BEATEN. Children are molested. Children grow up amid alcoholism and violence. Children are shipped from one relative to another, and from foster home to foster home. All too many children live through horrendous circumstances. Whereas the psychotic and psychopathic shooters in this study all came from intact families, the traumatized shooters all came from broken homes and suffered multiple types of abuse.

How does abuse affect a child? Common consequences include anxiety, depression, hostility, shame, despair, and hopelessness. These are features of posttraumatic stress disorder (PTSD). People who are traumatized often have a reduced capacity for feeling emotions and often feel detached from others. They may feel constantly threatened and have mild symptoms of paranoia. This is called "hypervigilance," meaning they are constantly on the lookout for threats to their security. They often become self-destructive, through substance abuse, self-mutilation, or suicidal urges. And sometimes they become violent.

"I Thought My Life Was at an End"

Mitchell Johnson was Drew Golden's partner in the attack in Jonesboro, Arkansas. Apart from that, the two boys had little in common. In fact, Mitchell's background was different from that of all the shooters discussed so far. All of the others—Drew Golden, Eric Harris, Dylan Klebold, Michael Carneal, Andrew Wurst, Kip Kinkel, and Seung Hui Cho—came from essentially stable, functioning families. There was no known physical abuse, sexual abuse, parental alcoholism, or parental criminal behavior. Mitchell's life was different.

Gretchen, Mitchell's mother, had been married once before she met Scott Johnson, and she had a daughter by her first husband. Gretchen and Scott married and lived in Minnesota, where they had two children together, Mitchell and Monte. Gretchen worked in a prison as a correctional officer. Scott worked at a grocery store in the small town of Spring Valley. They reportedly were financially stable, but a former neighbor recalled that the family lived in filth: "There was dog crap on the kitchen floor....Rotting food was lying on the counter for weeks. The yard was not cleaned or mowed."[1]

A dirty home was not the only problem Mitchell had to cope with. His father, Scott Johnson, was a difficult man to live with. Gretchen described him as a drinker with a bad temper, and Mitchell said his father smoked marijuana. Mitchell also smoked marijuana, dipping into his father's supply without the man's knowledge.[2] Scott Johnson yelled, punched holes in the walls of the house, and beat Mitchell. Mitchell stated that his father would "punch me in the face, slap me around, throw me against the walls."[3] His father's rages were so fierce that Mitchell would be left trembling in terror for hours. At times he became physically ill.

Perhaps to avoid the situation at home, Mitchell tended to disappear without telling his parents where he was going. Several times the Johnsons called the local police chief to help locate their missing son.

In 1993 Scott Johnson was arrested for stealing meat from his workplace. He was subsequently fired and became a truck driver. Scott's drinking and explosive temper had already strained the marriage. With Gretchen working long hours and Scott on the road as a truck driver, Mitchell and Monte began spending a lot of time at their maternal grandmother's home. She lived in a trailer park, and Scott Johnson did not like his children sleeping there. He complained that there was not enough room for them. One boy had to sleep on a sofa in the living room, and the other slept on the floor. Gretchen and Scott argued about the boys' living arrangements.

Although Mitchell's family life was difficult, it was not the worst thing he experienced. When Mitchell was eight years old, an older boy began raping him, a situation that went on for several years. In addition to the trauma of the sexual abuse, the rapist threatened to kill Mitchell's grandmother if the boy reported the abuse to anyone. Thus, sexual trauma was compounded by the terror of the threat to his grandmother. Making the situation even worse was the fact that Mitchell's younger brother, Monte, also became a victim of the rapist. Mitchell's inability to protect his brother probably left him with feelings of guilt, despair, and rage.

When Mitchell was 10 years old his parents divorced. According to a cousin, the boy's behavior deteriorated thereafter: "He'd get into fights, some physical, some verbal. He was easily pissed off."[4] Gretchen took Mitchell and Monte to live with her at her mother's during the divorce proceedings. Gretchen gave a vivid picture of how bitter the process was: "Scott was screaming, calling me…every name in the book. It was awful and ugly. He'd come busting through the door and he'd say… 'I'm going to keep these kids. It ain't a proper home for them here…I'll put them in a fucking foster home before they stay here with you,' and he slammed the door. Mitchell [began] throwing up."[5]

Despite the hardships at home and the sexual abuse, Mitchell managed surprisingly well. He was an honor roll student who enjoyed school, loved to sing, and was well behaved in the classroom. He was known as a mild-mannered boy.

Scott Johnson's threats to take the children came to nothing, and Gretchen moved with the boys to Arkansas, where she subsequently married a man named Terry Woodard; this was her third marriage. Woodard had been convicted of drug charges as well as the illegal use of a firearm. Despite his past, he was a good husband and father. Mitchell admired his stepfather and thought it was cool that he had been in prison.[6]

Mitchell made a remarkably good transition to life in Arkansas. He found friends. He went to church. He sang in the choir, performing for the elderly in nursing homes. He made the school football, baseball, and basketball teams. Not bad for a new kid, especially one with Mitchell's traumatic past.

In school, Mitchell received good grades and compliments for his politeness and manners. He addressed teachers as "ma'am" and "sir." A seventh-grade teacher sent a note to Mitchell's parents that said, "You can be very proud of your son. He is always so honest and polite to me. I want you and him to know I appreciate him."[7]

Even though his new home was in Arkansas, Mitchell returned to his father in Minnesota for his summer vacations. During the summer of 1997, he developed two obsessions: girls and gangs. The first was normal; the second was disturbing. In fact, according to his cousin Mike Niemeyer, Mitchell "said he'd give anything to be in a gang.... He'd kill anyone to be in a gang."[8] Why gangs and girls? They are both domains in which a boy can prove his masculinity. And Mitchell was entering puberty at this time.

His sexual awakening proved problematic. The onset of adolescence revived his memories of sexual abuse.[9] He was not able to control his sexual urges. During his summer vacation he was found in the presence of a two-year-old girl with his pants down. He said he had touched the girl's vagina. Sexual misbehavior is not unusual among victims of sexual abuse. During this same period Mitchell became suicidal. According to a friend, he was distraught after a girl he liked in Minnesota wanted nothing to do with him. He began crying and took a gun and a rope and was going to kill himself, but the friend talked him out of it.

Despite his sexual and romantic problems during the summer, Mitchell did well with girls at school. He was considered cute and dated a number of girls. Even so, there was something a little odd in his relationships. Mitchell took them very seriously—so seriously, in fact, that he talked to girls about marriage. At age 13, this was unusual behavior. Mitchell also seemed somewhat desperate to have numerous girls get their class photographs taken while they were wearing rings he had given them. He was trying hard—maybe too hard—but it was vitally important to him that he succeeded with girls.

This was not the only area where Mitchell tried too hard. Despite his politeness and good manners, he attempted to impress his peers as a dangerous kid. He tried to act cool and push kids around. Some described him as a bully with a bad temper who cursed at and threatened his classmates.

He bragged about being a gang member, only to have his peers dismiss his claims. (During a deposition in 2007, however, Mitchell insisted that he had been a member of the Bloods.) Thus, his attempts at being cool backfired; kids laughed at his gang talk and taunted him as a "wannabe" tough guy. Nevertheless, Mitchell was not an outcast. Between his athletic prowess, good grades, friendships, and girlfriends, he was doing quite well. All was not well behind the scenes, however.

The spring of 1998 became increasingly stressful for Mitchell. He racked up several hundred dollars' worth of charges calling telephone-sex lines. To make matters worse, he had used his father's credit card to do so. His father, furious, claimed Gretchen was not fit to raise Mitchell. He threatened to bring the boy back to Minnesota to live with him. The idea of living permanently with his father left Mitchell feeling frightened and hopeless.

Mitchell deteriorated even further. Just a couple of weeks before the shooting, he was kicked off the basketball team (or barred from joining—the sources do not agree) for carving his initials into his shoulder. Self-mutilation, or "cutting," is a common behavior in victims of sexual abuse, among others. There are many reasons why people hurt themselves. Some cut to induce a state of emotional numbness, using physical pain to distract themselves from psychological pain. Others cut to punish themselves. Mitchell's motivation remains unknown.

On top of losing status by being rejected from the basketball team, his girlfriend broke up with him. Around the same time, he was given an in-school suspension for getting into a struggle with teachers because he refused to remove his baseball cap indoors.

This was Mitchell's third in-school suspension. The first was in sixth grade, when he broke the glass case around a thermostat. Mitchell's second in-school suspension was for cursing at a teacher. He had also been paddled for cursing on the bus. None of Mitchell's misbehaviors was serious, however, and he was not viewed as a significant behavior problem in the school. Nonetheless, there were too many things happening to him.

One peer said that Mitchell had compiled a "death list" of people at the school, but no copy of this has been found, and Mitchell has denied writing anything about killing people. The same peer said that Mitchell complained of being "sick and tired" of everything. Another stated that the day before the attack, Mitchell said that he was going to shoot all the girls who had broken up with him. Someone else claimed that Mitchell said he was going to kill everyone who hated him and everyone he hated. Nine years later, Mitchell denied making any such threats the day before the attack. Nonetheless, over a dozen students reported having heard these threats firsthand. Regardless of what he may have said, there was no clear motive for the attack—it seems that Mitchell's frustration and anger built up to a point that he could not deal with it anymore. But why murder? Why not just kill himself?

Perhaps he wanted revenge. Shannon Wright, the teacher who was killed, was the one who put him on in-school suspension for breaking the glass around a thermostat. But that occurred when Mitchell was in sixth grade, two years before the attack. Was her death a result of vengeance or of simply being in the wrong place at the wrong time? In his 2007 deposition, Mitchell insisted that he did not target Ms. Wright and said that she was a good teacher whom he liked.

What about the other victims? According to a friend of Mitchell's, two of the girls had refused to go out with him. In addition, Candace, the girl who broke up with him shortly before the attack, was also a victim. Although the pattern of victims suggests revenge, this is not clear.

For example, Ms. Wright was protecting her students from the attack; a bullet that was aimed at someone else hit her instead. Also, ballistics could not always identify which boy shot which victim. Thus, the girls who would not go out with Mitchell could have been shot randomly by Drew rather than being targets of revenge by Mitchell. Mitchell denied that he aimed at anyone in particular and insisted he was quite upset when he saw that Candace had been hit. The questions of motive and intent remain ambiguous.

Who was the leader of the attack? The evidence, although not conclusive, points toward Drew. In an unguarded moment when first apprehended, Mitchell said that the attack was Drew's idea. Drew later told a worker in his detention program that he was the instigator. Thus, both boys identified Drew as the leader.

In addition, Drew was the one who had a preoccupation with guns and years of experience with firearms. He was the one who had access to the weapons they used; all the guns came from the homes of Drew's parents and grandparents. Drew was the one who pulled the fire alarm in the school to cause an evacuation. Finally, Drew was the more aggressive partner in the attack. The police investigation concluded that Mitchell fired 5 shots and Drew fired 25.[10]

The idea that Drew was the leader received a significant boost in 2007, when Mitchell was deposed. (Drew, unlike Mitchell, has not been deposed; we have no equivalent testimony from Drew to compare to Mitchell's account.)

He said that when Drew first mentioned the idea of the shooting, he refused to be part of it. At that point, Drew allegedly said that he wanted to scare people, not kill them. Drew brought up the topic again a few months later and asked Mitchell simply to provide the transportation. Mitchell agreed to do this, but expressed his concern that nobody would be hurt. This, of course, is at odds with the reports of students who claimed Mitchell made threats the day before the attack.

According to Mitchell's deposition, on the day of the attack, Drew asked him to join in the shooting. Mitchell acknowledged that he aimed and fired a rifle but said that he meant to shoot over people's heads. Even though he admitted to looking through the telescopic sight and being able to see people clearly, he denied any intent to kill. When pressed on this point, Mitchell simply repeated that he did not mean to hurt anybody and could not explain what happened.

How reliable is this testimony? Over a dozen students reported that Mitchell made threats prior to the attack. Thus, Mitchell's claim that Drew did not ask him to join in the shooting until the day of the attack is hard to credit. The same is true of his insistence that he did not mean to hurt anyone, especially since he acknowledged that he aimed through the rifle's scope.

Why did Mitchell participate in the attack? He tried to answer this question during his deposition: "Why I participated. I don't really know.... At the time of the shooting, I remember feeling like I was trapped, like no one understood me, you know what I mean? Like, I don't know. It just was—I felt cornered. I felt like I didn't have anywhere to go, nothing to do. I thought my life was at an end."[11] This passage suggests that Mitchell participated in the attack not because he was just going along with Drew, and not because he was angry with girls, but because he was desperate and depressed. He was also angry.

During his deposition, he denied that the attack had anything to do with in-school suspension or anything else that happened at school. Why then was he so angry?

One reason was his relationship with his father: "Me and my dad never got along, me and my real dad, Scott. I would go up there [to Minnesota], and I hated it."[12] Another reason was his history of sexual abuse: "After I hit puberty I recalled being molested. That had a lot to do with my anger, had a lot to do with why I was so mad all the time."[13] Victimization often creates a desire for revenge.

But why kill his peers? Perhaps he directed his rage at boys who rejected his gangster claims and girls who turned him down. These events may have triggered a deep sense of shame that was born in his history of abuse. If so, Mitchell was not the only traumatized boy to lash out against present targets rather than the deeper sources of his pain. (*This section's facts were drawn from Katherine Newman's research.*[14])

Son of Rambo

Evan Ramsey had a family curse. At least, he thought so. Eleven years before he committed a school shooting, his father, Don Ramsey, earned the nickname "Rambo of Alaska." When Evan was approximately five years old, there was a fire in the family's apartment. Don Ramsey reportedly blamed the fire on local politicians and bought space in the *Anchorage Times* in which to publish an open letter to a member of the government. When the paper refused to print the letter, Don Ramsey decided to take matters into his own hands. He showed up at the newspaper office like a soldier going to battle. In his own words, "I was armed and ready to go to war....I had an AR 180–223 semi-auto, something like 180 rounds of ammo for it. A snub barrel .44 magnum and about 30 rounds for it."[15]

Ramsey entered the newspaper building and chained the doors shut behind him. He set off smoke grenades and firecrackers, then fired into the ceiling and made his way to the publisher's office, where he held the man hostage. Despite stating that he was willing to die in his attempt to force the paper to print his letter, Ramsey was subdued by the publisher after a short standoff with police. Don Ramsey went to jail for approximately ten years. On January 13, 1997, Ramsey was released from prison. On February 9,

Ramsey called his son, Evan, and told him he was a free man. Ten days later, Evan went on a rampage of his own.

Being the son of the "Rambo of Alaska" was not Evan's only problem. Before the Rambo incident, the fire in the family's apartment resulted in a series of relocations. In addition, Evan's mother, Carol Ramsey, had a drinking problem, which predated her husband's imprisonment but apparently became worse after he was jailed: "Everything I did depended on alcohol. Every morning I would have beer for breakfast and drink all day," she said.[16] In 1995 Carol was charged with being drunk on a roadway; a year later she was charged with public drunkenness.[17]

Home life was unstable in other ways. Even before Don Ramsey went to prison, Carol had left him, moving with her three children to Fairbanks, where she led a life of "welfare and drinking."[18] Then Carol took up with a boyfriend in another town and moved her family in with him. She went from drinking beer to drinking whiskey. To make matters worse, the boyfriend was violent. She left him and moved her family in with yet another boyfriend in another town. Carol's drinking continued, and the new boyfriend was also violent.

The home situation deteriorated to the point that when Evan was seven years old, the Division of Family and Youth Services intervened. When a worker showed up at her home, Carol was too drunk to speak. Her three sons were huddled together in an unheated apartment. The temperature outside was 22 degrees below zero.

Evan and his brothers were removed from their mother's care and went through two or three years of being in and out of foster homes. Every now and then the boys would be returned to Carol. When she could not maintain her sobriety, they would be sent back to foster care. One night a boyfriend of Carol's hit her oldest son, John. John, who was perhaps all of nine years old at the time (Evan was approximately seven), decided that he had had enough. He led his two younger brothers out into an Alaskan winter night, in subzero temperatures, to escape the violence at home. The boys had to be desperate to risk their lives. They took refuge in the enclosed porch of their school principal's house. From there they were returned to foster care.

At this point things really went downhill. Over a period of two to three years, Evan and his younger brother, William, were placed in ten foster homes. This amount of instability can be overwhelming for a child, even if all the families are full of love and support. In Evan's case, the quality of care was perhaps the most traumatic factor in his life. In one of the homes, the biological son of the foster parents physically and sexually abused the boys. Evan was found to have bruises on his face and neck from the physical abuse. The sexual abuse was particularly degrading—the boy forced Evan and William to let him urinate in their mouths.

Very few preadolescents commit—or even attempt—suicide. It is not surprising, however, that Evan attempted suicide at age ten. He began walking into the ocean to drown himself; whether someone stopped him or he changed his mind remains unknown. Why would a ten-year-old want to die? We know that he lost his home in a fire and moved frequently after that. We know that his father was incarcerated for years. We know that his mother was an alcoholic and had violent boyfriends. We know that he bounced from foster home to foster home and that he was abused in at least one of them. Having experienced all of this by the age of ten, it is no wonder that Evan became suicidal.

Beyond what we know, more stresses than have come to light may have existed. Don Ramsey had been willing to consider killing people in order to get a letter printed; what kind of father and husband was he? What was life like in the Ramsey home when he was there? And when he was not there, how bad were things with Evan's mother? And what about all the foster homes besides the one where the abuse occurred—how stable and nurturing were they? An adopted son who was a convicted sex offender also lived in the home in which Evan was living at the time of the shooting. This does not mean that Evan was abused in that home, but he could have been an easy target. Thus, it is possible that there were far more traumas in Evan's life than have been made public.

There were other problems as well. Evan's older brother, John, engaged in criminal behavior starting at age 12, including theft and assault. Evan himself got into a conflict with his peers and was beaten up by a student named Josh Palacios. Evan's temper became a serious problem. In 1996 the police were called to his foster home because he had kicked a hole in a wall and threatened his foster mother's daughter. At school, there were multiple incidents of explosive anger in which he threw things and stormed out of the building. In the academic year of 1995 to 1996, he racked up a dozen disciplinary infractions. In 1995 Evan had again become suicidal.

He called a friend and said, "You've got five minutes to get over here or I'm going to shoot myself."[19] Somewhere along the way Evan began using drugs, presumably to ease his suffering and escape from the reality of his troubled life.

In the weeks leading up to the attack, several things happened that compounded Evan's rage and anguish. Ten days before the attack, his father called to say that he had been released from jail. What this meant to Evan is unknown; perhaps the prospect of living with his father was terrifying. Around the same time, his girlfriend of several months broke up with him and moved away. A week before the attack, the dean of students confiscated Evan's CD player. This was a minor event, but it added to the boy's anger. Also, a week before Evan's rampage, his brother John was arrested for armed robbery of a pornography shop. Perhaps he too was haunted by the family curse.

Eventually Evan reached the breaking point. On February 19, 1997, he went to school and shot Josh Palacios (the student who had beaten him up) and the principal (not the one who took him in years before), killing both. The same shotgun blast that killed Josh also wounded two other students. Then Evan walked the halls, firing into lockers. Finally he put his gun under his chin to kill himself, but did not pull the trigger. He went to jail and will likely remain there for the rest of his life.

The most disturbing aspect of Evan's attack is that initially he did not intend to commit murder but was goaded into it by his peers. Evan wanted to bring a gun to school to frighten the kids who picked on him and then kill himself. When Evan told two friends (one of whom was also a cousin) about his plans, instead of talking him out of it or going to an adult for help, they convinced him to kill people. With their encouragement, Evan made a hit list of 3 people. His friends gave him 11 more names to add to the list.

Evan was told he would become famous: "[My friend] said that my face and name would go across the world. He said I'll become famous. He said lots of people will know about me. He said I should live the fame."[20] One of Evan's friends actually taught him to use a 12-gauge shotgun, and another promised to bring his own gun to school to back Evan up in the attack. The conversation about killing himself happened four or five days before the attack itself. Evan was shown how to use a shotgun the day before the attack.

In addition to his two friends knowing about the upcoming attack, many other students knew something big was going to happen. A group of students even gathered to watch. One boy brought a camera for the occasion. At one point a girl told another student who was on a balcony to view the attack: "You're not supposed to be up here. . . . You're on the list."[21] Although many students knew about the planned attack, no one reported anything to parents or teachers. The police did not charge the students who simply knew about the attack ahead of time; they did arrest the two friends who encouraged Evan. One of them pleaded guilty to criminally negligent homicide, the other was convicted of second-degree murder.

Did Evan provide any insight into his behavior? A note was found in his bedroom after the attack; he expected to have committed homicide and suicide by the time the note was found. He wrote about killing the principal, though he did not say why. Later reports stated that it was one of Evan's friends who hated the principal and urged Evan to kill him. Evan also complained in his note about the "negative" treatment he received but did not provide any specifics: "The main reason that I did this is because I am sick and tired of being treated this way every day. . . . Life sucks in its own way, so I killed a little and kill myself."[22]

After the fact, Evan said, "My main objective of going into the high school was to check out. . . . To commit suicide."[23] Evan had been suicidal for several years prior to the shooting, and his note clearly indicated that he planned to kill himself. When it came time, however, he found he could not do it.

How badly had Evan's peers treated him? Josh Palacios (and others) threw wads of toilet paper at Evan. After the attack, Evan said, "I'd be called a piece of shit, a bastard. I—I've been called a spaz and a retard."[24] Does such harassment explain a murderous response? In retrospect, Evan does not think so. Reflecting on the boy he killed, Evan said, "Now I look back . . . and I wonder why did I let him get me so upset? Big deal that he said I was stupid."[25]

Although Evan was harassed at school, he was not friendless. Besides the two boys who encouraged his attack, he had other friends, both boys and girls. In fact, he was said to have been friends with some of the brightest students in the school. Thus, he was not a loner. It is worth noting, however, that Josh Palacios not only harassed Evan and beat him in a fight, he was also a popular boy who was attractive to girls and the star of the basketball team. In terms of status, he was everything that Evan was not. As with other shooters, we see the intersection of two issues: anger at mistreatment and envy regarding differential status.

In hindsight, Evan identified several issues that came together in driving him toward violence. Yes, he was angry about having his CD player confiscated. But it was more than that: "[My] girlfriend said 'fuck you' and disappeared. And everybody constantly coming at me and messing with me and messing with me. And I don't know who my parents are; that was another thing that hurts. It seemed like all my friends knew their fathers. And James and Matthew [his two friends] were getting me all riled up: 'yeah, it would be [expletive] awesome.'"[26] Even though Evan sought out and killed a boy who had harassed him, this was not simply an act of revenge. To say that the attack was caused by a desire for revenge ignores the devastating accumulation of stresses Evan endured year after year. It also ignores the fact that initially Evan planned to kill himself and no one else. His friends talked him into committing murder. A desire for revenge may have influenced Evan's choice of victim, but it was not the cause of his attack.

Yes, he was picked on, but the attack was not really about that. It was about everything else that had happened to him: his father in jail, his alcoholic mother, the foster homes, the abuse, his suicidal depression. And perhaps it was a matter of following in the footsteps of the Rambo of Alaska. Evan was aware of his father's bizarre attack at the newspaper. Did he look up to his father as some kind of macho warrior? Did he feel destined to follow in his father's footsteps? Whatever it was, Evan called it a family curse.[27]

"16 Years of Accumulated Rage"

If Evan Ramsey had a family curse, he was not alone. Jeffrey Weise had a similar family history and a similar "curse." In fact, Jeffrey's family history was perhaps more traumatic than that of any other school shooter. Although there are many gaps in the story, it is clear that trouble began early in Jeffrey's life.

Jeffrey was a Native American of the Ojibwa (Chippewa) tribe. He lived alternately in Minneapolis and Red Lake, Minnesota, which is a reservation of approximately 5,000 people. Although his parents were never married, he spent his first three months with his mother and father, Joanna Weise and Daryl Lussier, Jr. Then, for an undisclosed reason, from the age of three months to three years, Jeffrey lived with his father. His mother stayed in Minneapolis, while Jeffrey moved with his father to Red Lake.

At age three, Jeffrey moved back in with his mother. Life with her was far from stable. When Jeffrey was four, Joanna Weise was jailed for driving while intoxicated. A few months later she was jailed again, this time for assault. She later became involved with a man named Timothy DesJarlait and had two children with him.

Jeffrey was shuffled among family members, living for a time with his mother, a grandfather, and a grandmother. Occasionally he even spent the night at the house of a woman who was a "cultural coordinator" at the Red Lake Middle School. He was also in and out of foster homes. Apart from his mother's brief incarcerations, the frequent shifting of homes and caregivers was a result of two family tragedies.

On July 21, 1997, Jeffrey's father, Daryl Lussier, Jr., engaged in a daylong armed standoff with police. To make matters worse, Jeffrey's grandfather, Daryl Lussier, Sr., was one of the police officers involved. Jeffrey's grandfather tried to talk his son into surrendering without hurting anyone, but the attempt failed. Jeffrey's father chose not to surrender and killed himself. He was 31 years old. Jeffrey was 8. This was the first tragedy.

Approximately two years later, Jeffrey's mother and a cousin went out drinking. The cousin was driving drunk and got into a car accident; she was killed. Jeffrey's mother survived, but suffered brain damage. She went to a nursing home, where she was wheelchair bound and had to learn basic skills all over again. This was the second tragedy.

In between these traumatic events, Jeffrey's mother married Timothy DesJarlait, who was said to have had a drinking problem. He left her after she was in the car accident. When she could no longer function as a mother, the stepfamily took in the couple's two children, but did not take Jeffrey. Thus, within two years, Jeffrey lost his father to suicide, his mother to brain damage, and his stepfather and half-siblings to separation.

These losses were not the only sources of agony in young Jeffrey's life. Even before his mother's car accident, she had provided little in the way of love and nurturing: "My mom used to abuse me a lot when I was little. She would hit me with anything she could get her hands on, she used to drink excessively, too. She would tell me I was a mistake, and she would say so many things that it's hard to deal with them or think of them without crying."[28] In addition, Jeffrey's mother and an unidentified paramour mistreated the boy in other ways. For example, he was locked out of his house, locked in a closet, and forced to kneel in a corner for hours.

Jeffrey Weise was an abused child who had an alcoholic mother. He lived with a succession of family members and foster families. He lost his father to suicide and his mother to brain damage. Beyond what we know, what other stresses did Jeffrey endure? What kind of man was Jeffrey's father? Why was he involved in an armed standoff with police? What problems was he struggling with, and how did these affect his son?

Whatever the factors were, on March 21, 2005, Jeffrey carried out his long-planned attack. He killed his grandfather and his grandfather's girlfriend at their home. Then Jeffrey took his grandfather's police firearms and bulletproof vest and drove the police cruiser to school, where he gunned down a security guard and entered the school. Then he killed five students and one teacher and wounded seven other people.

As always, our first question is "Why?" Although Jeffrey wrote extensively, most of his available writings are fiction, with only minimal journal-type messages from his Web pages. He may have been somewhat isolated because he had not attended school for several weeks. The reason for this has been reported variously as a medical problem, a learning problem, a result of his behavior problems, and an attempt to protect him from being picked on. According to his grandmother, however, Jeffrey was being tutored at home on the recommendation of a counselor from the reservation hospital. Whatever the truth, Jeffrey had been out of school for approximately five weeks before the attack.

He had been suicidal for some time. He expressed his desperation vividly: "Most people have never dealt with people who have faced the kind of pain that makes you physically sick at times, makes you so depressed you can't function, makes you so sad and overwhelmed with grief that eating a bullet or sticking your head in a noose seems welcoming."[29]

Jeffrey reached the point where he tried to kill himself by cutting his wrist; the attempt was serious enough to get him hospitalized. Several months after the attempt he posted the following message online:

> I had went through a lot of things in my life that had driven me to a darker path than most choose to take. I split the flesh on my wrist with a box opener, painting the floor of my bedroom with blood I shouldn't have spilt. After sitting there for what seemed like hours (which apparently was only minutes), I had the revelation that this was not the path. It was my decision to seek medical treatment, as on the other hand I could've chose to sit there until enough blood drained from my downward lacerations on my wrists to die.[30]

Jeffrey was prescribed Prozac, an antidepressant medication, but it did not seem to help. He continued to struggle. He engaged in cutting his skin on several occasions, scratching wounds in his flesh with the metal at the end of a pencil. Marijuana was his drug of choice, and he smoked it frequently. He flunked eighth grade. He wrote violent stories, drew violent pictures, and made brief animated sequences of murder and suicide. He summed up his life in this way: "16 years of accumulated rage suppressed by nothing more than brief glimpses of hope, which have all but faded to black."[31]

Two months before the attack, Jeffrey wrote this on his Web page:

> So fucking naive man, so fucking naive. Always expecting change when I know nothing ever changes. I've seen mothers choose their man over their own flesh and blood. I've seen others choose alcohol over friendship. I sacrifice no more for others, part of me has fucking died and I hate this shit. I'm living every man's nightmare and that single fact alone is kicking my ass. I really must be fucking worthless. This place never changes, it never will. Fuck it all.[32]

The reference to mothers choosing "their man over their own flesh and blood" could well refer to his own mother. The reference to people choosing alcohol over friendship remains a mystery. Similarly, although Jeffrey's anger and desperation is clear, he does not explain what is driving him to the edge. What did he mean by "every man's nightmare?" Is he referring to the loss of his parents? The abuse he endured? Or was it something else?

A puzzling and disturbing aspect of Jeffrey was his interest in the Nazis. He posted this message on a neo-Nazi Web site: "I stumbled across this site in my study of the Third Reich as well as Nazism, amongst other things. I guess I've always carried a natural admiration for Hitler and his ideals."[33] He signed himself "Todesengel," which is German for "Angel of Death." Elsewhere online he referred to himself as a "Native American National Socialist" and "Native Nazi."

The idea of a Native Nazi seems like a contradiction, as the Nazis viewed "non-Aryan" races as inferior. How could a Native American be a neo-Nazi? Jeffrey wrote that he admired Hitler's "courage to take on larger nations."[34] Thus, as with Eric Harris, Jeffrey's identification with Hitler was an attempt to identify with a source of power.

There is another disturbing parallel with Eric Harris and his preoccupation with natural selection and the survival of the fittest. Jeffrey posted this quote from Hitler online: "The law of existence requires uninterrupted killing...So that the better may live."[35] Eric clearly articulated his desire to rid the world of inferior people. Did Jeffrey really share this ideology? Or was he clinging to it as a justification for murder? Was Jeffrey using Nazi ideology to rationalize revenge against his peers?

Jeffrey made an interesting comment online about his attraction to the Nazis: "I've been feeling a strong connection toward Nazi Germany, and it's not necessarily the most pleasing thought, though I can't help it."[36] This statement indicates that Jeffrey was troubled by his attraction to the Nazis, and although he wasn't happy about it, he felt it was beyond his control. Clearly, the attraction was filling some unmet need of his that he could not comprehend.

There are multiple reports that Jeffrey was teased or harassed by some of his peers, as well as multiple reports that he was not picked on. The evidence is so mixed that it is impossible to know for sure what really happened to him at school.

According to his aunt, Jeffrey was picked on because of his appearance, but this was not a daily occurrence, nor was it severe. Other people, however, said that Jeffrey was consistently picked on and that the harassment was excessive. Yet Michelle Kingbird, a friend, stated that Jeffrey was not a target of teasing.

Jeffrey himself noted that his size and appearance were deterrents to being picked on. He reportedly was six foot three and between 250 and 300 pounds, a formidable size. He also tended to dress in black and for a while wore bits of his hair in small horns. In his own words: "Because of my size and appearance people don't give me as much trouble as they would if I looked weak."[37]

Reports that describe Jeffrey as a loner are wrong. A girl named Jen commented that the people who said Jeffrey had no friends did not know what they were talking about: "They never talked to him. He was the nicest guy you'd ever want to meet."[38] Alicia, a girl who knew Jeffrey, said, "He seemed like a pretty good guy.... Whenever I talked with him, he seemed all friendly."[39] Michelle had this to say about Jeffrey: "He was funny. He was cool.... Any time I felt sad, he made me feel happy.... He always made me laugh."[40] Yet another girl stated, "He was always trying to help other people with their problems."[41]

Jeffrey played guitar and was part of a band. In one of his online postings, he commented that he had friends, although he wondered why they liked him and vice versa. These friends may have been the "Darkers," a group of boys outside the mainstream peer culture. The same month as the attack, Jeffrey watched the movie *Elephant*, about a school shooting, with a couple of male friends. Perhaps his best friend was his cousin Louis Jourdain. They were both 16, went to school together, and communicated regularly by e-mail. After the attack, 900 pages of their Internet conversations were reviewed as evidence. Thus, the reports that Jeffrey never spoke to anyone simply were not true. Although he was not in the mainstream of the local peer culture, he engaged with both male and female friends and acquaintances.

Perhaps even harder to understand than the random killing of his peers is the murder of his paternal grandfather. At the time of the attack, Jeffrey was living with his paternal grandmother (the grandparents were separated), although he spent time at his grandfather's house. Family members reported that Jeffrey and his grandfather loved each other and that they always got along well. This seems unlikely, given not only the fact that Jeffrey murdered him, but that he fired at least ten shots into his grandfather's head and chest. This suggests that Jeffrey felt overwhelming rage toward his grandfather. In addition, Jeffrey killed Michelle Sigana, his grandfather's girlfriend. Why? Are there any clues to Jeffrey's motivation for these murders?

According to law enforcement agents who investigated the shootings, Jeffrey was angry with his grandfather because he had left Jeffrey's grandmother for another woman, Michelle Sigana. Does this explain Jeffrey's rage toward the pair? Perhaps. But perhaps there was a deeper source of rage, one that Jeffrey's writings might reveal.

As noted, most of Jeffrey's writings that are available to the public are short stories. His stories were typically violent, with a special interest in zombies. Using fiction to understand someone is problematic, but in the absence of other clues, it is worth speculating.

In one of the stories, a character confronts a hit man and says, "You were the guy who killed my father."[42] The character then guns down the hit man. I cannot help wondering if Jeffrey said something similar to his grandfather before killing him. After all, his grandfather was involved in the armed standoff when Jeffrey's father committed suicide. Did Jeffrey blame his grandfather for his father's death?

Another story seems to echo Jeffrey's own life. In it, a man talks to his friends about growing up with a father who was a police officer. Jeffrey's father grew up with a father who was a police officer. Later in the story, the friends discover that the man has committed suicide. Jeffrey's father committed suicide. Thus, in both his life and his fiction, a man who was the son of a police officer killed himself. This story may have been Jeffrey's attempt to cope with his family trauma.

In a gruesome plot twist, however, the man who killed himself comes back to life as a zombie. He is gunned down with multiple shots to his head, neck, and chest. Perhaps this addition to the story expressed Jeffrey's rage at his father. How does a boy cope with the loss of his father by suicide? Confused feelings of anger and grief would not be surprising. Perhaps he was angry with his father for ending his life and with his grandfather for not being able to save the father.

Another piece of Jeffrey's creativity is worth mentioning. He made a 30-second animated video that shows a gunman killing people and then killing himself. Three aspects of this animation were prophetic. The most obvious is the cold-blooded shooting of innocent people. Another is the gunman's suicide by shooting himself in the head. In between these events, however, the killer blows up a police car with a grenade. Was this a foreshadowing of his murder of his police-officer grandfather?

Apart from feelings of rage, other feelings may have been involved. We do not know what Jeffrey thought of his father, what he knew about the circumstances of his father's death, and how he viewed his father's suicide. Did Jeffrey look up to his father? Was Daryl Lussier, Jr., his role model? Was the school shooting an imitation of his father's own armed standoff with police? Did he feel condemned to follow in his father's footsteps?

Jeffrey wrote a passage that suggests he may have admired his father for committing suicide. Or perhaps it was a way of preparing for his own death: "I think it takes a lot of courage to accept death.... It takes courage to turn the gun on yourself, takes courage to face death. Knowing you're going to die and actually following through takes heart."[43]

In addition to Jeffrey's traumatic family history and being picked on to some extent by his peers, there was another factor to consider in understanding the attack. Jeffrey did not plan it alone. He and his cousin Louis apparently had been planning the attack for months. Although their e-mail conversations have not been made public, they reportedly contained references to the upcoming attack.

On the day of the attack, before Louis saw that it was Jeffrey who was shooting, Louis told people that the attacker was Jeffrey. He *knew*. And because he knew and had been part of the planning, he was charged for his role in the attack. Although the initial charge of conspiracy to murder was dropped, Louis pleaded guilty to a charge of sending threatening messages over the Internet. His role in the planning remains unclear. It is also unknown why Jeffrey committed the attack without his cousin. Perhaps Jeffrey's rage became too great to contain and his desire to live had worn away. The end result? Another boy following in the footsteps of his father, but with more deadly results.

Traumatized Shooters

A single trauma can have a profound impact on a child; the traumatized shooters each endured multiple traumas. All three boys were emotionally and physically abused at home. Evan was beaten by a succession of violent men whom his mother lived with as well as by a boy in foster care. Jeffrey was beaten by his mother and mistreated by the men his mother became involved with. Mitchell was abused and terrorized by his father. Perhaps even worse than physical abuse, two of the three traumatized shooters were sexually abused. An older boy in the neighborhood raped Mitchell repeatedly over several years, and Evan was molested in a foster home.

Physical and sexual abuse can have devastating consequences, including anxiety, rage, depression, and suicide. Traumas affect people's identities and relationships. Due to the trauma, they may have a sense of being damaged and have trouble relating to others. Their ability to trust people is affected, as is their ability to love and feel connected to others.

In addition to traumas, the traumatized shooters lived with ongoing stresses and significant losses. All three had substance-abusing parents. This alone can severely impair family functioning. When this is combined with severe traumas, the damage is compounded. All three boys also moved around from one home to another. For Evan and Jeffrey, these moves were frequent, and often involved foster homes. Such moves can be highly stressful for children, as they repeatedly leave behind friends and caregivers and enter new environments.

A closer look at Evan and Jeffrey reveals a remarkable number of similarities. Both boys were Native American—Jeffrey on both sides, and Evan on his mother's (she was part Eskimo and part Athapascan).[44] Evan and Jeffrey both had lost their fathers, one to jail and one to suicide. They both had alcoholic mothers who were neglectful and/or abusive and who had abusive boyfriends. A year or two after losing their fathers, they each lost their mothers to some extent. In one case by being removed from her care due to her drinking, and in the other as a result of her brain damage. Both boys ended up in foster care. They both used drugs. They both became suicidal. They were both picked on at school to some extent. They both had friends who were involved in planning their attacks. In Jeffrey's case, this friend was also his cousin. Similarly, one of Evan's two friends who encouraged the attack was a cousin.

Although Mitchell also had a history of abuse, his life differed from Evan's and Jeffrey's in significant ways. His mother was not alcoholic or abusive. Mitchell's parents divorced and his mother relocated, but he was never in foster care. He spent time with his grandmother when things got bad between his parents, but he was never out of the care of a family member.

Nevertheless, the events leading up to Mitchell's and Evan's attacks have several parallels. Both had disciplinary issues at school shortly before their rampages. Both had break-ups with girls a week or two before the attacks. They both faced the prospect of living with their fathers again, which may been frightening. In Mitchell's case, his father was so angry at his misbehavior that he threatened to take him away from his mother. In Evan's case, his father was released from prison and called him to reestablish contact. Thus, on top of their histories of abuse, numerous events converged that contributed to their desperation, depression, and rage.

What was life like for the traumatized shooters? First of all, the world was unpredictable. Parental alcoholism and bad tempers meant that the boys never knew what each day would bring. Maybe they would be nurtured, maybe they would be abused. They moved from one family member to another and back again or from one foster home to another. Stability was unknown. Outside of their families, two of them endured cruel, degrading sexual abuse. They lost parents to separation, jail, and death.

They were depressed to the point of contemplating suicide. They were likely ashamed of themselves, their families, their abuse. Life was overwhelming. They began smoking marijuana. They tried to get along at school, but their social skills were not the best and they were teased. They engaged in self-mutilation and suicide attempts. Life was unfair and the world was cruel. People could not be trusted. On top of it all, they were angry. Angry at life. Angry for living in hell. Despite all this, they were not crazy or evil, just wounded. Badly. They sought a way to end their misery. Unfortunately, they created even more suffering.

THE BIGGER PICTURE

6

BEYOND THE TYPOLOGY

Many different kinds of people engage in violent acts; though their overt behavior seems similar, their psychological makeup may be at polar extremes.

—Dr. Aaron Beck

DYLAN KLEBOLD DROVE HIS own BMW and lived in a spectacular home with a swimming pool, tennis court, and basketball court; Evan Ramsey lived in an unheated apartment in Alaska. Michael Carneal was the son of respected, law-abiding, loving parents; Jeffrey Weise was the son of a father who committed suicide during a police standoff and an alcoholic, abusive mother. Despite their differences, however, all these boys—as well as the others presented in this book—engaged in similar acts of violence. The starting point for understanding school shooters is to recognize the three categories of shooters: psychopathic, psychotic, and traumatized.

A comparison of the similarities and differences among the three types can shed further light on rampage school shootings. Before proceeding, however, I must make two points:

1. The three types of shooters that I discuss are not necessarily the only types. Shooters not discussed in this book may not fit this typology.

2. Shooters could fit more than one type. For example, there is no reason why a psychotic child could not also be traumatized.

Among the ten shooters presented here, however, the types do not overlap.

In order to illustrate the typology, I have placed the school shooters into one of three categories. Exhibit 6.1 presents the classification scheme, with the shooters presented in chronological order within each type.

A couple of points need to be made about the exhibit. First, psychopathy is not simply the absence of trauma and psychosis but also the presence of narcissism, callousness, immorality, and other features. Second, the category of psychotic refers to schizophrenia-spectrum disorders, such as schizophrenia and schizotypal personality disorder. Of the five psychotic shooters, four were schizophrenic; only Dylan Klebold was schizotypal.

Even though Eric Harris's narcissism appears to have crossed the line into delusions of grandeur, he does not belong in the psychotic category. Psychotic symptoms can be seen in many diagnoses, including personality disorders. Thus, Eric may have been psychotic without having a schizophrenia spectrum disorder. His primary type was the psychopathic. Conversely, although Dylan imitated Eric's psychopathic behavior, his primary type was the psychotic.

Exhibit 6.1 The Typology and the 10 Shooters

Name	Trauma	Schizophrenia Spectrum	Category
Drew Golden	No	No	Psychopathic
Eric Harris	No	No	Psychopathic
Michael Carneal	No	Yes	Psychotic
Andrew Wurst	No	Yes	Psychotic
Kip Kinkel	No	Yes	Psychotic
Dylan Klebold	No	Yes	Psychotic
Seung Hui Cho	No	Yes	Psychotic
Evan Ramsey	Yes	No	Traumatized
Mitchell Johnson	Yes	No	Traumatized
Jeffrey Weise	Yes	No	Traumatized

Beyond the Typology

Most people who are psychopathic are not mass murderers. Most psychotic people do not commit murder. Most traumatized people never kill anyone. Thus, although the typology is a step forward in understanding the shooters, the labels by themselves do not explain why these youths became killers. We need to look beyond the typology for additional factors that make the shooters different from other people who are psychopathic, psychotic, or traumatized.

What makes psychopathic shooters different from other psychopathic kids? One key factor is the presence of sadism. Although it might seem natural to associate sadism with psychopaths, they do not necessarily go together. For example, Dr. Robert Hare has studied psychopaths for years and compiled a list of 20 traits that define psychopathy.[1] Sadism is not one of them. Callousness, or a lack of empathy, is a core psychopathic trait. This, however, is not the same as sadism.

Similarly, the diagnostic criteria for antisocial personality disorder—the psychiatric diagnosis that most resembles the psychopathic personality—do not include sadism. Antisocial people are indifferent to the pain they cause others. Not caring about hurting people, however, is different from actively seeking out opportunities for inflicting pain on people so that you can experience a sense of power. Thus, people who are antisocial are not by definition sadistic.

Neither are sadistic people necessarily antisocial or psychopathic. Many people with sadistic personalities are not criminals. They can be found in all walks of life. They may be corporate executives, college professors, or drill sergeants. They may threaten and intimidate their coworkers, spouses, or children. They may like to make people squirm with fear. Because they are sadistic, they derive a fulfilling sense of power from their harsh treatment of those around them. This kind of sadism, however, is not a crime.

Thus, psychopaths are not necessarily sadistic, and sadists are not necessarily criminal. It is when psychopathic features, such as antisocial and narcissistic traits, are blended with a sadistic personality that the combination is particularly dangerous. This combination existed in the psychopathic school shooters.

Another common feature in the psychopathic shooters is that both boys came from families in which weapons had been an accepted part of life for at least two generations. Eric Harris's father was a retired air force pilot who also owned guns as a civilian. Eric's paternal grandfather was a World War II veteran. Drew Golden's grandfather was a hunter and game warden, and his parents were leaders of a local pistol association. As discussed in chapter 2, Drew and Eric not only grew up in families with traditions of law-abiding gun use, but both boys had a gun fetish. Many children grow up in homes where firearms are a normal part of life but most do not develop a fetish for guns. What was different about Drew and Eric? They were narcissistic, antisocial, and sadistic; they wanted power. Given their personalities, perhaps the presence of firearms was an irresistible temptation.

The two psychopathic shooters also had peer support for the attacks. They were the leaders of the attacks and recruited nonpsychopathic peers to collaborate with them. Of all the attacks examined in this volume, only two involved a pair of boys. In both, one boy was psychopathic and one was not. Both pairs consisted of a boy with too much ego and a boy with too little ego. Eric, who was grandiose, teamed up with Dylan, whose schizotypal personality left him feeling extraordinarily inadequate. Drew, who was narcissistic, teamed up with Mitchell, whose traumatic history left him with severe insecurity.

Perhaps the psychopaths needed to play the role of leader, and thus recruited followers. Perhaps they would not have carried out the attacks on their own. Thus, beyond their sadism and narcissism, they may have needed the support of a partner or follower to become mass murderers.

What makes the psychotic shooters different from other psychotic kids? Although many people may think there is a connection between mental illness and violence, this is a misconception. Schizophrenics are no more prone to violence than the general population. Several factors, however, are correlated with violence among schizophrenics.

The first factor correlated with a higher incidence of schizophrenic violence is easy to identify: being male. All four schizophrenic shooters were male. Although it is unknown whether it is a result of biology or culture, or most likely a combination of the two, male schizophrenics are more likely to become violent than female schizophrenics.

Another factor correlated with violence among schizophrenics is excessive substance abuse. Most of the psychotic shooters used drugs and alcohol. Details about their substance abuse, however, are lacking. Thus, it is difficult to determine what—if any—influence substance abuse had on their attacks. None was found to have been drunk or high at the time of the shootings. Dylan, however, used alcohol and marijuana, as did Michael and Andrew. We know that Kip used alcohol. Whether Seung used drugs or alcohol is unknown.

Substance abuse can contribute to violence in a couple of ways. First, drugs and alcohol impair one's judgment and impulse control. People do things while under the influence that they would not ordinarily do. Second, substance abuse can impair one's sense of reality. For people who already are losing touch with what is real, drugs can push them even further into psychosis.

The third factor that is correlated with violence among schizophrenics is lack of compliance in taking their antipsychotic medication. None of the psychotic shooters had even been prescribed antipsychotic medications. Their symptoms had either gone undetected or were unrecognized as psychosis. Without medication, the shooters were at increased risk of violence.

The final factor related to violence in schizophrenia is youth. Younger schizophrenics are more likely to be violent than older ones. The median onset of schizophrenia among males is the mid-20s.[2] Schizophrenia is a devastating condition, even for adults. What is the impact when it begins in adolescence, or even earlier? In addition to all the stresses of growing up, imagine having to cope with hallucinations, delusions, and the inability to live a normal life. Perhaps it is not surprising that all five psychotic shooters were suicidal. In fact, the rate of suicide among schizophrenics is 1 in 10^3; the rate in the U.S. population as a whole is approximately 1 in 10,000. Thus, the rate of suicide among schizophrenics is 1,000 times higher than among the general population.

Beyond the four factors just discussed, however, other influences were at work. One factor is family structure. All five psychotic shooters were the youngest children in their families. All had higher-functioning siblings, some of whom were high-achieving "stars." What is the impact on identity when one is not only significantly impaired but has high-functioning parents and older siblings? This small sample suggests that the impact is devastating.

A further consequence of their impairment is significant conflict with parents. Several of the psychotic shooters clearly felt rejected by their fathers, and some displayed strange and/or hostile behavior toward their mothers. Michael Carneal wrote a story in which the narrator (named Michael) presented his mother a gift of five mutilated bodies. Andrew Wurst felt rejected by his father and told people his mother was a prostitute. Kip Kinkel had severe, ongoing conflict with his father. Seung Hui Cho's father—perhaps in frustration or anger over his son's strange behavior—refused to praise him.

What about the role of peer influence? This was not a significant factor among the psychotic shooters. In only one case was there significant peer influence to commit a school shooting: Dylan probably would not have committed homicide without Eric leading the way. It is interesting that Dylan, the least impaired of the psychotic shooters, was the one who had peer influence to commit murder. Perhaps Eric's influence compensated for Dylan's "lack" of schizophrenia. Thus, although Dylan was not as impaired as the other psychotic shooters, he experienced powerful peer influence to kill. In the other four cases, none of the shooters' peers took part, or were arrested for having a role, in the shootings.

Apart from peer influence, however, infamous people did influence the shooters. Dylan identified with Charles Manson and his "family." Michael Carneal was interested in the Unabomber. Andrew Wurst was quite taken by the two shooters in Jonesboro, Arkansas. Kip Kinkel was also a "fan" of the Unabomber and thought the Jonesboro shooting was "cool." Seung Hui Cho identified with Harris and Klebold, whom he referred to as "martyrs." Each of these shooters felt like a "nobody," and each found a more powerful "somebody" to identify with and, in some cases, emulate.

Finally, what are the salient factors that all three traumatized shooters had in common? First, simply having violent and/or criminal fathers might mean that the boys were genetically at risk for violence. The combination of genetic inheritance and environmental influences may have left these boys highly vulnerable to violent behavior. It is impossible to know how much of their behavior was due to biology versus experience.

For example, two of the three boys had fathers who engaged in armed standoffs with police. Evan's father, the Rambo of Alaska, was ready to go to war because a newspaper refused to print his letter. (In addition,

Evan's older brother committed armed robbery five days before Evan attacked the school.) Jeffrey's father killed himself in an armed standoff with police. Men who engage in such standoffs are extremely rare; the fact that two out of three of the traumatized shooters had such fathers is a remarkable parallel. How do we understand this parallel? Were Evan and Jeffrey genetically prone to violence? Or was the parallel a result of imitation? Did Evan and Jeffrey admire their fathers? Did they feel destined to follow in their footsteps? After the attack, Evan referred to his "family curse." We do not know, however, how he viewed his father's act prior to his own shooting. We also do not know Jeffrey's attitude toward his father.

Not only did Evan and Jeffrey end up in armed standoffs like their fathers but each came to the same end as his father. Evan's father was captured and went to jail; Evan was captured and went to jail. Jeffrey's father committed suicide in front of the police; Jeffrey committed suicide in front of the police. Like father, like son.

How does Mitchell Johnson fit into this pattern? Although Mitchell's father was never in an armed standoff with police, Scott Johnson had been arrested at least once for theft, and Mitchell's stepfather had been incarcerated for drug charges and a weapons violation. Mitchell reportedly admired his stepfather and thought that it was cool that he had been in prison. Thus, both his father and stepfather had committed crimes, and the stepfather had engaged in illegal behavior with firearms. Mitchell apparently saw his stepfather's incarceration as something admirable. Mitchell also tried to convince his peers that he was a gang member, seeking to establish a dangerous image for himself. These factors suggest that Mitchell aspired to criminality.

Another factor found among the traumatized shooters is peer influence to go on a rampage. All three attacks committed by traumatized shooters resulted in charges against their peers. In Mitchell's case, of course, Drew Golden went to jail for murder. In Evan's case, the two friends who egged him on and taught him to use a gun were arrested for their roles in the attack. In Jeffrey's case, his cousin, who planned the attack with him, was charged. Thus, in addition to the influence of the men in their lives, the three traumatized shooters were significantly influenced by peers to commit the attacks.

We can speculate further on Mitchell. It is perhaps significant that the boy who did not have a father involved in an armed standoff with police had a partner who recruited him for the attack. Thus, where the parental influence toward armed violence was weaker, the peer influence was stronger. It is as if, for Mitchell, the influence of Drew Golden made up for the "lack" of a father involved in an armed standoff.

Birth order is another factor that might have played a part in the dynamics of the traumatized shooters. This is pure speculation, but the pattern is so clear that it seems to warrant commentary. Whereas all five psychotic shooters and both psychopathic shooters were the youngest children in their families, none of the traumatized shooters was the youngest child. How might this be significant? Perhaps the traumatized boys felt some responsibility toward their younger siblings. Maybe they tried to protect them from abuse, only to fail and feel even worse about themselves and the world.

Jeffrey had two younger half-siblings. We do not know if they were abused. We also do not know anything about Jeffrey's relationship with them. In Mitchell's case, however, not only was his brother Monte exposed to their father's terrorizing rages, but he also was molested by the same boy who repeatedly raped Mitchell. Similarly, the boy who molested Evan also victimized Evan's younger brother. What impact does knowing that he cannot protect his younger brother have on a boy? Perhaps their inability to protect their younger brothers caused excruciating anguish and guilt, exacerbating their sense of helplessness and rage.

Among the factors that distinguish the three types of shooters, peer involvement and the use of firearms by father figures seem particularly important. Exhibit 6.2 shows how these factors vary across the typology.

Beyond the influence of family structure, perhaps there were larger community influences on the shooters. In chapter 1 I questioned why rampage school shootings typically occur in small towns or suburbs rather than in urban centers. Whether there is a connection between geography and school shootings cannot be answered with certainty, but we can speculate. Although there is no apparent pattern in the geography of the psychopathic shooters, there are trends among the traumatized and psychotic shooters.

Exhibit 6.2 Paternal Gun Use and Peer Influence

Name	Legal Gun Use by Fathers	Illegal Gun Use by Fathers	Recruited Peers	Influenced by Peers	Category
Drew Golden	Yes	No	Yes	No	Psychopathic
Eric Harris	Yes	No	Yes	No	Psychopathic
Michael Carneal	No	No	No	No	Psychotic
Andrew Wurst	No	No	No	No	Psychotic
Kip Kinkel	No	No	No	No	Psychotic
Dylan Klebold	No	No	No	Yes	Psychotic
Seung Hui Cho	No	No	No	No	Psychotic
Evan Ramsey	No	Yes	No	Yes	Traumatized
Mitchell Johnson	No	Yes	No	Yes	Traumatized
Jeffrey Weise	No	Yes	No	Yes	Traumatized

Among the traumatized shooters, all three came from small, isolated northern communities of 5,000 people or fewer. These areas were distressed to varying degrees. The county where Mitchell Johnson grew up had a poverty rate that was more than 50 percent higher than both state and national averages.[4] The region of Alaska that Evan Ramsey lived in had one of the state's highest rates of alcoholism and child abuse.[5] In addition, the year before Evan's attack, a local seventh grader shot himself to death, and a 16-year-old boy shot himself in the head.[6] Beltrami County, Minnesota, where Jeffrey Weise lived, had significant problems with poverty, drugs, alcoholism, violence, and suicide. A year before Jeffrey's rampage, a survey on the reservation revealed that 80 percent of ninth-grade girls had thought about suicide.[7] Between 1990 and 2005, the suicide rate for Native Americans in Beltrami County was approximately four times higher than the state's overall suicide rate.[8]

What is the impact of these factors? Poverty and violence have multiple adverse effects on children. In addition, suicides among schoolmates or in small towns significantly increase the risk of further suicides. Suicide, especially among youth, can have a devastating impact on a community, generating a sense of hopelessness and despair that can lead to subsequent suicides. Thus, both Evan and Jeffrey came from highly stressed communities with increased rates of violence and suicide. The traumas in the larger communities paralleled, and exacerbated, the traumas the boys experienced in their families.

In contrast, most of the psychotic shooters came from relatively prosperous towns or suburbs. The shooters were failures in families where everyone else, was successful. When they looked around at their classmates and neighbors, they probably felt like failures within their communities, too. Whereas cities provide abundant evidence of those who have not made it, perhaps the shooters' communities did not. Perhaps it seemed that everyone around them was succeeding in life, thereby increasing the shooters' own sense of failure. The macrocosm of their communities paralleled the microcosm of their families.

Second, the psychotic shooters' communities were relatively homogeneous. For people who do not fit into the mainstream culture, there are fewer options in finding a niche among your peers. A misfit in West Paducah would be expected to have a harder time than a misfit in New York City, because New York offers a wider range of social options.

But What Do They Have in Common?

Although the shooters were different, it is natural to wonder what they had in common. Finding features that are common among all school shooters is surprisingly difficult. There is the obvious fact that all 10 presented in this book were male, yet girls have been involved in foiled attacks, including a girl I evaluated who presented a high risk of going on a murderous rampage.

This does not mean that the shooters had nothing in common. Similar dynamics or traits existed among many rampage shooters. In some cases, however, a trait that was present in multiple shooters had a variety of origins. For example, all the shooters were angry. The reasons for their anger, however, varied according to whether the shooter was psychopathic, psychotic, or traumatized. The psychopaths had different reasons from the psychotic shooters and the traumatized shooters. Looking at why the three types of shooters manifested the same features can deepen our understanding of school shootings.

Failure of Empathy

A fundamental aspect of the shootings that has received little attention is the failure of empathy among the shooters. Lack of empathy has been mentioned previously in relation to the psychopathic shooters, but it is a significant issue among all the shooters. To kill innocent people at close range—including classmates and acquaintances—requires a profound lack of feeling for fellow human beings. How can we account for such a lack of empathy? There are three situations in which people commonly have failures of empathy; these situations occurred among the shooters, too. In addition, other factors are specific to the three types of school shooters.

Perhaps the most common reason people have a lapse of empathy is anger. People often say or do something in anger that they later regret. They may say something hurtful, yell at a spouse, hit a child, or engage in other regrettable behavior. This occurs because of a temporary loss of empathy. For many people, anger cancels out empathy, making us feel indignant and self-righteous. When angry, we feel justified in how we treat others. We feel that they deserve what we do to them, because, after all, we are only acting in response to their unacceptable behavior. This is a powerful dynamic, and the fact that the school shooters were full of rage helps to explain their failures of empathy. The different sources of their rage will be discussed later.

A second situation where people have decreased empathy is when they are divided into an in-group and an out-group: us versus them. This occurs in war, politics, sports, and elsewhere. When we have this perception of otherness, we tend to have less empathy for those who are not in our group. In sports, for example, we get a kick out of seeing "our team" demolish "their team." In war, we feel more concern for "our" casualties than "theirs."

This dynamic also occurred with school shooters. For example, Eric Harris said, "Our actions are a two-man war against everyone else."[9] He and Dylan set themselves apart from other people, claiming that their own status was higher than that of others. Part of this process involved dehumanizing others by calling them "robots" or "zombies." It is easier to kill people not only when they are different but also when they are seen as inferior or subhuman.

For other shooters, it was not "us versus them" but rather "me against the world." This was the case with Seung Hui Cho, who believed he was under attack by enemies who sought to destroy him. Thus, he viewed people as his enemies and killed them without mercy or empathy. This dynamic is relevant for the traumatized shooters, too. Trauma victims often feel chronically unsafe and mistrustful, and are continuously scanning their environments for threats. This can create a "me against the world" attitude.

A third situation in which people act contrary to their normal empathic feelings involves what I call desperate insecurity. What does this mean? Imagine a boy who wants to fit in with a group of peers. He sees them making fun of someone, and although he normally would not do so, he joins in the teasing in the hope that the group will accept him. In some cases, he will do something extreme in order to impress those whose acceptance or admiration he seeks.

Michael Carneal experienced this dynamic. When simply bringing a gun to school did not impress his peers, he felt he had to do more: "I was thinking that if I didn't pull out a gun and take over the school, they wouldn't like me."[10] Thus, Michael's desperate insecurity canceled his empathy and resulted in behavior that he later regretted.

Evan Ramsey also felt pressure to make an intimidating impression on his peers. When he was considering forgoing the attack, his friend said, "You can't go back, everybody would think you're nothing. Everybody would just have one more reason to mess with you."[11] Thus, Evan faced two sources of pressure: He wanted to impress his enemies, and he did not want to look weak in the eyes of his friend. He was so desperately insecure that his normal empathy gave way under the stress of these external pressures.

In addition to anger, in group/out group dynamics, and desperate insecurity, other failures of empathy are specific to the three types of shooters. For example, psychopathic shooters, by definition, lack empathy. They are callous, egocentric, and sadistic. Rather than being distressed by people's suffering, they are delighted by it. They especially enjoy having the power to make people suffer. The failure of empathy for them is a more or less chronic state.

Among psychotic shooters, hallucinations can temporarily override empathy. For example, Kip Kinkel reported hearing voices commanding him to kill. Although he was subsequently wracked with anguish for the pain he caused, the hallucinations (and other factors) overpowered his empathy. Similarly, delusional beliefs can block empathic feelings. Andrew Wurst believed that everyone in the world was already dead; thus, killing them was not really murder. His delusion overpowered any empathy he otherwise would have had. A psychiatrist who evaluated him after the attack said that Andrew had no idea that what he did was wrong: "He is detached.... He is in his own world."[12]

Failure of empathy among the psychotic shooters could also be caused by their emotional impairment. Schizophrenics often have deficits in their ability to experience emotions as well as severely impaired social skills. They tend to be detached from others. This lack of social connection and decreased emotional experience could further weaken their empathy.

Finally, traumatized people have a decreased capacity for experiencing closeness with others. Traumas tend to leave people feeling emotionally numb, with an impaired ability to experience feelings such as love and affection. This emotional numbness may contribute to deficits in empathy.

Existential Rage

All the shooters, across all three categories, were angry. Anger, however, is a weak word to apply to mass murderers. I prefer the term "existential rage." These were young men who were raging against the conditions of their existence. They were not just angry with a person or a group of people; they were angry at life, angry at the world.

The reasons for their rage, however, were not the same. The two psychopathic shooters, Drew Golden and Eric Harris, manifested a narcissistic rage in response to a world that did not recognize them as superior beings. Drew could not tolerate teachers who tried to control him. Eric could not tolerate a world that he viewed with contempt but had power over him.

Drew Golden reportedly was tired of his teachers' "crap." Why did he focus on teachers? Because they exercised authority over him. By attacking the school, he was attacking the institution that gave his teachers their power. He may also have been angry with a girl who rejected him—another situation in which someone exercised power over him and denied him what he wanted. To an extreme narcissist, this is intolerable.

Eric Harris had a special hatred for police. When asked online to name the one person he hated the most, he answered, "are cops one person?"[13]

Why did he hate the police? Because they exercised authority over him. In Eric's fantasies, he was a superior being. After he broke into a van, however, he was arrested and brought into court just like anybody else. This was intolerable. Eric identified his arrest as his "most embarrassing moment."[14]

Eric also made lists of students he wanted to kill. Who was on these lists? People who made him feel small, such as boys who teased him in gym class and girls who would not go out with him. Beyond these specific people, Eric felt rage toward society as a whole. He built an image of superiority, but the world did not support that image. Eric's rage was rooted in his need to be powerful: "My belief is that if I say something, it goes. I am the law, if you don't like it, you die."[15] In reality, however, he was not the law, a situation he found infuriating.

The psychotic shooters felt rage, too, but for different reasons. When Michael Carneal wrote that he hated being compared to his sister, he also wrote: "I am seriously mad at the world."[16] He was not simply angry with his sister for making him look bad by comparison, he was angry about the conditions of his existence. Similarly, a friend said of Andrew Wurst: "He hated his life. He hated the world."[17] It was rage against a world that was unfair and incomprehensible.

The psychotic shooters realized they were misfits. They could not measure up to their siblings who were normal and, in some cases, outstanding individuals. Their parents were disappointed in them and argued about how to treat them. Their teachers recognized that they did not follow in the footsteps of their older siblings. They struggled socially and felt isolated. They fell desperately in love but believed they could never achieve intimacy. They raged against the cruelty of fate that they were born impaired and could never be like other people.

And the traumatized shooters? They raged against a world that victimized them over and over again. Jeffrey Weise expressed this: "So fucking naive man, so fucking naive. Always expecting change when I know nothing ever changes…I really must be fucking worthless. This place never changes, it never will. Fuck it all."[18]

Whereas the psychotic shooters felt rage because of the unfairness of being born deficient, the traumatized shooters felt rage because of the unfairness of what the world did to them. To the psychotic shooters, everyone else was normal, and they themselves were the problem. To the traumatized shooters, they were innocent and other people were the problem. Victimization generates rage.

Thus, although existential rage was a common factor across the three types of shooters, the source of the rage was specific to the category of shooters.

Suicide and Existential Anguish

Just as existential rage was a driving force in the shooters' committing murder, existential anguish was a driving force in their suicidal thoughts. What do I mean by existential anguish? The term refers to severe depression: hopelessness, helplessness, and self-loathing. "Depression," however, is too common a term to convey the magnitude of suffering among the shooters. Thus, I will use the term "existential anguish" to suggest the intensity of the shooters' feelings.

The fact that the psychotic and traumatized shooters were suicidal is not surprising. They all had suffered significant distress for years. All five psychotic shooters felt anguish because of their social deficits and psychotic symptoms and had histories of suicidal thoughts. The traumatized shooters felt anguish because they had been so damaged by life. All three traumatized shooters had been suicidal prior to the attacks, and two were suicidal at the time of the shootings.

What about the psychopathic shooters? There is no known evidence of anguish or suicidal thinking in Drew Golden. Although suicidal thinking and behavior is relatively common among adolescents, it is rare among preadolescents. Drew, at 11, was much younger than the other shooters under discussion; perhaps his age at the time of the attack was a factor in his lack of suicidal thinking. Another possibility is that psychopaths are usually too narcissistic to kill themselves.

Yet Eric Harris killed himself. Why? Over a year before his attack, Eric reported being depressed and having suicidal thoughts.[19] That is why he was given antidepressant medication. His journal, however, does not articulate why he was suicidal. Nonetheless, numerous passages indicate profound disillusionment and pessimism. Eric referred to the world as "this worthless place."[20] Elsewhere he said, "we are all a waste of natural resources and should be killed off."[21] A few months later, he wrote, "it's all doomed."[22]

Although these passages do not constitute suicidal statements, they suggest that Eric was bitter, disillusioned, and hopeless. Perhaps these feelings were rooted in his self-hatred regarding his looks, his frustration at not being given the status he felt he deserved, and his lack of success with girls. Beyond this, consider the world from his perspective: He rejected conventional morality and values. Goodness did not exist, justice was a meaningless concept, and love was just a word. Apart from the attack, he had no goals. There was nothing he wanted to achieve, nothing to look forward to in life. Underneath Eric's narcissism and rage there could well have been a sense that life was utterly meaningless. If love and relationships are meaningless, there are no goals, and nothing matters, what is there to live for?

In addition, Eric saw murder and suicide as his ticket to everlasting fame. As he said on his Web site, "I want to leave a lasting impression on the world."[23] He was so desperate for status that this was a path he was willing to take. By dying in the attack, he found his way out of a meaningless existence at the same time that he achieved world fame.

Extreme Reactivity

As I explained in chapter 1, the idea that school shootings are retaliation for bullying is highly problematic. This is not to say that peer relationships are irrelevant. The shooters often had difficulties with male friendships as well as problems in their romantic pursuit of females. These difficulties contributed to both rage and anguish. Beyond this, however, the shooters exhibited "extreme reactivity," a term referring to an overreaction to normal peer experiences. To be teased is normal; to be turned down for a date is normal. The shooters, however, were often so emotionally unstable or had such vulnerable identities that normal events triggered highly abnormal responses.

This is perhaps clearest in Eric Harris. In ninth grade he went on a double date; when his date refused to go out with him again, he faked a suicide attempt in front of her by pretending he had bashed his head with a rock and covering his face with fake blood. This is not a normal reaction. He sent threatening e-mails to another girl who turned him down. Eric described his extreme responses in a paper he wrote in which he compared himself to Zeus: "Zeus and I also get angry easily and punish people in unusual ways."[24]

Not surprisingly, Eric sometimes had conflicts with his friends. Once he became enraged with his friend Brooks for being late in picking him up for school. Eric subsequently damaged the windshield of Brooks's car, vandalized his home, and posted a homicidal threat against him online. Eric also vandalized the home of Nick, another friend. Other students reported that simply bumping into Eric in the hallway could result in intimidation and threats. Eric clearly was highly reactive as a result of his fragile narcissism, which made him intolerant of being crossed, insulted, or rejected. As he said, anyone who crossed him or told him to do something he did not like would be killed.

Some psychotic shooters also exhibited extreme reactivity. Kip Kinkel, for example, routinely called kids "fags," but when somebody used the epithet about him, Kip felt murderous rage. When his friends played a joke on him and hid one of his knives, Kip went ballistic, terrifying his friends who locked themselves in another room until Kip settled down.

Among the traumatized shooters, Mitchell Johnson was highly reactive, although not to the extent of Eric Harris or Kip Kinkel. Mitchell liked to put on a tough-guy act and tried to convince his peers that he was in a gang. When his peers dismissed him with a laugh, he was devastated. He tried to bully or intimidate others but reacted badly to being teased or laughed at himself.

He also was desperate to have serious relationships with girls and was apparently devastated when these did not work out. Why was he so desperate? After having been raped for years by an older boy, Mitchell was probably struggling with questions about his sexuality and sexual orientation. This kind of abuse often results in boys' wondering if they are gay. One way to prove to himself—and the world—that he was not gay was to be successful with girls. Lack of success with girls threatened his sense of himself as a heterosexual male in the same way that ridicule by peers threatened his sense of himself as a macho male.

Across the three types, many of the shooters had such fragile identities that they were highly reactive to anything that threatened their stability. For the psychopathic shooters, their narcissism made them highly reactive to put-downs and frustrations. Among the psychotic shooters, their poor social skills and paranoia exacerbated their sense of being threatened. Among the traumatized shooters, the hypervigilance associated with posttraumatic stress disorder, as well as the emotional instability caused by trauma, increased their reactivity.

Further, the depression and self-loathing of many of the shooters made them highly vulnerable to teasing and rejection. A confident, secure person has an easier time ignoring an insult than a person who knows (or suspects) that the insult is true. If you already feel like a reject and a failure, any experiences that support those feelings will be magnified in your mind. Thus, the issue is not simply that the shooters were sometimes teased or rejected but that they were highly vulnerable, and therefore highly reactive, to these experiences.

There is yet one more factor to consider in terms of extreme reactivity. One reason that some shooters were so reactive is that they were not only reacting to events in the present but were carrying a storehouse of resentment that had built up over years. In its report on school shooters, the FBI noted that many shooters were "injustice collectors." In other words, they were kids who went through life holding grudges and accumulating an ever-growing collection of injustices they had suffered.[25] John Douglas, an expert on serial killers and other murderers, noted this same dynamic. In discussing assassins, Douglas noted their tendency to record "every slight done to them."[26]

In terms of personality dynamics, collecting injustices can be understood as an aspect of a masochistic personality. Although people may associate masochism with sexual behavior, I am not using the term in that way here. People with masochistic personalities are preoccupied with, and exaggerate, their own suffering. Masochism can result in self-pity and/or self-righteous rage. Eric and Dylan provide examples of masochistic tendencies.

According to Dr. David Shapiro, masochists "seem to work themselves up, to try to experience more suffering than they actually feel at the time."[27] Eric illustrated this in a video where he said, "More rage. More rage. Keep building it on,"[28] and motioned with his hands to indicate he was piling up his rage.

Eric also held on to grudges. Numerous people noted this, and Eric himself wrote about it in his journal. A masochistic personality is one that is aggrieved—that is, the person goes through life with a chronic storehouse of grievances. Eric's writings provide abundant evidence of his extreme sense of being aggrieved with people and the world. Not only do masochists hold grudges, but they also exaggerate the magnitude of the injustices they have suffered. For example, Eric wrote: "If you pissed me off in the past, you will die if I see you. Because you might be able to piss off others and have it eventually blow over, but not me. I don't forget people who wronged me."[29] In Eric's mind, an act that pissed him off was justification for murder. Thus, he not only did not forget anyone who wronged him, but he exaggerated his wrongs and reacted out of all proportion to them.

Dylan also had masochistic features. He complained about hating snobby kids who (in his mind, at least) mistreated him when he was in daycare.[30] His reference to his suffering in daycare as a rationale for blowing up his high school is noteworthy. He was holding on to experiences from perhaps 15 years before and keeping alive his sense of hurt and injustice. Shapiro describes masochism as "the chronic, usually bitter exaggeration and 'nursing' of humiliations, defeats, and injustices."[31] Dylan's holding on to his perceived mistreatment in daycare and reviving it shortly before the attack is a dynamic described by Shapiro in a masochistic person: "when an old grievance threatens to grow faint, he tries to retrieve it and revive the experience of it."[32]

Masochists not only exaggerate their suffering but tend to be obsessed with their misfortunes. This is what we find in Dylan's journal: "I am in eternal suffering, in infinite directions in infinite realities."[33] Elsewhere he wrote, "Let's sum up my life...the most miserable existence in the history of time."[34] Dylan clearly was preoccupied with, and exaggerated, his pain.

By holding onto grudges and distorting their memories of past suffering, some shooters built up their self-pity, their righteous indignation, and their rage. They were not only reacting to current stresses but also responding to what they perceived as a lifetime of wrongs they had suffered.

Shame, Envy, and the Failure of Manhood

As noted earlier, the shooters' extreme reactivity was rooted in their fragile identities, an issue that leads to a consideration of what Dr. Katherine Newman calls "the failure of manhood."[35] The shooters not only had fragile identities; more specifically, they had fragile male identities.

Perhaps their fragile male identities were connected to their physical bodies. Most shooters were not good physical specimens. Evan Ramsey was short and thin. Michael Carneal was short, thin, and wore glasses; he was so small that people teased him about his size. To gain a sense of power, Michael accumulated weapons. "More guns is better. You have more power. You look better if you have a lot of guns," he wrote.[36]

Andrew Wurst was too weak to do the same work as his brothers in the family landscape business; he was a disappointment to his father, and he knew it. Dylan Klebold was awkward and self-conscious about his lack of physical coordination and prowess. Jeffrey Weise was overweight and unathletic. Kip Kinkel had been small all his life; at age six or seven his parents enrolled him in karate classes in an effort to help him compensate for his small stature and develop his self-confidence. He played football but was not very good, and his father considered him a failure as an athlete.

Mitchell Johnson, however, played on three sports teams at school, which suggests that he was a good athlete. Also, girls in his class considered him attractive. In Mitchell's case, however, he felt insecure about his maleness due to the physical and sexual abuse he endured. Similarly, a good number of girls dated Eric Harris and/or considered him to be cute. In addition, Eric was a serious soccer player. Objectively speaking, he was not a poor physical specimen. Nonetheless, he thought he was too thin, was self-conscious about his looks, and may have had a strong sense of physical inadequacy due to his birth defects. He may have felt shame over his sunken chest, especially in gym class, when he had to take his shirt off. He may also have felt inadequate due to his inability to perform to the athletic standards set by his brother.

Drew Golden was short for his age; his size meant that he could not compete in sports with his peers. His grandfather told a reporter that though Drew wanted to play football and basketball, he was "too slight for one, too short for the other. Shooting was what he did best."[37] Thus, guns allowed him to overcome the deficiencies of his body.

Students reported that Seung Hui Cho sometimes worked out "with a certain frenzy at the gym."[38] He was trying to bulk himself up. All his life he had been frail and unusually thin—so thin, in fact, that his autopsy report noted a distinct lack of muscle for the body of a young man. In the end, however, he too found that no matter how weak he was, guns provided him with power.

We can extend the concept of the failure of manhood beyond the issue of physique and athleticism to include issues related to social difficulties, intimate relationships, and identity as a whole. Many of these issues generated agony in the shooters.

Being teased caused the shooters shame and humiliation. Even if the harassment was more in their own minds than in reality, and even if some brought the harassment on themselves, they felt the shame of it deeply. In response to this shame, they became full of rage at their peers.

There were yet other sources of shame. Kip Kinkel was ashamed that he heard voices, so he hid his psychosis from everyone. In addition, his parents were teachers who valued and expected academic excellence. Kip was dyslexic and even in eighth grade continued to misspell his own last name as "Kinkle." He was a disappointment to his parents, who were known to call him "stupid." Kip also had to repeat first grade, which may well have been humiliating. Similarly, Jeffrey Weise had to repeat eighth grade, which may have been an embarrassment. Andrew Wurst was a bed-wetter until age nine; his brothers harassed him about this, which must have caused ongoing humiliation. He also had a collection of Raggedy Ann dolls, which was not only odd but may have resulted in taunting. Dylan Klebold was ashamed of his sexual urges, including a foot fetish and attraction to bondage. Mitchell Johnson and Evan Ramsey both suffered sexual abuse, a deeply shaming experience. Finally, many of the shooters experienced failure in their relationships with girls. All of these experiences contributed to their sense of shame and their failures of manhood.

To understand the shooters' rage toward their peers, we need to look beyond teasing to the issue of envy. For kids who felt like they were failures as males, the presence of "normal" kids was highly disturbing. Eric Harris was acutely aware of status and expressed hostility to people who had status, whether because they were rich or because they were "cool." Dylan envied athletes, who seemed to be living the life he wished he could live. Although Dylan was teased at times, his envy of normal kids appears to have been more devastating.

Kip Kinkel felt murderous hatred toward the boy who was the star of the football team and who dated the girl he wanted to date. His rage was a result of envy and his inability to be the person he wanted to be: "I want to be something I can never be. I try so hard every day. But in the end, I hate myself for what I've become."[39]

Michael Carneal wrote a story in which the narrator (named Michael) killed his classmates. The protagonist's rage was focused on the "preps." In the story, Michael used the names of actual kids in his class. His sadistic story about mutilating and murdering preps was a product of his envy. After the attack, Michael acknowledged that he envied the popularity of the students in the prayer group whom he shot.[40]

Seung Hui Cho, despite his scathing comments about rich people and their decadent lifestyles, longed to be one of them. He hated them and yet wished he could join them: "Oh the happiness I could have had mingling among you hedonists, being counted as one of you."[41] In the story he wrote about a boy named Bud who contemplated going on a rampage, Bud viewed everyone else as living in "heaven-on-earth," while he was doomed to being an isolated outsider. He envied the lives of everyone around him.

As young men struggling to establish an identity as males, the shooters sought out role models such as Hitler, Charles Manson, the Unabomber, other school shooters, and possibly their fathers who engaged in the criminal use of firearms. These were figures of power—figures that are highly attractive to people who feel inadequate or powerless.

The shooters also found figures to emulate in violent films and video games. What these figures have in common is that, as Newman says, they used violence to enhance male status. This is an important point. The school shooters did not simply get a kick out of explosions or shoot-outs in movies and games; they learned that violence enhances the social standing of males.

How do you go from being a nobody to being a somebody? Through violence. Eric Harris wanted to make a lasting impression on the world. How did he do it? By violence. Evan Ramsey's friends told him he should not just kill himself; he should kill others too. They told him he should "live the fame." How could a nobody like Evan achieve world fame? By violence. Michael Carneal thought that bringing guns to school would result in his being elevated to a higher social status. The shooters tried to demonstrate manliness by killing innocent, unarmed people.

Thus, issues of manhood, shame, and envy were powerful factors among the school shooters. The boys were hostile toward their peers, their families, and the world. Hostile feelings, however, do not always make kids killers. There are other factors.

The Role of Fantasy: Rehearsal for Killing

The issue of fantasy is important in understanding school shooters. In fact, the FBI has reported that school shooters often are seriously involved in fantasy: books, movies, video games, or role-playing fantasy games. This is not unique to school shooters, however. John Douglas, a former FBI profiler, states that fantasy played a central role in the minds of serial killers. According to Douglas, "Probably the most crucial single factor in the development of a serial rapist or killer is the role of fantasy."[42] And John Hinckley, who attempted to assassinate President Reagan, commented: "You know a few things about me, dear sweetheart, like my obsession with fantasy; but what the rabble don't yet understand is that fantasies become reality in my world."[43]

Unfortunately, most of the shooters did not leave records of their fantasy lives. The writings of Eric Harris, however, provide documentation of the extent to which he mingled reality and fantasy. The primary focus of his fantasy life was the video game Doom, including new levels that he programmed. In posting his new levels online, Eric wrote: "I have been playing Doom since November of 1994, so it is basically my life. These levels are better than anything you have ever seen before. I don't want to brag about my own sh*t, but these levels come from the Herrgott of DOOM himself. . . . Lots of the rooms and secrets in this place come directly from my imagination, so you are basically running around in my own world. I live in this place."[44] Elsewhere he wrote, "I wish I lived in Doom,"[45] and "Doom is so burned into my head my thoughts usually have something to do with the game. . . . What I can't do in real life, I try to do in Doom."[46] What does Eric's preoccupation with the video game have to do with his rampage attack? Eric made the connection in his journal: "I have a goal to destroy as much as possible so I must not be sidetracked by my feelings of sympathy, mercy, or any of that, so I will force myself to believe that everyone is just another monster from Doom . . . so it's either me or them. I have to turn off my feelings."[47]

Eric Harris was losing touch with reality through his chronic fantasizing about Doom. As he said, he lived in Doom. This does not mean that he was not aware of what he was doing in the attack; he knew exactly what he was doing. In this regard he was like Hitler: "Hitler was a hard-headed pragmatist with a remarkable capacity to deal effectively with the realities of political life; he was also a person who lived in a fantastic dream world."[48] Eric also navigated the real world with exceptional skill, planning a large-scale attack while going about the activities of a typical teenager. At the same time, however, he was half living in a world of fantasy.

Fantasy served two purposes for Eric:

1. By living in his fantasy, the task he set himself became easier to execute. As he wrote, he could turn off his feelings by imagining his victims as creatures from Doom.
2. Doom provided years of rehearsal for killing.

Although none of the other shooters provided this much insight into his fantasy life, Eric Harris was not the only one to mentally rehearse a rampage. Michael Carneal wrote a story full of graphic and sadistic violence about a student with his own name who killed and mutilated other students. Dylan Klebold wrote a story about a cold-blooded killer who murdered a group of students. Jeffrey Weise wrote numerous stories of violence and murder. He also made an animated video of someone shooting others, killing police officers, and then blowing his own head off—an eerie foreshadowing of his own attack. Finally, Seung Hui Cho wrote a paper about the Columbine attack in high school, and during college he wrote a story about a would-be school shooter.

Thus, several shooters clearly fantasized about committing murder well before they carried out the actual attacks. These fantasies helped them prepare for the real thing both by serving as mental rehearsals and by contributing to desensitizing them to the pain they would inflict.

The Search for Answers

Why do school shootings happen? As much as we want to find a simple answer to this question, there is none. The rampage attacks presented in this book occurred due to complex combinations of environmental, family, and individual factors that varied from one perpetrator to another.

The psychopathic shooters came from families in which firearms were used lawfully; the shooters, however, were obsessed with weapons. They were boys with antisocial, narcissistic, and sadistic traits. They rejected morality, felt above others, and enjoyed inflicting pain and death. They played the role of leaders and recruited followers to join them in their attacks.

The psychotic shooters inherited the mental illnesses that ran in their families. They all had various manifestations of hallucinations and/or delusions. They all struggled socially and experienced profound alienation, sometimes to the point of believing they were not even human. They all had higher-achieving siblings who made them feel like failures, and some felt rejected by their parents. They sometimes endured peer harassment, although none targeted kids who picked on them. They seemed more consumed with rage that was born of envy of their peers than in anger at mistreatment.

The three traumatized shooters may have been genetically at risk for violence due to their violent parents. All three also had role models for violence and the misuse of firearms. They all grew up amid alcoholism and abuse at home. Two were molested outside of the home. On top of these historical factors, other events converged prior to the attacks: conflicts with the school staff, rejection by girls, the possibility of having to live with their fathers, peer harassment, and other stressful events. Even with all these factors combined, however, at least two of the attacks would not have happened without the traumatized boys being recruited or encouraged by their peers to commit murder.

Across the three types of shooters, common factors included homicidal rage, suicidal anguish, inadequate identities seeking to establish an image of manliness through violence, envy toward those with higher status, a desire for fame, fragile personalities that were highly reactive to commonplace slights and frustrations, and masochistic tendencies to hold grudges and magnify wrongs suffered. In all cases there were failures of empathy.

Many of these factors contributed to an overwhelming egocentricity. For example, a failure of empathy creates a distance between the self and everyone else. Narcissism involves an extreme preoccupation with the self, often at the expense of other people's welfare. Anger makes people self-righteous and insensitive to others. Depression and anguish constrict people's vision; consumed in a pervasive state of agony and helplessness, they lose all perspective of the larger world. Paranoia is an intense narrowing of experience focused on the preservation of the self, no matter what the cost to others.

The shooters' worlds shrank into the needs of the self: their friends did not matter; their parents did not matter; the rights and feelings of others did not matter; their own deaths did not matter. The shooters were in a state of psychological crisis.

Such a narrowing of the world is not necessarily permanent. Most shooters who survived the attacks have expressed consistent—and convincing—remorse, guilt, agony, and self-loathing for what they did. This is true for Evan Ramsey, Michael Carneal, Kip Kinkel, and Mitchell Johnson. The murders they committed were not inevitable outcomes of their personalities but actions they committed in a state of crisis. Had they been safely maintained through their crises, there is no reason to assume they would have become murderers later in life. Chapter 7 presents five potential school shooters; unlike actual school shooters, however, they were sent to a psychiatric hospital before they went on a rampage.

7

KIDS CAUGHT IN THE
NICK OF TIME

*I used to want to kill someone so bad, I'd go up to people and say, "I'll kill
someone for you for a pack of cigarettes."*

—A *former patient*

AS A PSYCHOLOGIST WORKING in a psychiatric hospital for children and adolescents, I am often asked to evaluate a youth's risk for violence. Every year, one or two of these cases involves potential school shooters. This chapter presents five such kids.

Talking with potential mass murderers is an intense and challenging experience. Sometimes they clam up, figuring the less they say, the better. Others are very smooth and casually minimize the threats they make. No matter how damaging the evidence against them, they demonstrate a remarkable facility for explaining it away as nothing more than a simple misunderstanding. Other potential killers are surprisingly open about their homicidal plans.

Were the teens I evaluated actually about to go on rampages, or were they just fantasizing about violence? If they had not been caught, would they have become killers? I cannot answer these questions with any certainty. Yet I can answer other questions: Do these would-be shooters fit into the three categories of school shooters? How similar and/or different are they compared to actual shooters? Do they highlight any of the facets of shooters discussed in previous chapters?

The Art of Creative Destruction

Jonathan worried me. He had plans; big plans. But not the kind of plans that warmed the hearts of his parents—or anyone else. He was a good-looking, intelligent, articulate, 17-year-old boy from an intact, middle-class family who lived in an upscale suburb in Connecticut. He had easygoing parents who trusted him and gave him a good deal of freedom. There did not seem to be anything significant he could complain about in his life. Jonathan, however, had his complaints. And he had his plans. Seven of them, to be specific. Seven variations on the same theme: mass murder of people at school.

Jonathan's plans ranged from burning down the school, to gunning down specific students, to shooting random people, to bombing the school. Some of his plans combined multiple elements of attack. For example, one involved placing bombs in strategic locations to bring the school down and then shooting people as they fled the building.

This last plan reminded me of what Eric Harris had planned to do at Columbine. In fact, many aspects of Jonathan reminded me of Eric Harris. It is not easy, however, to convince parents that their child is a potential mass murderer. In Jonathan's case, the parents regretted their decision to hospitalize their son, even though they were aware that he had both suicidal and homicidal thoughts. They were sure that they had overreacted. Despite Jonathan's preoccupation with murder, they insisted that he was a gentle boy who had never been violent. They simply could not accept that he would ever act on his thoughts. In their view, his violent plans were just a way for him to vent his anger.

They may have been right. Far more people have violent thoughts than commit violent acts. Maybe he would never carry out his plans. And how can a parent believe that a beloved son is a potential mass murderer? However, I was responsible for evaluating Jonathan's risk of violence, and to my mind, the fact that he had never been violent was meaningless. A common rule of thumb in predicting behavior is that past behavior is the best indicator of future behavior. Among school shooters, however, this rule has not been useful. Some school shooters had no prior history of violence and one day erupted. Was Jonathan likely to follow in their footsteps? It seemed quite possible.

I said that Jonathan resembled Eric Harris, but this is only partly true. He also resembled Dylan Klebold. Eric and Dylan were so different—how can one person resemble both? Furthermore, what can we learn from someone who did not kill anyone but who devoted considerable time to contemplating murder? Fortunately, Jonathan was not only articulate but also unusually open about his thoughts, feelings, and experiences.

There was no violence or abuse in the home. Both parents worked and maintained a home in a well-to-do area. They lived in the "poor" side of town, which was not poor at all—it just was not as strikingly wealthy as the rest of the town. Jonathan had been a shy, well-behaved child. There were no significant behavior problems through elementary school. During middle school, however, Jonathan became obsessed with girls. When rejected by rich girls, Jonathan became homicidal toward them. He stated, "I *know* the world would be a better place without these kids." He justified his hatred by saying that the girls cared only about money.

What about Jonathan's level of social acceptance? Was he picked on or marginalized? His parents said that Jonathan had always been well liked by his peers. Jonathan told me he was actually popular. He said, however, that he had "serious self-esteem issues" and saw himself as a failure. He reported being insecure and obsessive about his looks, and used "massive amounts of products" on his skin. Thus, Jonathan's sense of insecurity and low self-esteem was not a result of harassment by bullies but of his own troubled identity.

His social insecurity showed in his frequent changes of his image and his peer group. His mother said that Jonathan "becomes whoever he's with." This desperate insecurity and willingness to become someone else is reminiscent of Dylan's insecurity and transforming himself to be like Eric.

What about Jonathan's level of risk? He exhibited many traits seen in school shooters. For example, he had an interest in guns and weapons of destruction. His parents reported that he visited weapons sites on the Web. When asked about this, he said he was fascinated by "weapons and creative destruction—different ways to kill people." Jonathan's parents reported that he had used guns at a cousin's house. He knew how to shoot a gun and was a good shot. He told me that he could build a bomb if he wanted to. Jonathan said that although he did not think he could kill somebody by putting a gun to his head, he definitely could kill from distance, such as being a sniper or using bombs.

Like other school shooters, Jonathan dehumanized his intended victims. He said they have "no heart and soul" and "the world would be a better place without them." Regarding killing people, he said, "I have no moral issue with doing it." He clearly had a lack of empathy, not only for the targeted victims but also for innocent people who would be killed. Although he criticized the Columbine attack because innocent people died, his own plans included attacks that would kill innocent people. When confronted with this point, he simply shrugged it off as unavoidable. In fact, he told me that his initial interest in homicide took the form of thinking about "random killing." Also, like many school shooters, Jonathan "leaked," or shared his plans, with peers. He had at least one friend with whom he drew pictures and diagrams of how to carry out an attack on the school.

Jonathan was highly sensitive to rejection and issues of status. As noted earlier, school shooters are extremely reactive to anything that might threaten their identities or make them feel small. Jonathan's sensitivity to rejection was most severe with girls. His description of himself as a failure indicated issues with identity and status. Also, his focus on rich girls was another indication of his preoccupation with status. Jonathan's dislike of rich kids was reminiscent of Eric Harris's rants about wealthy people. Like Jonathan, Eric's family was not poor but solidly middle class. Nonetheless, Eric was preoccupied with people who were higher on the economic ladder.

Jonathan demonstrated ethnic prejudice. He had a fascination with neo-Nazi groups. He was also strongly influenced by Columbine, and said that he used to refer to himself as part of the Trench Coat Mafia, a group of students thought (mistakenly) to include Eric Harris and Dylan Klebold, and told me that he identified with the perpetrators. Regarding Columbine: "I was very for it," he said.

In addition, Jonathan had anger management problems: "definitely—I explode." He talked about having episodes in which "I punch everything in sight." Eric Harris also had problems with anger management, with explosive episodes of rage in which he punched walls.

Jonathan, like perhaps all school shooters, enjoyed violent video games and violent movies. Violence, in fact, was a significant source of entertainment for him. He was preoccupied with gory images and enjoyed "thinking about the sickest possible way to deform a human body." This attraction to mutilation was reminiscent of the writings of Eric Harris.

In summary, Jonathan was like Eric in his lack of empathy, his preoccupation with weapons and violence, his fascination with the Nazis, his sensitivity to status, his dehumanizing of others as inferior, and his sadistic pleasure in fantasizing about mutilating human bodies. He was like Dylan in his depression and profound insecurity, the malleability of his identity, his recurrent suicidal thoughts, his devastation at rejection by girls, and his sense of himself as a failure. He combined the rage and sadism of Eric with the anguish and depression of Dylan.

But was Jonathan really a threat? I believe so. On the positive side, he said that he would not act on his homicidal thoughts for two reasons. First, he didn't want to devastate his parents. He then added, however, "but take away my parents, and absolutely" he could kill people. This was not reassuring. What if, like Kip Kinkel, Jonathan killed his parents? Then the barrier would be removed. And even if his parents were alive, perhaps more rejections by girls would send him over the edge. His second reason for not killing people was that he was not sure that he was willing to give up his life to "make the world a better place" by killing people. He did not want to spend his life in jail. But what if he became more suicidal? If he no longer wanted to live and still was full of rage, what would keep him from carrying out his plans?

Thus, his assurance that he would not act on his plans carried little weight with me, especially in light of other comments he made. At one point, he said that although he would not attempt to carry out his plans, if someone gave him a gun he would use it. He knew at least one kid whose family had a gun at home. Finally, he stated that nothing changed in regard to his homicidal thoughts during his hospitalization: "when I leave I will have the same exact thoughts as before." This was not comforting.

To add to my concern, Jonathan's parents underreacted to the magnitude of his behaviors. Despite their awareness of his suicidal and homicidal thoughts, they stated "we are not certain that hospitalization was necessary." Although he had been suicidal for years, they said "we really don't think he would act on it." Additionally, despite knowing about his plans for murder, they stated "he is a very reasonable, loving, intelligent kid who never acted on any of this" (i.e., his homicidal thoughts). The parents said they did not want to be alarmists. Yet it is important to note that there are times when raising an alarm is not being alarmist.

How does Jonathan fit into the typology I presented in chapter 6? With no history of abuse or psychotic symptoms, he did not fit either the traumatized or psychotic categories. But was he psychopathic? Yes. He demonstrated a lack of empathy, a cold-hearted attitude toward innocent people he planned to kill. He said he had no moral scruples about ridding the world of people he viewed as undesirable and enjoyed thinking about ways to mutilate the human body. Jonathan also had explosive anger, a fascination with weapons, and bigotry that drew him to the neo-Nazi movement. In these ways, he resembled Eric Harris. He also appeared to be skilled in impression management. His parents were convinced that he was a sweet, gentle boy. Meanwhile, Jonathan was diagramming the school and figuring out where to put bombs and set up a sniper position. Even though they knew he was homicidal, it took persistent effort on my part to persuade his parents to continue his treatment.

Of course, Jonathan was a unique person who differed from Eric Harris in a number of ways. He lived with more ongoing distress than Eric. Jonathan did not have Eric's extreme narcissism, although he did feel superior to his intended victims. He also did not exhibit Eric's delinquent behaviors. Jonathan's case broadens the range of psychopathic shooters, but he still falls within the psychopathic category.

The Eyes that Did Not Blink

I have never met a person who did not blink, but Kyle came close. He had trained himself to blink as little as possible, because when you blink, you are vulnerable. Blinking is such an automatic and necessary behavior that there was something uncanny about Kyle's ability to maintain an unbroken stare. A short, thin, 14-year-old boy from a large family who lived in suburban New Jersey, Kyle had dark eyes that just stared and stared. Sitting with him in a hospital unit was unnerving. He fixed his unblinking eyes on me in a strangely intense gaze. He watched my eyes, and if I broke eye contact, he was instantly concerned about what was going on behind him that attracted my attention. He noted changes in light and shadow because they indicated that people were moving nearby. He had also trained himself to sleep lightly, because "I don't want to end up with a knife in my back."

This level of vigilance, called "hypervigilance," might be expected in a child who has been a victim of physical or sexual abuse. In Kyle's case, however, there was no such history. He complained he was severely picked on at school, but his reports were vague and the school contradicted his stories. Kyle said that he had been harassed for seven years, and although he had been in different schools, he claimed he was picked on wherever he went. There were probably two dynamics at work here. First, Kyle was odd. Even for me, a psychologist used to dealing with a wide spectrum of adolescents in crisis, being in Kyle's presence was an unusual experience. His strangeness could easily lead peers to avoid him or to tease him. Second, his hypervigilance and paranoia meant that he misperceived social situations and exaggerated negative reactions from his peers. In fact, he said that other kids at school were picked on the same as he, and they were able to handle it. Thus, he was aware that his reactions were not the same as those of most people. He was so disturbed by the alleged harassment that for a period he was home-schooled to avoid his peers.

Whatever the reality of problems with his peers, Kyle said he built a bomb the year before, which he was going to use to kill people at school. He told me he had planned a Columbine-style attack. No bomb was found, however, and it was never clear whether he had constructed one or not.

Kyle was hospitalized three times due to a variety of issues, including suicide risk, homicide risk, and psychotic symptoms. Although I had opportunities to assess him during each admission, psychological testing provided little information. He either refused to complete tests or completed them but reported virtually nothing in the way of symptoms. He revealed little during interviews and did not like my taking notes. He was too paranoid to trust me with personal information.

In an ironic twist, the one thing Kyle was comfortable talking about was his paranoia. He said that he read meanings into things that happened, held onto grudges, had frequent thoughts of being exploited or taken advantage of, and was careful not to reveal much about himself because he was afraid that it would be used against him. He said he was uncomfortable in crowds because he was preoccupied with the thought that he would be mugged or assaulted.

His mother noted that recently Kyle thought he was being watched or followed. When he walked into a room where his parents were talking, he suspected them of talking about him. Kyle accused his girlfriend's mother of following them to a restaurant because he saw the same model car that she drove pull into the restaurant parking lot. In Kyle's mind, this obviously meant that his girlfriend's mother had followed them.

Kyle said he wondered if he were "crazy" because he was different from other people. He also talked about having problems thinking straight, saying that his thoughts were "scattered." By his third hospitalization, his functioning seemed to have deteriorated further. He reported having visual hallucinations of the kids at school whom he said harassed him. He also heard voices telling him to kill those kids. Despite his preoccupation with being victimized, he did not provide any details about the harassment, and the school continued to maintain that there was no significant mistreatment. Thus, it seemed likely that Kyle was either misinterpreting social interactions or exaggerating the extent of his peers' behavior.

Where does Kyle fit in the typology? His odd presence and markedly impaired social functioning suggest that he had a schizotypal personality. Schizotypals not only are highly anxious and ineffective in social situations, but their social discomfort often manifests as paranoia. Kyle also reported low-level visual and auditory hallucinations, and schizotypals can have mild psychotic symptoms. He may have been disturbed enough for a diagnosis of schizophrenia and his fear about his own sanity and the disorganization of his thoughts suggest that perhaps he was headed in that direction. He made it clear that he was withholding a great deal of information. More disclosure would certainly have been helpful, but there are sufficient details to place Kyle in the psychotic category.

All five psychotic shooters discussed in this book were paranoid. None of them, as far as can be determined, was as hypervigilant as Kyle. Others had more paranoid delusions than Kyle, however. For example, Michael Carneal, Kip Kinkel, Andrew Wurst, and Seung Hui Cho had well-developed paranoid delusions. Of course, it is possible that Kyle had elaborate paranoid delusions that he simply did not disclose. Based on what he did reveal, Kyle exhibited a different balance of symptoms from the psychotic shooters, but he clearly belongs in the psychotic category.

Bombs Are Fun

Graham was innocent. Yes, he was fascinated by explosives and built bombs, but that was just for fun. And yes, he had a hit list of people he did not like and wrote about using bombs to kill people, but this was just self-expression, a way to vent his anger. Unlike patients who admit their homicidal plans, Graham insisted he was wrongly accused of posing a danger. His parents, however, did not think so. They not only had him hospitalized but they also called the police. After all, bombs are illegal and a hit list suggests a risk of mass murder.

Graham was a bright, good-looking, 14-year-old boy. He was from an intact family that lived in a small town in upstate New York. As far as I could determine, there was no violence or other serious problems in the home. Yet something was not right. Graham made death threats to his sister and his parents. Of course, within a family, people might say "I'm going to kill you" without truly having homicidal intent. Obviously, in Graham's case, the parents were not taking any chances.

Historically, Graham's mother said she had a good relationship with him. Graham also did well with his peers—until he hit puberty. At 13, he quickly changed his peer group and began hanging out with older kids. He gave up some of his hobbies and began listening to violent music and drawing swastikas and satanic symbols. Then he began isolating himself in his room, smoking marijuana, and having angry outbursts. He also became disrespectful in general, but particularly to his mother, frequently calling her "bitch" to her face. Calling her names, however, was minor compared to the time he assaulted her and pinned her to the ground. It was this event, along with his homicidal threats, that brought him to the hospital.

Graham was a mechanically skilled young man who had built a pipe bomb. Although he denied being homicidal, he was quite open about his love of fires and explosions. Graham rationalized his love of explosives as being perfectly natural. He said he made and detonated bombs strictly for entertainment, not destruction.

Besides amusing himself with explosives, Graham compiled a hit list of people he could not stand. His sister's name was on the list, along with names of kids at school. He said he hated his sister, but his only explanation was that she liked disco music. He also said he hated his father because of his "stupid rules." The only rule he could cite that bothered him, though, was a limit on how late he could stay out on weekends. There was no substantive reason for his hatred of his sister or his father. Graham gave no reasons for why the other kids' names were on the hit list; he simply could not stand them. There was no indication that Graham was a victim of bullying or any other mistreatment at school.

And assaulting his mother? What did he say about that? Well, they were having an argument, and she began to lay down consequences for behavior that he found unreasonable. He pushed her and wrestled her to the floor. Graham said that this really was not all his fault and rationalized his behavior. First, he justified the assault by saying that "she fought back," as if he expected her to respond passively to an attack. Second, he said that if his mother were larger than he was, "she would have treated me the same way." There was no evidence, however, that she had ever treated him in such a way when he was younger.

Graham did regret what he had done, but not in the way he should have. When I asked him how he felt about the incident, he said he felt "pretty bad" about what happened. When asked why he felt bad, he said it was because "I don't want to be in here [the hospital], I don't need to be in here." Thus, he exhibited no remorse or guilt for having assaulted his mother. The only reason he felt bad was because he was put in a psychiatric hospital.

Finally, beyond making death threats toward family members, writing a hit list, and building bombs, Graham also wrote a story for school about gunning down and bombing people he did not like. According to Graham, writing such a violent story was simply a means of venting his anger. He was adamant that he could not kill anyone.

He may have been telling the truth. Perhaps he had no intention of carrying out an attack. Too often, however, school shooters have written stories about murderous assaults that they later enacted in real life: Consider Michael Carneal, Eric Harris, Dylan Klebold, Jeffrey Weise, and Seung Hui Cho. Also, like Graham, Kip Kinkel built and detonated explosives to vent his anger. There were too many warning signs to ignore.

What did Graham's psychological assessment reveal? His personality profile indicated prominent antisocial tendencies and delinquent behavior as well as narcissistic features. He said that he felt superior to most people, that he liked to be the center of attention, and that he went out of his way to be different so he could stand out from the crowd. Although his profile did not indicate depressive symptoms, Graham had struggled with depression in the past. When a girlfriend broke up with him, for example, he became depressed to the point of having suicidal thoughts.

One thing that struck me about Graham was that for a boy of his intelligence, he demonstrated a remarkable lack of awareness regarding the seriousness of his behavior. He was furious that his parents turned him in to the police, yet he admitted to making bombs, knowing full well that this was illegal. He was completely nonchalant about breaking the law but enraged that his parents involved the police. He refused to take any responsibility for his behavior and blamed his parents for the fact that he was hospitalized.

Graham clearly fit the psychopathic type, although with some differences from others we have explored. Like others, he had antisocial and narcissistic traits. He was obsessed with explosives. He lacked empathy and remorse. He was angry and hateful toward family members and peers. There was no indication, however, of sadism. He was remorseless about assaulting his mother, but that act seemed to be an impulsive act of rage that he felt justified in carrying out rather than an incident that provided him with a thrill of power.

Also, there was much less indication of vulnerability. He showed no current depression or anxiety. The only evidence of vulnerability was in his depression in the wake of a breakup. Thus, whereas Jonathan clearly had ongoing distress, Graham seemed relatively free of psychological pain. He was in touch with his anger but did not appear to be in touch with much else—in himself or others.

A Taste for Killing

Roger was scary—just plain scary. He calmly articulated the most cold-blooded statements I have ever heard from a patient. He talked casually about contemplating a killing spree "just as something to do," as if for the entertainment value. He said, "I used to want to kill someone so bad, I'd go up to people and say, 'I'll kill someone for you for a pack of cigarettes.'" He stated that he was not interested in getting paid for it, he just wanted the experience of killing. When I asked him how he thought he would feel if he killed someone, he said, "I don't think I'd feel anything." Then he considered the matter further and said, "I'd probably like it too much and want to do it again. I'd probably develop a taste for it." Roger was 17 years old at the time.

A rather short, overweight young man, Roger was admitted to the hospital for a couple of reasons. First, he had assaulted his mother so severely that it took two people to get him off her. She said that if the others had not been present, she believed Roger would have killed her. Roger also thought about buying an automatic weapon, taking it to school, shooting his classmates, and then killing himself.

Roger was from a small town in West Virginia. As a child, he had no friends—not because he was ostracized, but because he had no use for them. When children came to his house and asked him to play, he told them to go home. He just was not interested.

Roger was fascinated by war and loved military movies. Eventually his interest in war resulted in his finding a use for other children. He engaged a group of younger kids in military games and reenactments. Roger, the drill sergeant, was quite strict with his "recruits."

Roger also played the drill sergeant at home. His mother was divorced, and Roger did his best to control her dating. He disapproved of her working as a clerk in a convenience store because it embarrassed him and tried to get her to change jobs. He laughed at her attempts to discipline him. Finally, when she tried to maintain her authority, he assaulted her. In short, Roger ruled the roost.

To be fair, Roger was not always cold and controlling. When his mother was sick, he was caring and helpful. He also claimed to have apologized to his mother for assaulting her. He told me, "I'm really sorry that I hurt her." His mother, however, said Roger had not apologized for the assault. In fact, she said he rarely apologized or seemed remorseful for anything.

What was Roger like at school? By his own report, he was a bully. He said he had bullied kids for five years. He picked on them, intimidated them, and started fights simply because he enjoyed doing so. He said that he derived pleasure from physically hurting people.

In eleventh grade, however, he encountered someone who bullied him. Suddenly, the tables were turned, and he did not like it. He said that if someone gunned down the bully, the boy would be getting what he deserved. He also said that if any of the victims at Columbine had teased the killers, then they deserved to die. Roger's homicidal thoughts, however, pre-dated his experience of being bullied. Long before he was picked on, Roger daydreamed about killing sprees and school shootings.

Roger cooperated with psychological testing. His personality was strik-ing for its extreme sadism and lack of empathy. He was someone who could nonchalantly violate social norms and the rights of others. He would meet his own needs at the expense of other people. Not only would he do it, but he would enjoy doing it. This part of his profile was not surprising, given how candid he had been about his homicidal urges.

But there was more. Roger showed an extreme level of social insecurity. He was not comfortable with his peers; he felt socially lost and left out. A part of him wanted to be close to people, but he did not know how to achieve intimacy and was too afraid of rejection to risk getting close. It seemed that the only way he knew to interact with others was through power and intim-idation. Although this gave him a momentary thrill, it failed to provide him with a meaningful existence.

In fact, testing indicated that Roger had significant symptoms of depres-sion and self-devaluation. He did not think much of himself. In fact, he saw himself as someone who chronically engaged in self-defeating behaviors. He was his own worst enemy, and instead of doing things that helped him meet his needs, he kept digging himself deeper into a hole. Three years earlier he had held a knife to his wrist, although he had not actually tried to kill himself. More recently, his planned school shooting was to end with his suicide.

Behind the swagger of the bully, Roger was an insecure boy who was anxious and socially inadequate. Like Eric Harris, he used domination to deal with his sense of weakness. Eric sought the experience of playing God and having the power of life and death. So did Roger. Fortunately, people intervened before he could reach his goal.

Was Roger a victim of abuse? No. Was there any evidence of psychotic symptoms? None at all. Was there evidence of a lack of empathy and sadistic traits? Absolutely. Roger fits into the typology as a psychopath. And yet, like

Eric Harris, Roger was not lacking in feeling. In fact, it was his ability to feel vulnerable that drove him to desire power.

The Childless Girl with Children

Many people think that all school shooters are male. Depending on how school shooters are defined, this may be true. In 1979 16-year old Brenda Spencer opened fire on an elementary school across the street from her home. This, however, may not have been a school shooting. Brenda did not attend the school she attacked; it appears to have been a target of convenience. If she had lived across the street from a restaurant or playground, she may have opened fire on those targets. I have found no indication that she knew anyone she shot or targeted the people for any reason. She committed a murderous assault at a school, but it differed from the rampage school shootings discussed in this book.

In 2001 a girl in Williamsport, Pennsylvania, took a gun to school. She shot and wounded a classmate. This, too, was not a rampage school shooting as I define the term. The attack was not a rampage attack but a targeted shooting of a girl with whom the perpetrator had an ongoing feud.

An exploration of why the perpetrators of murder and other violent acts are overwhelmingly male is beyond the scope of this book. There are numerous factors to be considered, including biology, parenting differences across genders, peer influences, and the relationship between masculinity and power. Our culture is awash with portrayals of violence enhancing male status. This is not true for females. Nonetheless, females are not immune from committing violence, and I have evaluated a potential female school shooter. What can we learn from her? Is she similar to the boys we have reviewed?

Shalisa was 14 years old and lived in a suburb outside of Washington, D.C. She was admitted to the hospital because of a plan to stab her parents, kill people at school, and then kill herself. She had shared this plan with a friend who reported it to a guidance counselor. During a search of her bedroom, her parents found a large hunting knife. Increasing the danger, Shalisa had a hunting license and knew how to use a gun. The family had multiple firearms in the home. These had been removed as Shalisa's behavior deteriorated—except for one that could not be found. When her father searched the house, he found the missing gun under the mattress in his daughter's bedroom. Having acquired a knife and a gun, she had been close to carrying out her plan.

But why? Shalisa said she had been mistreated at home, but this statement was not substantiated. The only allegation she made was that her father had once punched her in the head. According to the father, however, he had slapped her in the face for cursing at him. Regardless of what happened, this incident did not justify killing her parents. She said that all her problems would disappear if her family was dead. Her rationale for killing people at school was that she had been picked on and one boy had made a sarcastic comment to her. Her murderous plans were extraordinary responses to minimal provocations.

The situation was complicated by Shalisa's severe depression and suicidal urges. On one hand, she said that her problems would vanish if her family were dead. On the other hand, she believed that "everyone would be happier" if she were dead. She said that she was hopeless about her future and had nothing to live for. Was the family really the problem, or was the problem within Shalisa?

Based on what Shalisa disclosed, the problems were within her mind. She reported having heard male and female voices inside her head since she was young, voices that "definitely [are] not my own thoughts." The voices were sometimes encouraging, sometimes insulting, and sometimes commanding. They told her to hurt the people who hurt her. She also had visual hallucinations of people and demons. Although such experiences could be drug related, no history of drug use was reported, and a drug screen conducted by the hospital was negative.

Shalisa also had unusual ideas. For example, she believed that her thoughts floated about her head and that people could see them. And her thoughts themselves were odd. Despite her strong suicidal feelings, she also said that she had three reasons for living: her children. She was old enough to have children, but nothing in her record indicated that she had borne any. After many doubts on my part and much questioning, Shalisa admitted that her "children" were really stuffed animals. This was not a delusion, because she knew the animals were not really her children. She played with them and pretended they were little boys and girls. Nevertheless, telling a psychologist in a psychiatric hospital that she had three children that were really stuffed animals was odd behavior.

What was Shalisa like socially? Her personality profile from a psychological assessment indicated that she was someone who did not get close to people and who had a high level of insecurity with her peers. She was ambivalent about relationships. Part of her simply had no interest in personal relationships. Another part, however, wanted intimacy but was too fearful of rejection to allow herself to experience emotional closeness.

Shalisa clearly fit the psychotic category. Her symptoms included her social aloofness, her odd thoughts, hearing voices, and seeing demons.

How Dangerous Were They?

How did I determine the level of threat posed by these patients? The key issue was what they had done that constituted attack-related behavior. Attack-related behavior includes anything that involves taking steps toward carrying out a murderous assault. This can include developing plans, drawing a diagram of the school, sharing a plan with friend, obtaining bombs or guns, and practicing with the weapons.

Had Jonathan engaged in attack-related behavior? He had not obtained any weapons, but he said he had a friend with a gun. He had also developed seven different plans, and although some of them seemed unrealistic, he was obviously spending a good deal of time contemplating an attack. In addition, he had drawn diagrams of the school to figure out where to put bombs so that they would do the most damage and where he might set up a good sniper position. Thus, the ideas were no longer confined to his thoughts; he had begun to take steps toward their execution. He had also talked to a friend about his plans. Jonathan presented a substantive threat.

Whereas Jonathan was remarkably disclosing about himself and his plans, Kyle was remarkably guarded. He claimed that he had built a bomb, but no one had seen it and he could not (or would not) tell me how he built it. Thus, there was ambiguity regarding whether he had engaged in attack-related behavior. Kyle did not disclose any current plans, although this does not mean that he did not have any. He made no direct threats about carrying out an attack, but his psychosis had reached the point that he was having visual hallucinations of kids at school and hearing voices telling him to kill his perceived tormentors. Thus, even in the absence of attack-related behavior, Kyle presented a serious risk.

And what about Graham, the boy who made explosives for fun? Was he a threat? He swore that he had no intention of killing anybody. He insisted that he blew things up for pleasure, not to hurt anyone. Despite his protestations of innocence, I saw him as a potential danger.

Was there attack-related behavior? He had compiled a hit list of people he could not stand. That did not present as imminent a threat as obtaining a gun, but it suggested that he was moving toward taking action. He also wrote a scenario in which he killed people with guns and bombs. There was also the fact that he had built a pipe bomb. Playing with fireworks may be innocent. Building a pipe bomb, especially by someone with a hit list and a written narrative about killing people with bombs, is not so innocent.

What about Roger? He was preoccupied with war and violence. He longed to have the experience of killing someone. As disturbing as these factors are, they did not necessarily constitute attack-related behavior. True, he had thought about buying a gun and committing a school shooting. According to his mother and grandmother, however, Roger had no easy access to guns, and as far as could be determined, he had not taken any steps toward obtaining one. This does not mean that he did not pose a risk, only that he did not present with as imminent risk as someone with a more developed plan who has taken steps toward executing it. Like Shalisa.

Shalisa had written about stabbing her parents in their hearts and dismembering their bodies. She also wanted to kill people at school. Not only did she have plans, but she had taken steps toward acting on them. Her parents found a knife stashed in her bedroom and a gun hidden under her mattress. Here were clear examples of attack-related behavior.

It is noteworthy that Shalisa presented the most imminent threat of violence. First of all, she was a girl, which is not what people expect. Second, she had no obsession with weapons or violence; she did not idolize Hitler or play violent video games; she did not wear a trench coat or listen to violent music. The lesson to be learned is that there is no profile of a school shooter that we can compare kids to in order to determine how dangerous they might be. A threat assessment is based on behavior, not taste in music, fascination with violence, or negative role models. Shalisa did not fit the popular picture of a school shooter, but she was the one who had obtained the weapons necessary to carry out mass murder.

Although a full explanation of threat assessment is beyond the scope of this book, the basic point is that it is based on what a person has done, not what a person is like. A boy may resemble Eric Harris in terms of a having a fascination with Hitler, playing the same video games, and liking to play with fireworks, but these similarities do not constitute a threat. He may be narcissistic and sadistic, but if his behaviors do not demonstrate movement toward carrying out mass murder, he does not present an imminent danger.

Potential Shooters and Actual Shooters

These cases of foiled shooters tell us several things. First, one factor is conspicuous by its absence. None of the foiled shooters presented here, and none of the foiled shooters I have worked with, fit the traumatized category of school shooters. This is particularly noteworthy because many of the patients who pass through the hospital I work at have significant histories of abuse. In fact, the hospital treats far more traumatized teens than schizophrenic or psychopathic teens. Why then, if traumatized patients are so prevalent, were all the potential school shooters I encountered psychotic or psychopathic?

The lack of potential shooters in the traumatized category highlights the importance of other factors in the actions of people like Evan Ramsey, Mitchell Johnson, and Jeffrey Weise. As noted previously, there were two significant factors in the lives of the traumatized shooters: father figures who used firearms illegally, and, in two cases, engaged in armed standoffs; and prominent peer influence to carry out the attacks, including encouragement and/or collaboration. Trauma in children is unfortunately all too common. Although trauma is part of the picture among traumatized shooters, it cannot be the whole story, or else the country would be full of children committing murder. In addition to trauma, other factors play a determining role in creating traumatized school shooters. The lack of these factors among the many traumatized children who pass through the hospital appears to account for the lack of traumatized kids planning school shootings in this sample.

The patients discussed here are also interesting because they highlight the issue of extreme reactivity. There may have been conflicts at home or school, but nothing that constituted abuse. Nonetheless, they all contemplated murder. Their homicidal urges were a result of either psychopathic personalities or psychotic functioning.

Another point worth noting is that all the potential shooters fit into the existing typology. There were variations, of course, because everyone is a unique individual. All psychotic and psychopathic shooters share features with other psychotic and psychopathic shooters, but they have their own personalities. Still, it is interesting that no new types emerged from this sample.

What other types might exist? Perhaps a shooter could simply be depressed. People often associate depression with self-harm rather than violence toward others, but this is not always accurate. Depressed people, especially adolescents, can become aggressive. Despite this, none of the actual or potential shooters was simply depressed. Depression figured prominently in most of the cases, but always in combination with other factors. Thus, shooters were traumatized and depressed, psychotic and depressed, or psychopathic and depressed. None of the shooters discussed in this book suffered solely from depression. This fact suggests that depression, in isolation from other personality features or psychiatric symptoms, is not enough to cause a school shooting.

Beyond the issue of the typology, the psychopathic patients discussed in this chapter broaden our knowledge of this type of shooter. The common view of psychopaths is that they are people without feelings. Not only do they not feel guilt or remorse, but they also experience no fear, no anxiety, and no depression. They may experience anger, but often when they kill it is not done in a rage, but simply as a necessary action to meet the need of the moment.

Dr. Robert Hare describes psychopaths as "two-dimensional characters without the emotional depth and the complex and confusing drives, conflicts, and psychological turmoil that make even ordinary people interesting.... Virtually all investigations into the psychopath's inner world paint an arid picture."[1]

The psychopathic school shooters, however, are not psychopathic to this extent. They are narcissistic and lack empathy, but they do have feelings. It is their feelings, in fact, that make them so dangerous. Because they feel small and inadequate, they need to dominate others. Because they are socially anxious and do not fit in, they become miserable. Because they are insecure, they become enraged toward those they envy.

Since little is known about Drew Golden's inner experiences, most of our understanding of psychopathic shooters has been based on Eric Harris. The three psychopathic potential shooters discussed in this chapter, however, provide confirmation of the inner workings of the psychopathic school shooter. Jonathan was narcissistic and sadistic, but he was also depressed and self-loathing. Being rejected by girls made him feel powerless. In response, he felt the need to dominate them by killing them. Roger was a bully who used intimidation and strength to feel good about himself. Behind the tough exterior, however, was a depressed boy who was socially anxious and felt left out of life. Graham revealed significantly less vulnerability than Jonathan or Roger, yet even he became depressed and suicidal following a breakup with a girlfriend.

Classic psychopaths are often said to be untreatable. They like who they are and see no reason to change. The psychopathic shooters and potential shooters are not necessarily like this. Their narcissism is an attempt to compensate for their inadequacy. Their rage is a response to their social and personal frustration. There are thus opportunities for intervention. Depression can be treated. Self-esteem can be improved. Social skills can be developed. Empathy can be learned. A boy who presents as a potential psychopathic school shooter is not a lost cause.

Similarly, traumatized kids who are potential school shooters can be treated. They need to process the impact of their traumas on their identities, their relationships, and their attitudes toward life. They need to develop healthy coping skills that allow them to deal with stress without becoming dangerous.

Potential psychotic shooters need to have their psychotic symptoms treated with medication and individual therapy. They also need help with their depression, their emotional isolation, their poor self-esteem, and their social deficits.

Speaking broadly, many school shooters were driven by a sense of desperate hopelessness. In treating potential shooters, a primary task is to develop hope for the future. If they can see a way out of their crises besides homicide and/or suicide, they will be less likely to become violent.

What happens to potential school shooters who are stopped before they can carry out their plans? Are they only temporarily thwarted, destined to commit violence at some other point? And what of actual shooters? If they had been stopped from killing as adolescents, would they have committed even greater atrocities as adults?

This latter point has been made regarding Eric Harris—that if he had been foiled in high school, he might have done far more damage as an adult. It is certainly possible. He wanted to join the marines and study weapons and demolitions. Imagine Eric Harris as an adult—ex-marine, military expert in explosives. At Columbine, none of Eric's major bombs detonated. As a demolitions professional, he would have built bombs that worked. The thought is frightening.

But that is not the only possible scenario. Let us say he did get into the marines. He longed for status, and being a marine carries a high level of status. Beyond status, he would have had a place he belonged, a place where he was accepted. He was a bright, studious boy who might have excelled in the military. And being a marine might have given his life meaning. As he wrote in his journal: "I would have made a fucking great Marine—it would have given me a reason to do good."[2] Apart from the military, other factors might have enabled Eric to change his course. He wrote that maybe getting compliments would be enough for him to cancel the attack. Or having sex might have been enough. He was desperate—in a state of crisis. Perhaps just finding a girlfriend could have turned things around for him.

For many people, adolescence is a time of crisis. For example, many teens contemplate, or even attempt, suicide. The vast majority of them survive the crisis and go on to lead fulfilling lives. The same can be true for those who contemplate homicide. If they are kept safe and supported through the crisis, they can go on to have productive—and safe—lives. An at-risk teen does not necessarily remain at risk for life.

I know people who look back at their homicidal thoughts and wonder, "What on earth was I thinking?" At the time, violence seemed like the solution. Even a short time later, however, they are able to see things from a completely different perspective. Thus, it is crucial to stop young people in crisis before they become violent. Chapter 8 presents guidelines on how to do so.

8

WHAT CAN BE DONE TO PREVENT SCHOOL SHOOTINGS

Kids are suspended and/or expelled, sent away from us, and I think rejecting them is a huge piece [of their anger and pain]. *Gathering them in makes more sense.*

—*Brenda Cumming*

SINCE COLUMBINE, THERE HAVE been many foiled school attacks. This is both good news and bad news. The good news is that people have become more alert to warning signs of homicidal violence. Instead of dismissing threats, students are now more likely to report their concerns. Their actions have prevented numerous potential attacks.

The bad news is that many more kids than we hear about are on the edge of violence. Besides the foiled attacks that are reported in the media, many others do not reach public awareness. For example, none of the patients discussed in the previous chapter made the headlines. Thus, we need to do whatever we can to maintain the safety of our schools.

What can we learn from actual and foiled attacks? In reviewing these events, a number of points stand out that can guide us in the future.

Lesson #1: The Limits of Privacy

Parents of school shooters get a lot of blame. They are blamed for raising hateful children. They are blamed for not seeing the warning signs. They are blamed for creating monsters who kill. This blame is misguided. No parents encouraged their children to commit murder or helped them plan their attacks. In hindsight, it is easy to criticize them for what they did or did not do. Doing this, however, is not productive. A more useful approach is to learn from past tragedies in the hope that we can prevent future ones.

What is the role of parents in preventing school shootings? Parents can do several things to minimize the risk not only of school shootings but dangerous behavior in general. Perhaps the most important task is to know your child. This, of course, is easier said than done, especially with teenagers. Adolescents are remarkably good at living private lives that their parents never see. Nonetheless, maintaining a supportive and nurturing relationship is important. Open communication can allow you to respond promptly as problems arise. Knowing your children's friends, where they go, what they do, what Web sites they visit, what they are posting on their own web pages, and so on, can prevent many problems.

But what about privacy? Parents often want to give their teens increasing privacy as they mature. The need for monitoring your children varies according to their behavior. Most teens do not need to have their rooms inspected on a regular basis. But if you catch your son with a pipe bomb, then routine inspections are in order. If you know your daughter is angry and obsessed with weapons, that she visits weapon-related Web sites and seems preoccupied with death and violence, it would be a good idea to keep close tabs on her and to seek professional assistance.

For example, Eric Harris's parents knew he had built a pipe bomb. In hindsight, it may seem obvious that they needed to be more vigilant, but they were living in a pre-Columbine world. Eric liked to set off fireworks and homemade explosives in a field; to those around him, this may not have raised any red flags. We, however, are living in a post-Columbine world. Times have changed. If parents know that their son or daughter is building bombs, or reading books on bomb making such as *The Anarchist's Cookbook*, they need to investigate.

Similarly, Kip Kinkel gave an oral report on how to build a bomb. He made and detonated bombs. He begged and pleaded with his parents to buy him guns. Guns, guns, guns. They were all he wanted. His parents recognized things were not going well, but his father continued to buy Kip guns in the hope of being able to monitor his weapons use and perhaps improve their father-son relationship. In retrospect, it is easy to see the warning signs. If today children or students seem preoccupied with weapons, talk openly about building bombs, and are desperate to have guns, they are not necessarily potential murderers, but it is crucial that people deny them access to weapons and look into the situation.

Both Kip and Eric manufactured and stored a large number of bombs in their homes. They also had multiple firearms hidden in their rooms or elsewhere in the house. When children are preoccupied with weapons, parents need to monitor their behavior and personal space to see what might be going on.

In the case of Shalisa from the last chapter, her parents were concerned about her and had her hospitalized. They searched her room and found a knife and a gun. Not all parents need to search their houses, but when there is a reason to be concerned, a house search is essential. If there is reason to think there might be bombs in the home, it is best to notify law enforcement and let them conduct the search. First, they will be better at recognizing a bomb when they see one, and second, the bombs may pose a danger. After Kip went on his rampage at school, the police searched his home. Not only did they find his parents' bodies, but they found so many sophisticated bombs that they had to evacuate the neighborhood while the bombs were removed.

Parents should also be alert to warning signs of potential violence. If they read a short story or a journal written by their child and have concerns about the content, they need to know what to do. Depending on the nature of the concern, it should be reported to the school, to a mental health professional, or to the police. Imminent threats of violence should be reported to law enforcement. Concern about someone's rage and depression, in the absence of a clear threat, should result in an appointment with a mental health professional. Other threats may warrant notification of school personnel. If your child reports that a peer is considering an attack, you must pass this information along immediately to the school and law enforcement.

Lesson #2: Do Not Lie to Protect Your Child

The day before Kip's rampage at school, he was suspended for having a gun at school and was taken to the police station. When Mr. Kinkel went to the police station, he told the officer that his son would be safe at home. He assured the officer that there were no more guns in the house. This was a lie, and Mr. Kinkel knew it. He had bought guns for Kip; obviously, he knew that there were other guns. Mr. Kinkel's apparent motivation was to minimize the scandal. Even though Kip had been found with a loaded gun in his locker, his father focused on Kip's grades and getting him through the school year. The gravity of the situation did not seem to register, or if it did, Mr. Kinkel's reaction was to think about Kip's academic career, not people's safety. This failure to tell the police about Kip's other weapons cost the lives of Mr. and Mrs. Kinkel and two students.

Long before the murders, Mrs. Kinkel also told a lie that may have had damaging consequences. She was concerned enough about Kip to take him to a psychologist. When the psychologist asked her if there was any family history of mental illness, however, she said no. Serious mental illness was rampant on both sides of Kip's family; relatives had been dangerous, and numerous relatives had been hospitalized. Psychologists ask about family history because many psychological problems have a genetic basis. Perhaps if the psychologist had known the extreme nature of the family's psychological history, he might have proceeded differently. Perhaps he would have probed Kip more deeply or urged the parents to more carefully monitor the boy's behavior. Lying to professionals when a child is in crisis just makes things worse.

Lesson #3: Follow through with Due Process, No Matter Who Is Involved

There is yet another twist to the Kinkel story. Kip's parents were teachers, and his father had taught in Kip's school for years. The fact that the school knew Kip's family influenced the course of events. Policies and procedures were not followed, and Kip was treated differently from how students were supposed to be treated when they brought a loaded gun to school.

No matter who presents a threat, a proper threat assessment needs to occur. This must apply to everyone, whether it is the son of the principal or the daughter of the police chief. Policies and procedures exist for a reason, and bypassing protocol because the family is well known or has a good reputation can be a grievous mistake. Dick Doyle, the assistant principal at Kip's school, said, "The rules we set up were ignored when the moment of truth arrived. They were not followed because, quite simply, he was Kinkel. Instead of considering the fact of the gun, they considered the family of the boy who was caught with it."[1]

Lesson #4: If the School Is Concerned about Your Child, Pay Attention

It is not always easy for parents to hear negative information about their children. This is understandable. Nonetheless, if someone from the school calls with a concern that a child's behavior might pose a threat, parents should take this seriously. It might be a false alarm, but it could also turn out to be a matter of life and death.

Several weeks before Columbine, Dylan Klebold wrote a story about a man who brutally murdered a group of students. His English teacher was so upset by the story that she talked to Dylan and called the Klebolds to discuss it. Dylan's explanation was that it was "just a story." His parents accepted this, having no reason not to. How could they know that Dylan was planning to act out the story?

A similar situation played out when Kip Kinkel did a class presentation on making bombs. A school counselor heard about it and urged Mrs. Kinkel to get professional help for her son. Mrs. Kinkel apparently resented the suggestion and requested that Kip be assigned to a different counselor.[2]

The lesson here is that parents should give the school the benefit of the doubt. Teachers read thousands of papers without contacting a parent. If a teacher does contact a parent because of something a child has written, there might be a very good reason for concern. This does not mean that the child needs to be suspended or arrested in the absence of a more substantive threat, but there should be some kind of follow-up. If parents do not know how to address the situation with their child, they can seek guidance from the school or take their child for a psychological evaluation.

A related point for teachers is that they should pay attention to their own reactions. They deal with hundreds of students and read thousands of papers. If a particular paper strikes them as disturbing or threatening, there may be a good reason. Dylan Klebold's English teacher was right to be concerned by his story about a man who went on a rampage of murder against students. Unfortunately, no one listened.

Lesson #5: Eliminate Easy Access to Guns

Easy access to guns is a critical concern. Most school shooters get their weapons from their own homes, from their grandparents' homes, or from friends and neighbors. Drew Golden was 11 years old and able to quickly amass an arsenal of weapons. Michael Carneal took guns from a neighbor. Andrew Wurst brought his father's pistol to the dinner-dance. And Kip Kinkel not only convinced his father to buy him guns but knew where they were kept.

It is not enough for guns to be secured somewhere in the house. Children often know where weapons are hidden or where to find the key to the gun cabinet. When Drew Golden wanted guns, he knew exactly where to find them at home and at his grandparents' house. His grandfather had a gun rack in which the guns were secured by a wire. Drew simply cut the wire and had an instant arsenal. If children, using every tool at their disposal, including hammers, screwdrivers, crowbars, and power tools, can get at the guns, then the weapons are not secure. The weapons need to be kept at a gun club or some other place that is unknown to and/or out of reach of adolescents.

What if parents are absolutely confident that their children would not misuse firearms? They should remember that it is possible that their trust is misplaced. This certainly happened in the families of several school shooters. Even if their children are trustworthy, what about their peers? If kids in the neighborhood know where a family keeps its guns, the guns may not be secure. Michael Carneal took weapons from a neighbor's garage. If the kids in the home know where the guns are, it is likely that other kids also know.

Lesson #6: Assume Threats Are Serious until Proven Otherwise

After all the shootings that have occurred, it would be reassuring to think that everyone recognizes by now that a death threat cannot be ignored. Unfortunately, that is not the case. In 2007 a student named Asa Coon in Cleveland, Ohio, threatened to come to school and kill everybody. Numerous students heard him make his threats. No one took him seriously. A few days later, he showed up with a gun and went on a rampage.

Students need to be trained to know what to look for and to know what to do when they observe a potential threat. This is the foundation of preventing school shootings and will be discussed later in this chapter.

Lesson #7: Anyone Can Stop a School Shooting

Numerous students have prevented possible attacks because they knew enough to report what they heard to parents or to school personnel. Students are not the only people, however, who have prevented school shootings. Anyone who is alert to warning signs can be a hero by coming forward and saving people's lives.

In 2001 Al Deguzman, a 19-year-old student at De Anza College in Cupertino, California, planned to commit mass murder at the college with guns and bombs. Shortly before the attack, Deguzman took photographs of himself with his arsenal of weapons. A clerk in the shop where the photographs were developed became worried and notified her father, a police officer. This led to a raid of Deguzman's room and the discovery of his guns, bombs, a map showing where the bombs were to be placed, and a tape recording of Deguzman apologizing for what he was about to do. The attack was planned for the following day.

In July 2007, just three months after the attack at Virginia Tech, a gun dealer stopped a possible attack. A customer by the name of Olutosin Oduwole seemed overly eager for his shipment of semiautomatic weapons. Oduwole was a student at Southern Illinois University. Something about him made the dealer nervous; there was an urgency, a desperation, in his behavior. The dealer reported his concern to the police. When Oduwole's vehicle was searched, police found a written document threatening to carry out an attack similar to that at Virginia Tech.

Also in July 2007, someone found a notebook in the parking lot of a McDonald's restaurant on Long Island, New York. The notebook contained comments about an upcoming attack at Connetquot High School. Included in the notebook was the statement, "I will start a chain of terrorism in the world." The would-be killer wrote: "Take everyone down, turn the guns on the cop, take out myself. Perfecto."[3] An investigation discovered that two students were involved in the planned attack, they had made a video about their plans, and they had attempted to purchase an Uzi automatic rifle, an AK-47 assault rifle, and five pounds of black powder explosives. Their plans were foiled because of a notebook in a parking lot and an alert citizen.

As these examples show, school shootings can be prevented by anyone who notices a possible threat and takes prompt action.

Lesson #8: Recognize Possible Rehearsals of Attacks

A common behavior among school shooters is the imaginary rehearsal of what they are going to do. This can take the form of drawings, animation, a video, or a short story. Eric Harris and Dylan Klebold were in a video production class at Columbine. One of their productions was called "Hitmen for Hire," which portrayed a harassed student who hired Eric and Dylan to kill the people picking on him. Besides this project, which was actually filmed, they talked about making a video of themselves going into the cafeteria and gunning people down.[4]

Dylan also wrote a short story about a man who kills a group of students. Michael Carneal wrote a story about a boy who mutilates, tortures, and kills students. Jeffrey Weise made an animated video of a person who guns down innocent people, blows up a police car, and then shoots himself in the head.

In hindsight, it is easy to see these works as obvious warning signs. However, schoolwork involving war, crime, or horror is commonplace in our culture. So how do you tell a potential school shooter from a student following in the footsteps of Stephen King?

There is no guaranteed way to identify potential killers by what they write in a story. We need to use caution in inferring warning signs of murder from creative works. Because of the frequency with which school shooters have provided such creative rehearsals, however, it seems prudent to attempt to identify possible warning signs.

One such sign is the student's identification with the perpetrator of violence. For example, in Michael Carneal's story, the killer is named Michael. In addition, the names of the victims were the names of actual students at the school. These factors increase the sense of imminent danger. A student writing about the murder of other students who are named in the story needs to be investigated.

Similarly, in Dylan's story, although the narrator is not the murderer, there is an obvious identification with the killer. Dylan was left-handed, approximately six foot four, and wore a black trench coat; the killer in the story was left-handed, six foot four, and wore a black trench coat. In addition, the narrator expressed understanding for the killings and admiration of the murderer bordering on worship. The story ends with this passage: "If I could face an emotion of god, it would have looked like the man. I not only saw in his face, but also felt emanating from him power, complacence, closure, and godliness. The man smiled, and in that instant, through no endeavor of my own, I understood his actions."[5]

Thus, Dylan created the killer in his own image, wrote that the narrator understood the act of mass murder, and granted godlike status to a cold-blooded killer. These are indicators that may help teachers or parents identify potential warning signs of violence in the work of their students.

One other behavior is worth mentioning. School shooters sometimes feel the need to record themselves with their weapons. Harris and Klebold made videos of themselves talking about the upcoming attack and holding their guns. They also filmed themselves engaging in target practice with their illegal weapons.

Kimveer Gill, a 25-year-old who shot 20 students in Montreal in 2006, posted 51 photographs of himself on his Web site, all of which showed him in various poses with his guns. Seung Hui Cho made a multimedia manifesto that included photographs of himself posing with a variety of weapons. In 2007 a Finnish student named Pekka-Eric Auvinen posted a video on YouTube about his upcoming attack. And as noted, a clerk who noticed photographs of a young man posing with an arsenal of weapons prevented an attack. Such recordings or photographs can be clues to upcoming attacks.

Student projects that suggest a desire to carry out a murderous attack should be investigated. The stories or videos may turn out to be innocuous, but they might be the red flag that enables us to save lives.

Lesson #9: Punishment Is Not Prevention

Over the last 10 years, many schools have adopted a zero-tolerance approach to violence. Theoretically, this seems like a good idea. In practice, however, it often results in inappropriate responses to innocuous situations. This occurs because of the failure to distinguish actual threats from nonthreats. Suspending a student because he brings a plastic figure holding a rifle to school is not a meaningful response.

Punishment in the form of suspension or expulsion for a threat of violence is not effective in preventing violence. In fact, this type of punishment can have several undesirable effects. It can increase students' rage and the desire for revenge. It can also increase their sense of isolation. They may feel rejected and experience a loss of status. For people who are already on shaky ground emotionally, such punishment can make things even worse. Additionally, suspension or expulsion can result in decreased supervision in that students have unstructured time all day long. The lack of supervision may make preparing for an attack easier. In some families, suspension may enrage the parents to berate or beat their child, exacerbating the crisis. Finally, punishment does not resolve the problem. Suspending or expelling students does nothing to address whatever forces are driving these violent thoughts.

The main problem with punishment, however, is that it does not prevent school shootings. Both the Secret Service and the Department of Education have recognized this fact: "The response with the greatest punitive power may or may not have the greatest preventive power."[6] If the goal is to prevent violence, schools need to consider doing more than punishing students who engage in inappropriate or threatening behavior. The shortcomings of punishing students can be demonstrated by numerous cases, including several school shooters not discussed previously in this book.

In the United States, the most significant attack following a suspension was the case of Kip Kinkel. Kip was caught with a gun at school. He was immediately suspended pending a formal expulsion hearing. Later that day

Kip shot his father and then his mother. The next day he went to school and shot 27 people. No one conducted a threat assessment to see if Kip had other weapons at home, if anyone knew of a planned attack, or if Kip's writings suggested a risk of homicide. Punishment did not result in prevention.

Similar incidents have occurred both in and out of the United States. In 1995 a boy in South Carolina named Toby Sincino was suspended for making an obscene gesture. A week later he went to school with a gun, shot two teachers, then killed himself. In 2005 a Canadian student named Peter Keatainak was expelled. He returned to school, shot a teacher, and then killed himself. In Germany, in 2002, an expelled student named Robert Steinhauser returned to his school and killed 17 people before committing suicide. And the list goes on.

A student threatening mass murder is a student in crisis. Simply getting such youths out of school by suspension or expulsion does not resolve the crisis. These students need attention, not rejection. This does not mean that there should be no consequences for serious threats of violence. Students may need to be out of school for a variety of reasons, including their own mental health, as well as for the safety of the school. While out of school, however, students on the verge of violence need to be monitored and receiving treatment.

There are two points being made here:

1. Suspensions or expulsions need to be used in the appropriate situations, not as knee-jerk responses to any possible threat.
2. Suspending or expelling a student does not necessarily prevent violence. It may be a necessary response, but it should not be the only response.

Lesson #10: The Limits of Physical Security

In the wake of shootings, schools often increase their physical security measures by giving students identification badges, adding surveillance cameras, and installing metal detectors, among other measures. These measures, however, do not prevent school shootings.

When students commit school shootings, they typically do so at their own schools. Identification badges might help prevent strangers from entering a school, but that is not a relevant factor in the kind of acts discussed in this book. Identification badges and other forms of physical security might help prevent mass murder by strangers that takes place at schools, but that is a different issue.

Similarly, surveillance cameras can have a deterrent effect on people who might try to commit a crime secretly, but they do not stop school shootings. Unlike most killers, school shooters are not concerned with hiding their identities. They commit public acts with no attempt at secrecy. The presence of a camera does not stop an attack. There were cameras at Columbine and at Red Lake, Minnesota, but they were not a deterrent.

Finally, metal detectors can prevent students from sneaking guns or knives into school. They will not, however, prevent school shootings. There was a metal detector and security guards at Red Lake. Jeffrey Weise shot one of the guards and walked into the building. The presence of a metal detector meant nothing. If you expect to die in the attack, it does not matter if you set off an alarm at the metal detector. It does not matter if people see you with a gun, because you are there to kill and to die.

So what can be done? The best defense is early detection. By the time shooters are approaching the school with a gun, it is too late. Even if they can be kept from entering the building, they still can go on a rampage. They can shoot people in the morning as they arrive at school, or wait until school lets out. If a door is locked, they may be able to shoot their way through. Shooters have to be stopped before they can get to the school with weapons. This means a different style of prevention than physical security.

Threat Assessment

Schools today need to establish threat assessment procedures. The details on designing and implementing threat assessment programs are beyond the scope of this book, but a few introductory comments can be made.

A fundamental premise of threat assessment is that there are different kinds of threats. The FBI divides them into low, moderate, and high levels of risk. Dr. Dewey Cornell divides them into transient and substantive threats. Whatever terminology is used, however, the aim is to distinguish an imminent threat from a nonimminent (or even nonexistent) threat.

What makes a threat substantive or high risk? Generally, the more detailed it is in terms of time, place, or method, the greater the risk. A student who says "If things don't change, I'm going to do something drastic someday" is making a vague threat. Not only is it vague, but it is conditional; it is dependent on whether things get better for him or her. Perhaps the student will act on the threat, but perhaps he or she will not.

If, however, a student tells a friend, "Don't be in the cafeteria tomorrow at noon because I'm going to blow the place up," this implies a detailed plan that poses a high level of risk. Not only is there a time, place, and method specified, but the attack is scheduled for the next day. This is imminent.

The existence or nonexistence of a threat, however, is not always a good predictor of violence for two reasons:

1. Many people make threats that they never intend to carry out. The threat could be made jokingly, or it could be made impulsively in anger, but with no intention of acting on it.
2. The absence of a direct threat does not mean there is no danger. In many school shootings, no one received a direct threat. Thus, whether a threat has been made is not a reliable guideline for evaluating potential danger.

Threat assessment does not focus on students who *make* a threat but on students who *pose* a threat. Students can pose threats through their behavior even if they do not directly threaten anyone. What kind of behavior poses a threat? Attack-related behavior, which refers to anything a person does that provides a clue to intentions to perpetrate an attack. Perhaps the most important type of attack-related behavior is what the FBI calls leakage, which refers to the revealing of one's plans.

One type of leakage occurs when perpetrators try to recruit a friend to join in the attack. Andrew Wurst and Kip Kinkel both asked friends to join them. If the friends had reported this, the attacks might have been prevented. In 2007 a 14-year-old boy in Plymouth Meeting, Pennsylvania, tried to recruit a friend. The friend told an adult, and the police investigated. The potential perpetrator turned out to be someone who admired Harris and Klebold, wanted to start his own army, and had convinced his mother to buy him a rifle. Because the friend reported the attempted recruitment a potential shooting was prevented.

Another kind of leakage occurs when perpetrators tell people to stay away from school on a certain day. Mitchell Johnson told a girl he was friends with not to come to school the day of the attack. Alternatively, perpetrators might give only a vague intimation of intentions by saying "Something big is going to happen on Monday." This is what Michael Carneal did. He let people know that something was in the works but did not spell out what he planned to do. In the case of Evan Ramsey, many students knew that there was going to be a big event, and one student even brought a camera to take pictures when it happened.

Sometimes it is hard to tell if a comment is leakage or not. Kids may routinely talk about wishing they could kill someone or make comments like "Wouldn't it be cool to blow up the school?" This could be leakage, or it could be completely innocent. If you are not sure what to make of a possible threat, it is always best to investigate it.

What else constitutes attack-related behaviors? Making plans and drawing diagrams of the school are attack-related behavior. Obtaining guns or materials for making bombs are attack-related behaviors. Target practice and testing homemade explosives are attack-related behaviors. A boy I worked with wanted to kill his family and people at school. He planned to stab his family. He got a knife and tested its sharpness on a piece of wood. When it penetrated the wood easily, he thought, "This will work on flesh." This was attack-related behavior.

When a threat assessment procedure is in place, threats and other attack-related behavior can be evaluated properly. In order for the system to work effectively, however, people have to report their concerns about potential violence. Schools need an early detection system. The most effective system is to utilize the eyes and ears of students. If anyone is likely to know what is going on, it is the students. By training students to recognize the warning signs of potential violence, we can significantly increase the safety of our schools.

To lay the groundwork for this effort, students should be taught the difference between snitching and reporting. Snitching, or tattling, is done to get someone in trouble. Reporting is done to keep people safe. Even if students understand this difference, however, reporting a friend is not easy. Students should have an opportunity to discuss the issues involved. Role-playing situations can be helpful. Students need to understand that although reporting a friend might endanger the friendship, it is better to have an angry friend than risk having people killed. If they fail to stop an attack and have to live with a sense of guilt for not having taken action, that agony will be far worse than making a friend temporarily angry. In addition, reporting their concerns may save their friend's life. School shooters either end up dead or in jail. If they care about their friend, they need to do what they can to prevent such an outcome.

Besides teaching students the warning signs of school shootings, schools should have multiple methods for students to report their concerns including voicemail, e-mail, a mailbox, and designated people who can meet with students regarding safety issues. Students are not the only ones who need to be educated, however. Teachers, administrators, and other school staff also should know what to look for and what to do when they see it.

The material presented here on threat assessment is drawn from several excellent resources that I highly recommend. The Secret Service and Department of Education collaborated on two documents that are available from the Web site of the Secret Service: *The Final Report and Findings of the Safe School Initiative: Implications for the Prevention of School Attacks in the United States* and *Threat Assessment in Schools: A Guide to Managing Threatening Situations and to Creating Safe School Climates*.[7] The FBI also conducted a major study of school shooters and published a paper that is available on its Web site: "The School Shooter: A Threat Assessment Perspective."[8] Dr. Dewey Cornell and Dr. Peter Sheras have published a book that provides clear, comprehensive guidelines on the assessment not only of potential school shootings but any threat of violence: *Guidelines for Responding to Student Threats of Violence*.[9]

Good Communication and Positive Culture

A threat assessment system can prevent school violence by intervening in response to early warning signs. This is a crucial function, but it is not the only way to prevent school shootings. Dr. Katherine Newman investigated the schools and communities of West Paducah, Kentucky, and Jonesboro, Arkansas, the sites of the shootings perpetrated by Michael Carneal, and Drew Golden and Mitchell Johnson respectively. She identified a number of things that schools can do to improve communication, documentation, and the ways they meet the students' needs. These recommendations are from Newman's book, *Rampage: The Social Roots of School Shootings*.[10]

One issue that Newman identifies is the fragmentation of documentation. In Michael Carneal's case, different teachers witnessed disturbing events, but in isolation, each event seemed minor. No one had the whole picture. By changing the way academic, counseling, and disciplinary records are kept across grades and bureaucratic boundaries, schools can better identify warning signs of potential violence. Other efforts to improve communication can include the use of team teaching as well as ensuring that parent-teacher conferences cover behavioral as well as academic concerns.

As noted, physical security measures do not prevent school shootings. Newman recommends that instead of spending money on metal detectors or other types of physical security, schools would derive greater benefit from employing more mental health or counseling staff. She also advocates the use of school resource officers. These are people who combine the functions of maintaining security and enhancing communication between students and staff.

To minimize the number of students who are struggling socially, Newman encourages schools to make sure that every student is connected with at least one adult. If school personnel identify students who appear to have no meaningful connection to any teachers, coaches, or other staff, the school should make an effort to reach out and create a connection. She suggests that a diversity of teachers provides a range of role models for students to connect with. Diversity is not confined to racial/ethnic diversity, but includes a range of interests, talents, and other variables. In addition, local businesses, civic leaders, and parent groups should extend support to recognize more than sports-related student achievements. To make this effort most effective, schools need to provide a range of activities for students.

Students need to feel safe in school. Although bullying itself does not cause school shootings, anything that contributes to students' misery, fear, and rage can play a part in driving them to violence. The administration must take seriously student safety, including physical and emotional safety.

Newman also recommends that schools periodically conduct programs on school shooters to remind students about what to look for and how to report their concerns. For the threat-detection system to be effective, students must trust that what they say will remain confidential. They also need to know that their concerns will be addressed. If these conditions do not exist, then the likelihood that students will come forward is diminished.

The reports by the FBI and the Secret Service and Department of Education go beyond threat assessment and make recommendations on preventing violence by maintaining positive school environments. Schools can take many approaches, from establishing student assistance and peer assistance programs, to empowering students to take an active role in creating a safe school culture and offering training to parents on how to recognize when their children are showing signs of psychological problems.

There are still other options to be considered, including mediation programs to reduce conflicts among students and teach conflict-resolution skills. Examples of such programs are discussed in Dr. Ralph Larkin's book, *Comprehending Columbine.*[11] Other initiatives aim at building emotional resilience by teaching stress management and/or social skills. Another approach focuses on restructuring the classroom to enhance positive peer relationships and improve self-esteem among students, a method discussed in Dr. Elliot Aronson's book, *Nobody Left to Hate: Teaching Compassion after Columbine.*[12]

The factors that contribute to school shootings are a complex mix of genetics, family environment, personality traits, psychiatric symptoms, and peer relationships. Although this book has emphasized numerous factors beyond teasing and bullying that may drive youths to violence, I do not mean to imply that school experiences are irrelevant. Any events that cause stress, humiliation, frustration, depression, or rage add fuel to the fires that are already burning inside. By creating positive peer cultures, reducing student conflict and harassment, and taking steps to improve the social connectedness of students, schools can be proactive in preventing school shootings.

Notes

Chapter 1

The Jefferson County Sheriff's Office documents can be ordered through that organization's Web site: www.co.jefferson.co.us/sheriff/.

1. Cybelle Fox, Wendy D. Roth, and Katherine Newman, "A Deadly Partnership: Lethal Violence in an Arkansas Middle School." In National Research Council, ed., *Deadly Lessons: Understanding Lethal School Violence*, pp. 101–131 (Washington, DC: National Academies Press, 2003), p. 114.
2. Jefferson County Sheriff's Office, *Columbine Documents*, pp. 26,317, 26,232, 26,325, 26,331.
3. Jefferson County, *Eric Harris Diversion Documents*.
4. Loren Coleman, *The Copycat Effect: How the Media and Popular Culture Trigger the Mayhem in Tomorrow's Headlines* (New York: Simon & Schuster, 2004), p. 168.
5. Joseph Lieberman, *The Shooting Game: The Making of School Shooters* (Santa Ana, CA: Seven Locks Press, 2006), p. 225.
6. Jefferson County, *Columbine Documents*, p. 16,418.
7. Ibid., pp. 483, 1,069–1,070, 1,090, 1,140, 2,038, 2,476, 5,036, 5,707, 5,931, 6,281, 7,068, 7,260, 7,380, 8,888, 8892, 8,897.
8. Ibid., pp. 247, 483, 1,069–70, 1,074, 1,090, 1,246, 1,593, 2,038, 2,476, 2,522, 6,001–2, 7,068, 7,312, 7,380, 8,897, 10,286, 23,450, 25,053. See also Ralph Larkin, *Comprehending Columbine* (Philadelphia: Temple University Press, 2007), pp. 92–93.
9. Jefferson County, *Columbine Documents*, pp. 1,069, 1,663–4, 2,813, 3,788, 3,907, 4,650, 5,036, 5,647, 5,995, 6,271, 6,545, 10,509, 24,407.
10. After I had developed my typology of school shooters, I came across a similar typology of violent youth in the work of Cornell and Sheras. Though I focused on rampage school shooters and Cornell and Sheras focused on youth violence in general, it is interesting to note the overlap between the two models. See Dewey Cornell and Peter Sheras, *Guidelines for Responding to Student Threats of Violence* (New York: Sopris West, 2006).

Chapter 2

Eric's journal was a handwritten work that was found after the attack. The quotes from the journal are my transcriptions. The Jefferson County Sheriff's Office documents can be ordered through that organization's Web site: www.co.jefferson. co.us/sheriff/.

1. Robert Hare, *Without Conscience: The Disturbing World of the Psychopaths among Us* (New York: Guilford Press, 1999).

2. This discussion of psychopaths drew from several sources, with the most significant being a chapter by Theodore Millon and Roger Davis titled "Ten Subtypes of Psychopathy," and Robert Hare's book *Without Conscience: The Disturbing World of the Psychopaths among Us.*

3. Nadya Labi, "The Hunter and the Choirboy," *Time Magazine,* April 6, 1998; www.time. com/time/magazine/printout/0,8816,988083,00.html.

4. Cybelle Fox, Wendy D. Roth, and Katherine Newman. "A Deadly Partnership: Lethal Violence in an Arkansas Middle School." In National Research Council, ed., *Deadly Lessons: Understanding Lethal School Violence,* pp. 101–131. (Washington, DC: National Academies Press, 2003), p. 117.

5. Katherine Newman, *Rampage: The Social Roots of School Shootings* (New York: Basic Books, 2004), p. 45.

6. Fox, Roth, and Newman, "A Deadly Partnership," p. 113.

7. T. Trent Gegax, Jerry Adler, and Daniel Pedersen, "The Boys Behind the Ambush," *Newsweek,* April 6, 1998, p. 20.

8. Rick Bragg, "Judge Punishes Arkansas Boys Who Killed 5," *New York Times,* August 12, 1998; http://query.nytimes.com/gst/fullpage.html?res=9A03E5D6143AF931A2575BC0A96E958260.

9. Andy Lines and Emily Compston, "In Dock with a Smile on His Face: Boys Charged with Jonesboro Killings Make First Court Appearance," *The Mirror* (UK), March 26, 1998; www.mirror.co.uk/.

10. The primary sources of facts about Drew Golden were Katherine Newman's book, *Rampage: The Social Roots of School Shootings,* and the chapter by Cybelle Fox, Wendy D. Roth, and Katherine Newman, "A Deadly Partnership: Lethal Violence in an Arkansas Middle School."

11. Jefferson County, *1997 Documents.*

12. Ibid.

13. Jefferson County, *Columbine Documents,* p. 10,411.

14. Ibid., p. 26,052.

15. Ibid., p. 26,004.

16. Ibid., pp. 10,377–10,378.

17. Ibid., p. 10,096.

18. Ibid., pp. 10,094–10,095.

19. www.acolumbinesite.com/autopsies/eric3.gif.

20.   Dirk Johnson and Jodi Wilgoren, "Terror in Littleton: The Gunmen; A Portrait of Two Killers at War with Themselves," *New York Times*, April 26, 1999; http://query. nytimes.com/gst/fullpage.html?res=9905E5DA163DF935A15757C0A96F958260& scp=1&sq=johnson+wilgoren+terror+in+littleton&st=nyt.

21.   Lynn Bartels and Carla Crowder, "Fatal Friendship: How Two Suburban Boys Traded Baseball and Bowling for Murder and Madness," *Denver Rocky Mountain News*, August 22, 1999; http://denver.rockymountainnews.com/ shooting/0822fatal.

22.   Raphael Ezekiel, *The Racist Mind: Portraits of American Neo-Nazis and Klansmen* (New York: Viking, 1995).

23.   Ann Imse, Lynn Bartels, and Dick Foster, "Killers' Double Life Fooled Many," *Denver Rocky Mountain News*, April 25, 1999; http://denver. rockymountainnews.com/shooting/0425shool.shtml.

24.   Jefferson County, *Columbine Documents*, p. 26,017.

25.   Ibid., p. 26,018.

26.   Ibid., p. 10,427.

27.   Ibid., p. 6,623.

28.   Ibid., p. 1,290.

29.   Dan Luzadder and Kevin Vaughan, "Amassing the Facts: Bonded by Tragedy, Officers Probe Far, Wide for Answers," *Denver Rocky Mountain News*, December 13, 1999; http://denver.rockymountainnews.com/shooting/1213 col1.shtml.

30.   Nancy Gibbs and Timothy Roche, "The Columbine Tapes," *Time Magazine*, December 20, 1999; www.time.com/time/magazine/article/0,9171,992873,00. html. Columbine Review Commission, *The Report of Governor Bill Owens' Columbine Review Commission* (Denver, CO, 2001); www.state.co.us/ columbine/.

31.   Jefferson County, *Columbine Documents*, p. 26,013.

32.   Ibid., p. 26,344.

33.   Ibid., p. 26,011.

34.   Ibid., pp. 26,343, 6,106, 26,007.

35.   Ibid., p. 26,004. For additional passages on natural selection in Eric's writings, see pp. 10,411, 26,004, 26,005, 26,203, 26,343.

36.   Ibid., p. 26,010.

37.   Ibid., p. 26,575.

38.   Ibid.

39.   Ibid., p. 26,010.

40.   Robert G. L. Waite, *The Psychopathic God: Adolf Hitler* (New York: Basic Books, 1977), p. 85.

41.   Jefferson County, *Columbine Documents*, p. 26,012.

42.   Ibid., p. 10,411.

43.   David Shapiro, *Neurotic Styles* (New York: Harper & Row, 1965), pp. 81–82.

44. Jefferson County, *Columbine Documents*, p. 26,004.

45. Ibid., p. 26,005. For additional passages in Eric's writing on the themes of originality and influence, see pp. 26,009, 26,189, 26,204, 26,593 (two passages), 26,723, 26,784.

46. Theodore Millon, Roger D. Davis, Carrie M. Millon, Andrew Wenger, Maria H. Van Zullen, Marketa Fuchs, and Renee B. Millon, *Disorders of Personality: DSM-IV and Beyond* (New York: John Wiley & Sons, 1996), p. 703.

47. Jefferson County, *Columbine Documents*, p. 10,415.

48. www.acolumbinesite.com/profiles2.hmtl.

49. Jefferson County, *Columbine Documents*, p. 10,382.

50. Shapiro, *Neurotic Styles*, p. 85.

51. David Shapiro, *Autonomy and Rigid Character* (New York: HarperCollins, 1981), p. 137.

52. Jefferson County, *Columbine Documents*, p. 26,006.

53. Ibid., p. 26,007.

54. Ibid., p. 26,005.

55. Ibid., p. 26,009.

56. Ibid., p. 26,012.

57. Ibid., p. 26,010.

58. Ibid., p. 10,376.

59. Ibid., p. 26,013.

60. Dave Cullen, "Goodbye, Cruel World," *Salon*, December 14, 1999; www.salon.com/news/feature/1999/12/14/videos/print.html.

61. Alan Prendergast, "Doom Rules: Much of What We Think We Know about Columbine Is Wrong," *Westword*, August 5, 1999; www.westword.com/issues/1999-08-05/feature2_full.html.

62. Jefferson County, *Columbine Documents*, p. 26,116.

63. Ibid., p. 26,525.

64. Ibid., p. 26,005.

65. Millon et al., *Disorders of Personality*, p. 452.

66. http://columbine.free2host.net/quotes.hmtl.

67. Jefferson County, *Columbine Documents*, p. 26,343.

68. Ibid., p. 26,005.

69. Ibid., p. 10,415.

70. Ibid., p. 26,006.

71. Ibid., pp. 960, 2,234, 10,713, 26,087; Art Harris, "From Little League to Madness: Portraits of Littleton Shooters," CNN, April 30, 1999; www.cnn.com/SPECIALS/1998/schools/they.hid.it.well/index.html.

72. Millon et al., *Disorders of Personality*, p. 411.

73. Jefferson County, *Columbine Documents*, p. 26,343.

74. Ibid., p. 26,011.

75. Ibid.

76. Ibid., p. 10,432

77. Ibid., p. 10,383.
78. Ibid., p. 26,014.
79. Ibid., p. 26,015.
80. Ibid.
81. Ibid., p. 26,024.
82. Ibid., p. 26,018.
83. Ibid.
84. Ibid., p. 26,009.
85. Ibid., p. 26,004.
86. Ibid., p. 26,006.
87. Ibid., p. 26,016.
88. Millon et al., *Disorders of Personality*, p. 489.
89. Ibid.
90. Erich Fromm, *The Anatomy of Human Destructiveness* (New York: Holt, Rinehart and Winston, 1973), pp. 288–289.
91. Jefferson County, *Columbine Documents*, p. 26,573.
92. Fromm, *Anatomy of Human Destructiveness*, p. 290.
93. Ibid., p. 292.
94. John Douglas and Mark Olshaker, *The Anatomy of Motive: The FBI's Legendary Mindhunter Explores the Key to Understanding and Catching Violent Criminals* (New York: Pocket Books, 1999), p. 276.

Chapter 3

Dylan's journal was handwritten and not always legible. The quotes from it are my transcriptions. The Jefferson County Sheriff's Office documents can be ordered through that organization's Web site: www.co.jefferson.co.us/sheriff/.

1. Lisa Belkin, "Parents Blaming Parents," *New York Times Sunday Magazine*, October 31, 1999; http://query.nytimes.com/gst/fullpage.html?res= 9401E2 DD1438F932A05753C1A96F95826.
2. Brooks Brown and Rob Merritt. *No Easy Answers: The Truth Behind Death at Columbine* (New York: Lantern Books, 2002), p. 30.
3. Lynn Bartels and Carla Crowder, "Fatal Friendship: How Two Suburban Boys Traded Baseball and Bowling for Murder and Madness," *Denver Rocky Mountain News*, August 22, 1999; http:// denver.rockymountainnews.com/ shooting/0822fatal.shtml.
4. Jefferson County Sheriff's Office, *Columbine Documents*, p. 26,486.
5. Ibid., p. 26,389.
6. Ibid., p. 26,390.
7. Ibid., p. 26,389.
8. Ibid., p. 26,416.
9. Ibid., p. 26,390.
10. Ibid., p. 26,388.

11. Ibid., p. 26,389.

12. Ibid., p. 26,405.

13. Ibid., p. 26,388.

14. Ibid., p. 26,396.

15. Ibid., p. 26,390.

16. Ibid., p. 26,388.

17. Ibid., p. 26,397.

18. An online search did find that the band "Nine Inch Nails" has used the word "Infinince." The abbreviation of the band's name is NIN, and "Infinince" was written with the letters "NIN" capitalized. It is possible that Dylan found the word through his interest in the band. This, however, does not make it a real word, or account for the many other improper word usages found in Dylan's journal.

19. Jefferson County, *Columbine Documents*, pp. 26,390, 26,393, 26,397, 26,399, 26,412.

20. American Psychiatric Association. *Diagnostic and Statistical Manual of Mental Disorders, Fourth Edition, Text Revision* (Arlington, VA: American Psychiatric Association, 2000), p. 698.

21. Jefferson County, *Columbine Documents*, p. 26,406.

22. Ibid., p. 26,410.

23. Ibid., p. 26,397.

24. Ibid., p. 26,399.

25. Ibid., p. 26,392.

26. Ibid., p. 26,396.

27. Ibid., p. 26,400.

28. Ibid.

29. Ibid., p. 26,390.

30. Ibid., p. 26,405.

31. Ibid., p. 26,404.

32. Ibid., p. 26,390.

33. Ibid., p. 26,397.

34. Ibid., p. 26,397.

35. Ibid., p. 26,389.

36. Ibid.

37. Ibid., p. 26,414.

38. Ibid.

39. Ibid., p. 26,487.

40. Ibid., p. 26,410.

41. Theodore Millon, Roger D. Davis, Carrie M. Millon, Andrew Wenger, Maria H. Van Zullen, Marketa Fuchs, and Renee B. Millon, *Disorders of Personality: DSM-IV and Beyond* (New York: John Wiley & Sons, 1996), p. 629.

42. Ibid., p. 623.

43. Ibid., p. 625.

44. Jefferson County, *Columbine Documents*, p. 26,393.
45. Ibid., p. 26,406.
46. Ibid., p. 26,397.
47. Ibid., p. 26,400.
48. Ibid., p. 26,405.
49. http://columbine.free2host.net/quotes.html.
50. Millon et al., *Personality Disorders*, pp. 618–619.
51. Millon et al., *Personality Disorders*, p. 629.
52. Ibid., p. 26,402.
53. Jefferson County, *Columbine Documents*, p. 26,388.
54. Ibid., p. 26,414.
55. Ibid., pp. 172, 444, 556, 785, 5,036, 7,231, 9,820, 16,408.
56. Ibid., pp. 19, 3,931, 4,650, 7,504.
57. Jefferson County Sheriff's Office, *Dylan Klebold's Diversion Documents*, p. 55.
58. Jefferson County, *Columbine Documents*, pp. 1,779, 1,780, 4,084, 6,207, 6,974.
59. Ibid., p. 1,828.
60. Ibid., p. 6,135.
61. Ibid., p. 26,394.
62. Ibid.
63. Ibid., p. 18,459.
64. Ibid., p. 4,436.
65. Ibid., p. 10,763. Also, during ninth and tenth grades, Dylan spent a great deal of time at Zach's house; in fact, he often slept there. After Zach became involved with his girlfriend, the intensity of his friendship with Dylan declined. Members of Zach's family noticed that Dylan was changing: "At some point in junior year, he [Dylan] picked up one of those black duster coats. This year, we hardly saw Dylan at all." (Peter Wilkinson, "Humiliation and Revenge: The Story of Reb and VoDkA," *Rolling Stone*, June 10, 1999, p. 49).
66. Jefferson County, *Columbine Documents*, pp. 328, 1,450, 5,282, 6,574, 16,408, 23,546.
67. Ibid., p. 26,400.
68. Bartels and Crowder, "Fatal Friendship"; Alan Prendergast, "Doom Rules: Much of What We Think We Know about Columbine Is Wrong," *Westword*, August 5, 1999; www.westword.com/issues/1999-08-05/feature2_full.html; Paul Duggan, Michael Shear, and Marc Fisher, "Shooter Pair Mixed Fantasy, Reality," *Washington Post*, April 22, 1999; www.washingtonpost.com/wp-srv/national/daily/april99/suspects042299.htm.
69. Eric Pooley, "Portrait of a Deadly Bond," *Time Magazine*, May 10, 1999; www.time.com/printout/0,8816,990917,00.html.
70. Millon et al., *Personality Disorders*, p. 339.
71. Ibid.
72. Jefferson County, *Columbine Documents*, p. 26,770.

73. Ibid., p. 26,724.
74. Ibid., p. 20,368.
75. Ibid., p. 2,628.
76. Ibid., p. 19,519.
77. Ibid., pp. 174, 8,926.
78. Ibid., p. 556.
79. Ibid., p. 470.
80. Ibid., p. 317.
81. Ibid., pp. 3,421, 20,313.
82. Ibid., p. 24,409.
83. Ibid., p. 26,400.
84. Ibid., p. 26,405.
85. Ibid., p. 10,380.
86. Ibid., p. 26,415.
87. Ibid., p. 26,485.
88. Ibid., p. 26,237.
89. www.acolumbinesite.com/quotes.html.
90. Jefferson County, *Columbine Documents*, pp. 16,023–16,034.
91. Ibid., p. 16,023.
92. Ibid., p. 16,028.
93. Ibid., pp. 16,033–16,034.
94. Ibid., p. 10,636.
95. Ibid., p. 16,025.
96. David Brooks, "Columbine: Parents of a Killer (Dylan Klebold)," *New York Times*, May 15, 2004; www.nytimes.com/.
97. Jefferson County, *Columbine Documents*, p. 16,025.
98. Ibid., p. 16,027.
99. Ibid. p. 16,026.
100. Vincent Bugliosi and Curt Gentry, *Helter Skelter: The True Story of the Manson Murders* (New York: W. W. Norton and Company, 1994), p. 203.
101. Ibid., p. 315.
102. Jefferson County, *Columbine Documents*, pp. 16,027–16,028.
103. Eric identified Indigo as his nickname on a Web page (Jefferson County, *Columbine Documents*, p. 26,859). Dylan addressed Eric as Indigo in his yearbook inscription, and signed himself as both VoDkA and Green (ibid., p. 26,241). Finally, on a page of doodles, there is a small notation that reads "DK Green" (ibid., p. 25,989).
104. Ed Sanders, *The Family* (New York: Avalon, 2002), p. 482.
105. Jefferson County, *Columbine Documents*, p. 26,241. The signs of Manson influence in the use of colors as nicknames, as well as pig terminology occur in Eric's yearbook from the spring of 1998. This suggests that Dylan did not simply study Manson for a research paper in the fall semester of 1998, but was already immersed in Manson at least as early as the spring of his junior year.

106. Ibid., p. 10,467.

107. Ibid., p. 19,642. This occurred in the fall of 1998, when Eric was writing a paper on the Nazis and Dylan was writing his on Manson. The two boys were seen spray-painting graffiti on a pawnshop. Two phrases were found. One was "Nazis Rule." This, presumably, was Eric's contribution. It seems reasonable to conclude that the phrase "Death to Pigs" was Dylan's work.

108. Bugliosi, *Helter Skelter*, pp. 263; opposite p. 301; 485; 487; 537.

109. www.acolumbinesite.com/quotes.html. Also, on the day before the attack, Dylan wrote, "About 26.5 hours from now the judgment will begin" (Jefferson County, *Columbine Documents*, p. 26,486).

110. It may also be of interest that the album that appears to have been Dylan's favorite was *Downward Spiral* by Nine Inch Nails (he referred to it in his journal and doodled *Downward Spiral* repeatedly). This album was recorded in the former home of Sharon Tate, where the first mass murder by Manson's followers took place. The album includes songs titled "Piggy" and "March of the Pigs." Similarly, Dylan was a fan of Marilyn Manson, who not only took his stage name from Charles Manson, but also recorded songs in the former Tate home (Bugliosi, *Helter Skelter*, p. 667). Though there have been contradictory reports about whether or not Dylan was a Marilyn Manson fan, there is clear evidence that he was. A classmate stated that Eric and Dylan did a psychology project on Marilyn Manson and Jeffrey Dahmer (Angie Cannon, Betsy Streisand, and Dan McGraw, "Why?" *U.S. News & World Report*, May 3, 1999, p. 16). When Dylan's house was searched following the attack, law enforcement officials found a Marilyn Manson CD (Jefferson County, *Columbine Documents*, p. 25,730). Friends who talked regularly with Dylan affirmed that he liked Marilyn Manson (ibid., pp. 3,420; 10,826–10,827). Finally, his mother reported that Dylan liked Marilyn Manson, had talked with her about liking the music (he told her he didn't listen to the lyrics), and had a poster of Marilyn Manson in his bedroom (ibid., p. 10,511).

Chapter 4

1. Katherine Newman, *Rampage: The Social Roots of School Shootings* (New York: Basic Books, 2004), p. 26.

2. See ibid. for the identification of the writing as a school assignment. See *Kentucky Post*, "Inside Carneal's Bedroom," December 5, 1997, p. 5K, and Daniel Pedersen and Sarah Van Boven, "Tragedy in a Small Place," *Newsweek*, December 15, 1997, pp. 30–31, for references to the writing as a note.

3. Newman, *Rampage*, p. 98.

4. Ibid., p. 64.

5. David Harding, Jal Mehta, and Katherine Newman, "No Exit: Mental Illness, Marginality, and School Violence in West Paducah, Kentucky." In

National Research Council, ed., *Deadly Lessons: Understanding Lethal School Violence*, pp. 132–162 (Washington, DC: National Academies Press, 2003), p. 150.

6. Newman, Rampage, p. 94.
7. Ibid.
8. Ibid.
9. Ibid., p. 32.
10. Ibid.
11. Andrew Wolfson, "Michael Carneal Tells His Story," Courier-Journal (Louisville, KY), September 12, 2002.
12. Jim Adams and James Malone, "Outsider's Destructive Behavior Spiraled into Violence," Courier-Journal (Louisville, KY), March 18, 1999.
13. Ibid.
14. Dewey Cornell, School Violence: Fears Versus Facts (Mahway, NJ: Lawrence Erlbaum Associates, 2006), p. 41.
15. Newman, Rampage, p. 22.
16. Ibid., p. 134.
17. Ibid., p. 24.
18. Wolfson, "Michael Carneal Tells His Story."
19. The primary sources of facts about Michael Carneal were Katherine Newman's book, *Rampage: The Social Roots of School Shootings*, and the chapter by David Harding, Jal Mehta, and Katherine Newman, "No Exit: Mental Illness, Marginality, and School Violence in West Paducah, Kentucky."
20. William DeJong, Joel C. Epstein, and Thomas E. Hart, "Bad Things Happen in Good Communities: The Rampage Shooting in Edinboro, Pennsylvania, and Its Aftermath." In National Research Council, ed., *Deadly Lessons: Understanding Lethal School Violence*, pp. 70–100 (Washington, DC: National Academies Press, 2003), p. 73.
21. Ibid., p. 76.
22. Ibid., p. 78.
23. Ibid., p. 77.
24. Ibid., p. 80.
25. Ibid., p. 87.
26. Ibid., p. 73.
27. Ibid., p. 85.
28. Ibid., p. 78.
29. Ibid., p. 85.
30. The primary source of facts about Andrew Wurst was the chapter by William DeJong, Joel C. Epstein, and Thomas E. Hart, "Bad Things Happen in Good Communities: The Rampage Shooting in Edinboro, Pennsylvania, and Its Aftermath."
31. Joseph Lieberman, *The Shooting Game: The Making of School Shooters* (Santa Ana, CA: Seven Locks Press, 2006), pp. 269–270.

32. Ibid., p. 27.

33. Ibid., p. 185.

34. www.pbs.org/wgbh/pages/frontline/shows/kinkel/trial/bolstad.html.

35. Lieberman, *The Shooting Game*, p. 141.

36. www.pbs.org/wgbh/pages/frontline/shows/kinkel/trial/bolstad.html.

37. Ibid.

38. Ibid.

39. Lieberman, *The Shooting Game*, p. 172.

40. Ibid., p. 28.

41. Ibid., p. 131.

42. Ibid., p. 132.

43. Ibid., pp. 26–28.

44. Ibid., pp. 3–4.

45. Ibid., p. 144.

46. Ibid., p. 148.

47. www.pbs.org/wgbh/pages/frontline/shows/kinkel/trial/.

48. Alex Johnson, "Gunman Sent Package to NBC News," April 19, 2007; www.msnbc.msn.com/id/18195423/.

49. Ibid.

50. Ibid.

51. www.msnbc.msn.com/id/18186085/.

52. Johnson, "Gunman Sent Package."

53. www.msnbc.msn.com/id/18186072/.

54. Virginia Tech Review Panel, "Mass Shootings at Virginia Tech: April 16, 2007. Report of the Review Panel Presented to Governor Kaine, Commonwealth of Virginia" (August 2007), p. 50; www.governor.virginia.gov/TempContent/techPanelReport.cfm.

55. Ibid., p. 46.

56. www.thesmokinggun.com/archive/years/2007/0417071vtech4.html.

57. Johnson, "Gunman Sent Package."

58. www.msnbc.msn.com/id/18186064/.

59. Johnson, "Gunman Sent Package."

60. Bob Drogin, Faye Fiore, and K. Connie Kang, "Bright Daughter, Brooding Son: Enigma in the Cho Household," *Los Angeles Times*, April 22, 2007; www.latimes.com/.

61. www.msnbc.msn.com/id/18186053/.

62. Johnson, "Gunman Sent Package."

Chapter 5

1. Nadya Labi, "Mother of the Accused," *Time Magazine*, April 13, 1998; www.time.com/time/magazineprintout/0,8816,988117,00.html.

2. Circuit Court of Craighead County, Arkansas. Deposition of Mitchell Johnson, April 2, 2007.

3.   Ibid.

4.   Nadya Labi, "The Hunter and the Choirboy," *Time Magazine*, April 6, 1998; www.time.com/time/magazine/printout/0,8816,988083,00.html.

5.   Katherine Newman, *Rampage: The Social Roots of School Shootings* (New York: Basic Books, 2004), pp. 34–35.

6.   John Cloud, "Of Arms and the Boy," *Time Magazine*, June 24, 2001; www.time.com/time/magazine/printout/0,8816,139492,00.html.

7.   Newman, *Rampage*, p. 35.

8.   Labi, "The Hunter and the Choirboy."

9.   Circuit Court, *Deposition of Mitchell Johnson*.

10. Newman, *Rampage*, p. 12.

11. Circuit Court, *Deposition of Mitchell Johnson*.

12. Ibid.

13. Ibid.

14. The primary sources of facts about Mitchell Johnson were Katherine Newman's book, *Rampage: The Social Roots of School Shootings*, and the chapter by Cybelle Fox, Wendy D. Roth, and Katherine Newman, "A Deadly Partnership: Lethal Violence in an Arkansas Middle School."

15. "Rage: A Look at a Teen Killer." *CBS News*. March 7, 2001; www.cbsnews.com/stories/1999/08/17/60II/main58625.shtml.

16. Steve Fainaru, "Killing in the Classroom: Alaska School Murders: A Window on Teen Rage," *Boston Globe*, October 18, 1998; www.boston.com/bostonglobe/.

17. www.courtrecords.alaska.gov/.

18. Sheila Toomey, "Brothers Testify to Hard Life, Then Ramsey Defense Rests," *Anchorage Daily News*, February 3, 1998.

19. Steve Fainaru, "Killing in the Classroom: A Tragedy Was Preceded by Many Overlooked Signals," *Boston Globe*, October 19, 1998; www.boston.com/bostonglobe/.

20. Ibid.

21. Bill Dedman, "Deadly Lessons: School Shooters Tell Why," *Chicago Sun-Times*, October 15, 2000, p. 1.

22. *Ramsey v. State* (10/11/2002) ap-1832. Court of Appeals No. A-7295. Available at www.touchngo.com/ap/html/ap-1832.htm.

23. CBS News, "Rage."

24. Carol Marin, "Portrait of High School Killer, *60 Minutes* (CBS News Transcript), March 6, 2001; www.cbsnews.com/stories/1999/04/27/broadcasts/main44660.shtml?source=search_story.

25. Jenifer Hanrahan, "No Way Out," *San Diego Union-Tribune*, May 14, 2001; www.signonsandiego.com/.

26. Fainaru, "Many Overlooked Signals."

27. The information on Evan Ramsey was drawn from many sources, the most significant of which was a series of three articles by Steve Fainaru: "Killing in the Classroom: Alaska School Murders: A Window on Teen Rage," "Killing

in the Classroom: Many Struggle to Put Their World Together," and "Killing in the Classroom: A Tragedy was Preceded by Many Overlooked Signals."

28. www.jeffweise.com/who.html.
29. Frank J. Zenere III, "Tragedy at Red Lake: Epilogue," *Communique* 34, no. 1 (2005); www.nasponline.org/publications/cq/cq34lredlake.aspx.
30. www.abovetopsecret.com/forum/viewthread.php?tid=95648.
31. www.thesmokinggun.com/archive/032405lweisel.html.
32. weise.livejournal.com/.
33. http://cryptome.quintessenz.org/mirror/jeff-weise.htm.
34. Ibid.
35. http://profiles.yahoo.com/verlassen4_20.
36. Chris Maag, "The Devil in Red Lake," *Time Magazine*, April 4, 2005, p. 35.
37. Jodi Rave, "Family Still Struggling to Understand Teenager's Rampage in Minnesota," *Missoulian*, July 10, 2005; www.missoulian.com/articles/2005/07/11/ jodirave/rave40.prt.
38. Maag, "The Devil in Red Lake."
39. Chuck Haga, Howie Padilla, and Richard Meryhew, "Teen Was a Mystery in a Life Full of Hardship," *Minneapolis-St. Paul StarTribune*, March 23, 2005.
40. Heron Marquez Estrada, Ron Nixon, and John Stefany, "An Internet Trail of a Boy's Death Wish," *Minneapolis-St. Paul StarTribune*, March 23, 2005; www.startribune.com/local/11574851.html.
41. Maag, "The Devil in Red Lake."
42. http://cryptome.sabotage.org/jeff-weise2.htm.
43. Estrada, Nixon, and Stefany, "An Internet Trail."
44. Fainaru, "A Window on Teen Rage."

Chapter 6

1. Robert Hare, *Without Conscience: The Disturbing World of the Psychopaths among Us* (New York: Guilford Press, 1999).
2. American Psychiatric Association, *Diagnostic and Statistical Manual of Mental Disorders, Fourth Edition, Text Revision* (Arlington, VA: American Psychiatric Association, 2000), p. 308.
3. Ibid., p. 304.
4. 1996 Children's Report Card: Fillmore County. www.lmic.state.mn.us.
5. Steve Fainaru, "Killing in the Classroom: Alaska School Murders: A Window on Teen Rage," *Boston Globe*, October 18, 1998; www.boston.com/bostonglobe/.
6. Ibid.
7. Chuck Haga and Terry Collins, "Did Friendship Spiral into Conspiracy?" *Minneapolis-St. Paul StarTribune*, November 19, 2005; www.startribune.com/.

8. Molly Miron, "Program Aims to Cut Beltrami County's High Youth Suicide Rate." *Bemidji* (MN) *Pioneer,* September 20, 2007; www.bemidjipioneer.com/.

9. http://Columbine.free2host.net/quotes.html.

10. Katherine Newman, *Rampage: The Social Roots of School Shootings* (New York: Basic Books, 2004), p. 32.

11. Steve Fainaru, "Killing in the Classroom: A Tragedy was Preceded by Many Overlooked Signals," *Boston Globe,* October 19, 1998; www.boston.com/bostonglobe/.

12. Ed Palattella, "Testimony: Wurst Is Psychotic," *Erie Times-News,* March 10, 1999; www.goerie.com/.

13. Jefferson County Sheriff's Office, *Columbine Documents,* p. 26,859.

14. Ibid.

15. Ibid., p. 10,415.

16. Newman, *Rampage,* p. 134.

17. Ed Palattella, "Friend: Suspect Threatened to Go to the Dance 'And Kill Some People,'" *Erie Times-News,* April 26, 1998; www.goerie.com/.

18. htttp://Weise.livejournal.com/.

19. Jefferson County Sheriff's Office, *Eric Harris's Diversion Documents.*

20. Jefferson County, *Columbine Documents,* p. 26,007.

21. Ibid., p. 26,012.

22. Ibid., p. 26,015.

23. Ibid., p. 26,343.

24. Ibid., p. 26,770.

25. Critical Incident Response Group, *The School Shooter: A Threat Assessment Perspective* (Quantico, VA: National Center for the Analysis of Violent Crime, FBI Academy, 2000).

26. John Douglas and Mark Olshaker, *The Anatomy of Motive: The FBI's Legendary Mindhunter Explores the Key to Understanding and Catching Violent Criminals* (New York: Pocket Books, 1999), p. 276.

27. David Shapiro, *Autonomy and Rigid Character* (New York: HarperCollins, 1981), p. 113.

28. Nancy Gibbs and Timothy Roche, "The Columbine Tapes," *Time Magazine,* December 20, 1999; www.time.com/time/magazine/article/0,9171,992873,00.html.

29. Jefferson County, *Columbine Documents,* p. 26,007.

30. http://Columbine.free2nost.net/quotes.html.

31. Shapiro, *Autonomy and Rigid Character,* p. 109.

32. Ibid., p. 113.

33. Jefferson County, *Columbine Documents,* p. 26,388.

34. Ibid., p. 26,396.

35. Newman, *Rampage.*

36. Newman, *Rampage,* p. 6.

37. John Kifner, "From Wild Talk and Friendship to Five Deaths in a Schoolyard," *New York Times*, March 29, 1998.

38. N. R. Kleinfield, "Before Deadly Rage, a Lifetime Consumed by a Troubling Silence," *New York Times*, April 22, 2007; www.nytimes.com/.

39. Joseph Lieberman, *The Shooting Game: The Making of School Shooters* (Santa Ana, CA: Seven Locks Press, 2006), pp. 26–27.

40. Associated Press, "Boy Says He Was 'Mad at the World' When He Shot Classmates," Oak Ridger, April 6, 2000; www.oakridger.com/stories/040600/stt_0406000085.html.

41. www.msnbc.msn.com/id/18186053/.

42. John Douglas and Mark Olshaker, *Mindhunter: Inside the FBI's Elite Serial Crime Unit* (New York: Scribner, 1995), p. 114.

43. Lincoln Caplan, *The Insanity Defense and the Trial of John W. Hinckley, Jr.* (New York: Dell, 1987), p. 62.

44. Jefferson County, *Columbine Documents*, p. 26,845.

45. Ibid., p. 26,496.

46. Ibid., p. 26,189.

47. Ibid., p. 26,012.

48. Robert G. L. Waite, *The Psychopathic God: Adolf Hitler* (New York: Basic Books, 1977), p. 40.

Chapter 7

1. Robert Hare, *Without Conscience: The Disturbing World of the Psychopaths among Us* (New York: Guilford Press, 1999), pp. 140–141.

2. Jefferson County Sheriff's Office, *Columbine Documents*, p. 26,017.

Chapter 8

1. Joseph Lieberman, *The Shooting Game: The Making of School Shooters* (Santa Ana, CA: Seven Locks Press, 2006), p. 110.

2. Ibid., p. 104.

3. David Schoetz, "Samaritan Helps Foil Columbine-Style Shooting," ABC News, July 13, 2007; http://abcnews.go.com/print?id=3374965.

4. Jefferson County Sheriff's Office, *Columbine Documents*, p. 2,236.

5. Ibid., p. 10,468.

6. Robert A. Fein, Bryan Vossekuil, William S. Pollack, Randy Borum, William Modzeleski, and Marissa Reddy, *Threat Assessment in Schools: A Guide to Managing Threatening Situations and to Creating Safe School Climates*. U.S. Department of Education, Office of Elementary and Secondary Education, Safe and Drug-Free Schools Program, and U.S. Secret Service (Washington, DC: National Threat Assessment, 2002), p. 65. Available at www.ustreas.gov/usss/ntac.shtml.

7. Ibid.; and Bryan Vossekuil, Robert A. Fein, Marisa Reddy, Randy Borum, and William Modzeleski, *The Final Report and Findings of the Safe School Initiative: Implications for the Prevention of School Attacks in the United States.* (U.S. Department of Education, Office of Elementary and Secondary Education, Safe and Drug-Free Schools Program, and U.S. Secret Service. Washington, DC: National Threat Assessment Center, 2002). Available at www.ustreas.gov/usss/ntac.shtml.

8. Critical Incident Response Group, *The School Shooter: A Threat Assessment Perspective* (Quantico, VA: National Center for the Analysis of Violent Crime, FBI Academy, 2000). Available at www.fbi.gov/filelink.html?file=/publications/school/school2.pdf.

9. Dewey Cornell and Peter Sheras, *Guidelines for Responding to Student Threats of Violence* (New York: Sopris West, 2006).

10. Katherine Newman, *Rampage: The Social Roots of School Shootings* (New York: Basic Books, 2004).

11. Ralph Larkin, *Comprehending Columbine* (Philadelphia: Temple University Press, 2007), pp. 217–227.

12. Elliot Aronson, *Nobody Left to Hate: Teaching Compassion After Columbine* (New York: Henry Holt and Co., 2001).

Bibliography

In order to facilitate the study of particular shooters, sources that provide information about each perpetrator are arranged alphabetically by shooter (or by pairs of shooters, in the cases where two shooters were involved in the same incident), with specific Web sites listed alphabetically at the end of each entry. General sources are included at the end of the bibliography. Articles without complete citations that come from online sources are listed with their URLs whenever possible. The Jefferson County Sheriff's Office documents can be ordered through that organization's website: www.co.jefferson.co.us/sheriff/.

Michael Carneal

Adams, Jim, and James Malone. "Outsider's Destructive Behavior Spiraled into Violence." *Courier-Journal* (Louisville, KY), March 18, 1999, p. 17A.

Associated Press. "Boy Says He Was 'Mad at the World' When He Shot Classmates." *Oak Ridger*, April 6, 2000; www.oakridger.com/stories/040600/stt_0406000085. html.

Belkin, Lisa. "Parents Blaming Parents." *New York Times Sunday Magazine*, October 31, 1999; http://query.nytimes.com/gst/fullpage.html?res= 9401E2DD 1438F932A05753C1A96F958260.

Blank, Jonah, Warren Cohen, and Mark Madden. "Prayer Circle Murders: In Paducah, Heroism, Forgiveness, and the Search for a Motive." *U.S. News & World Report*, December 15, 1997, pp. 24–27.

"Carneal's Signals Went Unnoticed." *Kentucky Post*, September 6, 1999, p. 1K.

Collins, Michael. "Carneal: I Saw It in Movie." *Kentucky Post*, December 5, 1997; www.kypost.com/.

Cornell, Dewey. *School Violence: Fears versus Facts*. Mahway, NJ: Lawrence Erlbaum Associates, 2006.

Gutierrez, Karen. "Torment of a Teen Killer." *Cincinnati Enquirer*, September 14, 2002, p. 1B.

Harding, David, Jal Mehta, and Katherine Newman. "No Exit: Mental Illness, Marginality, and School Violence in West Paducah, Kentucky." In National

Research Council, ed., *Deadly Lessons: Understanding Lethal School Violence*, pp. 132–162. Washington, DC: National Academies Press, 2003.

"Inside Carneal's Bedroom and Ammo Box." *Kentucky Post*, December 5, 1997, p. 5K.

Newman, Katherine. *Rampage: The Social Roots of School Shootings*. New York: Basic Books, 2004.

"Paducah Killer Still Can't Explain Motives." *Join Together*, September 16, 2002; www.jointogether.org/.

Pedersen, Daniel, and Sarah Van Boven. "Tragedy in a Small Place." *Newsweek*, December 15, 1997, pp. 30–31.

Popyk, Lisa. "Teen Lives Out Murderous Dream." *Cincinnati Post*, November 10, 1998, p. 1A.

Simon, Stephanie. "Flashbacks: The 1997 Rampage in West Paducah, KY, Was the First School Shooting to Grab National Attention. Five Years Later, There Still Are No Answers—For the Victims or the Shooter." *Los Angeles Times*, December 8, 2002, p. A11.

"Teen Flashed Warning Signs before Rampage." *Kentucky Post*, December 16, 1997, p. 20A.

Wolfson, Andrew. "Michael Carneal Tells His Story." *Courier-Journal* (Louisville, KY), September, 12, 2002, p. 1A.

Seung Hui Cho

Alvis-Banks, Donna, and Anna Mallory. "A Cold and Blustery Morning." *Roanoke* (VA) *Times* April 21, 2007; www.roanoke.com/clicks/default.aspx?url=/vtnarrative/narrative.doc.

Apuzzo, Matt. "Va. Tech Gunman Writings Raised Concerns." *San Francisco Chronicle*, April 17, 2007; www.sfgate.com/cgi-bin/article.cgi?file=/n/a/2007/04/17/national/a094055D47.DTL.

Apuzzo, Matt. "Va. Tech Shooter Was Laughed At." Associated Press, April 19, 2007; www.breitbart.com/article.php?id=D8OJPBU00&show_article=1.

Baram, Marcus. "A Daughter Who Succeeded, a Son Who Found Trouble." *ABC News*, April 18, 2007; www.abcnews.go.com/US/print?id=3053725.

Breed, Allen G., and Chris Kahn. "Those Closest to Cho Return to School." *Washington Post*, April 22, 2007; www.washingtonpost.com/wp-dyn/content/article/2007/04/22/AR2007042200878.html.

Depue, Roger L. "A Theoretical Profile of Seung Hui Cho: From the Perspective of a Forensic Behavioral Scientist." In "Mass Shootings at Virginia Tech: April 16, 2007. Report of the Review Panel Presented to Governor Kaine, Commonwealth of Virginia" (August 2007): N1-N5; www.governor.virginia.gov/TempContent/techPanelReport.cfm.

Drogin, Bob, Faye Fiore, and K. Connie Kang. "Bright Daughter, Brooding Son: Enigma in the Cho Household." *Los Angeles Times*, April 22, 2007; www.latimes.com/.

Fernandez, Manny, and Marc Santora. "Massacre in Virginia: In Words and Silence, Hints of Anger and Isolation." *New York Times*, April 18, 2007; www.nytimes.com.

Gardner, Amy, and David Cho. "Isolation Defined Cho's Senior Year." *Washington Post*, May 6, 2007; www.washingtonpost.com/wp-dyn/content/article/2007/05/05/AR2007050501221.html.

Gibbs, Nancy. "Darkness Falls. One Troubled Student Rains Down Death on a Quiet Campus." *Time Magazine*, April 30, 2007, pp. 36–52.

Green, Frank. "The Killer: Who Was He?" *Richmond* (VA) *Times-Dispatch*, April 18, 2007; www.timesdispatch.com/.

Horwitz, Sari. "Paper by Cho Exhibits Disturbing Parallels to Shootings, Sources Say." Washington Post, August 29, 2007; www.washingtonpost.com/wp-dyn/content/article/2007/08/28/AR2007082801948.html.

Johnson, Alex. "Gunman Sent Package to NBC News." April 19, 2007; www.msnbc.msn.com/id/18195423/.

Kleinfield, N. R. "Before Deadly Rage, a Lifetime Consumed by a Troubling Silence." *New York Times*, April 22, 2007; www.nytimes.com/.

Potter, Ned, and David Schoetz. "Va. Tech Killer Ruled Mentally Ill, but Let Go after Hospital Visit." *ABC News*, April 18, 2007; http://abcnews.go.com/US/Story?id=3052278& page=2.

Santora, Marc, and Christine Hauser. "Anger of Killer Was on Exhibit in His Writings." *New York Times*, April 20, 2007; www.nytimes.com.

Thomas, Evan. "Tragedy at Virginia Tech: Quiet and Disturbed, Cho Seung-Hui Seethed, Then Exploded. His Odyssey." *Newsweek*, April 30, 2007; www.msnbc.msn.com/id/18248298/site/newsweek/page/0/print/1/displaymode/1098/.

Urbina, Ian. "Virginia Tech Criticized for Actions in Shooting." *New York Times*, August 30, 2007; www.nytimes.com/.

"Virginia Tech Killer's Sister Speaks." *ABC News*, April 20, 2007; www.abcnews.go.com/US/print?id=3057057.

Virginia Tech Review Panel. "Mass Shootings at Virginia Tech: April 16, 2007. Report of the Review Panel Presented to Governor Kaine, Commonwealth of Virginia" (August 2007); www.governor.virginia.gov/TempContent/techPanelReport.cfm.

www.msnbc.msn.com/id/18186053/.

www.msnbc.msn.com/id/18186064/.

www.msnbc.msn.com/id/18186072/.

www.msnbc.msn.com/id/18186080/.

www.msnbc.msn.com/id/18186085/.

www.thesmokinggun.com/archive/years/2007/041707lvtech1.html.

Andrew Golden/Mitchell Johnson

Bonner, Brian. "Tragedy Adds to Family Turmoil: Portrait of Boy's Minnesota Years Is of Hardship, Search for Normalcy." *St. Paul Pioneer Press*, March 27, 1998.

"Boy's Reported Role Shocks His Minnesota Hometown." *St. Paul Pioneer Press*, March 26, 1998.

Bragg, Rick. "Judge Punishes Arkansas Boys Who Killed 5." *New York Times*, August 12, 1998; www.nytimes.com.

Bragg, Rick. "'Why?' Still Echoes in Jonesboro's Quiet Streets." *New York Times*, April 18, 1998; www.nytimes.com.

"Choirboy to Killer?" *BBC News*, March 26, 1998; http://news.bbc.co.uk/1/hi/special_report/1998/03/98/us_shooting/70064.stm.

Circuit Court of Craighead County, Arkansas. Deposition of Mitchell Johnson, April 2, 2007.

Cloud, John. "Of Arms and the Boy." *Time Magazine*, June 24, 2001; www.time.com/time/magazine/printout/0,8816,139492,00.html.

"Complex Portraits Emerge of Jonesboro Shooting Suspects." CNN, March 26, 1998; www.cnn.com/US/9803/26/shooter.profiles/.

"Counselor: 'It Sounds Like a Middle School': Jonesboro Students Return to Classrooms." CNN, March 30, 1998; www.cnn.com/US/9803/30/jonesboro.shooting.folo/index.html.

Davis, Sandy, and Jeff Porter. "Illness Faked, the Weapons Were Gathered." *Arkansas Democrat-Gazette*, March 26, 1998; www.ardemgaz.com/prev/jonesboro/absuspect26.asp.

Davis, Sandy, and Linda Satter. "Differing Views Depict Character of Suspect, 11." *Arkansas Democrat-Gazette*, March 29, 1998; www.ardemgaz.com/prev/jonesboro/Aamain29.asp.

"Divorce Files Show Parents Fought over Mitchell, Brother." *Arkansas Democrat-Gazette*, March 29, 1998; www.ardemgaz.com/prev/jonesboro/afminn29.asp.

Encyclopedia of Arkansas History. "Westside School Shooting." www.encyclopediaofarkansas.net/encyclopedia/entry-detail.aspx?search=1&entryID=3717.

Fox, Cybelle, Wendy D. Roth, and Katherine Newman. "A Deadly Partnership: Lethal Violence in an Arkansas Middle School." In National Research Council, ed., *Deadly Lessons: Understanding Lethal School Violence*, pp. 101–131. Washington, DC: National Academies Press, 2003.

Gegax, T. Trent, Jerry Adler, and Daniel Pedersen. "The Boys Behind the Ambush." *Newsweek*, April 6, 1998, p. 20.

Heard, Kenneth. "Shooter's Anger at Teacher Drove School Ambush, Reports Suggest." *Arkansas Democrat-Gazette*, March 27, 1999; http://www.ardemgaz.com/prev/jonesboro/aestfiles27.asp.

"Judge Orders Boys Held in Arkansas Shooting." CNN. March 26, 1998; http://www.cnn.com/US/9803/26/school.shooting/.

Kifner, John. "From Wild Talk and Friendship to Five Deaths in a Schoolyard." *New York Times*, March 29, 1998. Accessed through www.lexisnexis.com.

Labi, Nadya. "The Hunter and the Choirboy." *Time Magazine*, April 6, 1998; www.time.com/time/magazine/printout/0,8816,988083,00.html.

Labi, Nadya. "Mother of the Accused." *Time Magazine*, April 13, 1998; www.time. com/time/magazineprintout/0,8816,988117,00.html.

Lines, Andy, and Emily Compston. "In Dock with a Smile on His Face: Boys Charged with Jonesboro Killings Make First Court Appearance." *The Mirror* (UK), March 26, 1998; www.mirror.co.uk/.

Lines, Andy, and Emily Compston. "Son of a Gun Nut: Family Filmed as Dad Taught Playground Killer to Shoot Aged Just Six." *Daily Record* (UK), March 27, 1998; www.dailyrecord.co.uk/.

Newman, Katherine. *Rampage: The Social Roots of School Shootings*. New York: Basic Books, 2004.

1996 Children's Report Card: Fillmore County; www.lmic.state.mn.us.

Schwartz, John. "Ambush at Arkansas School Leave 5 Dead." *Washington Post*, March 25, 1998; www.washingtonpost.com/wp-dyn/content/article/2007/04/16/AR2007041601495_pf.html.

Usborne, David. "Jonesboro Massacre: Two Macho Boys with 'a Lot of Killing to Do.'" *The Independent* (UK), March 27, 1998; www.independent.co.uk/.

Verhovek, Sam Howe. "Bloodshed in a Schoolyard: The Suspects." *New York Times*, March 26, 1998; www.nytimes.com.

Whitely, Michael. "Boys Locked Up, but for How Long?" *Arkansas Democrat-Gazette*, March 27, 1998; www.ardemgaz.com/prev/jonesboro/AAmain27.asp.

Eric Harris/Dylan Klebold

Achenbach, Joel, and Dale Russakoff. "Teen Shooter's Life Paints Antisocial Portrait." *Washington Post*, April 29, 1999; www.washingtonpost.com/wp-srv/national/daily/april99/antisocial04299.htm.

Adams, Lorraine, and Dale Russakoff. "Dissecting Columbine's Cult of the Athlete." *Washington Post*, June 12, 1999; www.washingtonpost.com/wp-srv/national/daily/june99/columbine12.htm.

Anton, Mike, and Lisa Ryckman. "In Hindsight, Signs to Killings Obvious." *Denver Rocky Mountain News*, May 2, 1999; http://denver.rockymountainnews.com/shooting/0502why10.shtml.

Bartels, Lynn. "Neighbors Repeatedly Alerted Sheriff's about Harris' Menacing Behavior." *Denver Rocky Mountain News*, April 26, 1999; http://denver.rockymountainnews.com/shooting/0426brow2.shtml.

Bartels, Lynn, and Carla Crowder. "Fatal Friendship: How Two Suburban Boys Traded Baseball and Bowling for Murder and Madness." *Denver Rocky Mountain News*, August 22, 1999; http://denver.rockymountainnews.com/shooting/0822fatal.shtml.

Bartels, Lynn, and Ann Imse. "Friendly Faces Hid Kid Killers: Social, Normal Teens Eventually Harbored Dark, Sinister Attitudes." *Denver Rocky Mountain News*, April 22, 1999; http://denver.rockymountainnews.com/shooting/0422bdag7.shtml.

Belkin, Lisa. "Parents Blaming Parents," *New York Times Sunday Magazine*, October 31, 1999; http://query.nytimes.com/gst/fullpage.html?res=9401E2DD1438F932A05753C1A96F958260.

Belluck, Pam, and Jodi Wilgoren. "Parents' Agony: Did Columbine Killers' Families Miss Clues—or Just Look Away?" *New York Times*, July 14, 1999; www.nytimes.com/.

Brooks, David. "Columbine: Parents of a Killer (Dylan Klebold)." *New York Times*, May 15, 2004; www.nytimes.com/.

Brown, Brooks, and Rob Merritt. *No Easy Answers: The Truth behind Death at Columbine*. New York: Lantern Books, 2002.

Carnahan, Ann. "Girl Turned Down Harris for Prom Date." *Denver Rocky Mountain News*, May 1, 1999; http://denver.rockymountainnews.com/shooting/0501bran7.shtml.

Carnahan, Ann. "Hatred for Jocks Stuns Harris' Ex-Teammate." *Denver Rocky Mountain News*, May 2, 1999; http://denver.rockymountainnews.com/shooting/0502soc80.shtml.

Columbine Review Commission. *The Report of Governor Bill Owens' Columbine Review Commission*, Denver, CO, 2001; www.state.co.us/columbine/.

Crowder, Carla. "Harrises Didn't See a Monster in Their Midst." *Denver Rocky Mountain News*, June 21, 1999; http://denver.rockymountainnews.com/shooting/0621harr1.shtml.

Cullen, Dave. "The Depressive and the Psychopath: At Last We Know Why the Columbine Killers Did It." *Slate*, April 20, 2004; http://slate.msn.com/toolbar.aspx?action=print&id=2099203.

Cullen, Dave. "Goodbye, Cruel World." *Salon*, December 14, 1999; www.salon.com/news/feature/1999/12/14/videos/print.html.

Cullen, Dave. "'Kill Mankind. No One Should Survive.'" *Salon*, September 23, 1999; www.salon.com/news/feature/1999/09/23/journal/print.html.

Cullen, Dave. "New Clues in Columbine Killings." *Salon*, November 22, 2000; http://archive.salon.com/news/feature/2000/11/22/columbine/print.html.

Cullen, Dave. "The Rumor that Won't Go Away: Jocks Say Littleton Killers Were Gay, but Friends Deny It." *Salon*, April 24, 1999; www.salon.com/news/feature/1999/04/24/rumors/print.html.

Duggan, Paul, Michael Shear, and Marc Fisher. "Shooter Pair Mixed Fantasy, Reality." *Washington Post*, April 22, 1999; www.washingtonpost.com/wp-srv/national/daily/april99/suspects042299.htm.

Foster, Dick. "Eric Harris, Dad a Study in Contrasts." *Boulder Daily Camera*, April 28, 1999; www.dailycamera.com/.

Gibbs, Nancy. ". . . In Sorrow and Disbelief." *Time Magazine*, May 3, 1999; www.time.com/time/magazine/printout/0,8816,990870,00.html.

Gibbs, Nancy, and Timothy Roche. "The Columbine Tapes." *Time Magazine*, December 20, 1999; www.time.com/time/magazine/article/0,9171,992873,00.html.

Harris, Art. "From Little League to Madness: Portraits of Littleton Shooters." CNN, April 30, 1999; www.cnn.com/SPECIALS/1998/schools/they.hid.it.well/index.html.

Hubbard, Burt. "Online Friend Didn't See Evil Side of Harris." *Denver Rocky Mountain News*, April 26, 1999; http://denver.rockymountainnews.com/shooting/0426mafi3.shtml.

Imse, Ann, Lynn Bartels, and Dick Foster. "Killers' Double Life Fooled Many." Denver Rocky Mountain News, April 25, 1999; http://denver.rockymountainnews.com/shooting/0425shool.shtml.

Jefferson County Sheriff's Office. *Columbine Documents*, pp. 1–27,000.

Jefferson County Sheriff's Office. *Eric Harris's Diversion Documents.*

Jefferson County Sheriff's Office. *Dylan Klebold's Diversion Documents.*

Jefferson County Sheriff's Office. *1997 Columbine Documents.*

Jefferson County Sheriff's Office. *1998 Columbine Documents.*

Johnson, Dirk, and Jodi Wilgoren. "Terror in Littleton: The Gunmen; A Portrait of Two Killers at War with Themselves." *New York Times*, April 26, 1999; http://query.nytimes.com/gst/fullpage.html?res=9905E5DA163DF935A15757C0A96F958260&scp=1&sq=johnson+wilgoren+terror+in+littleton&st=nyt.

Kiely, Kathy, and Gary Fields. "Colo. Killers' Last Days Gave No Hint of Plans." *USA Today*, May 3, 1999; www.usatoday.com/news/index/colo/colo137.htm.

Kurtz, Holly. "Columbine Like a Hologram: Life at School Depends on Angle of One's View." *Denver Rocky Mountain News*, July 25, 1999; http://denver.rockymountainnews.com/shooting/0725cult1.shtml.

Kurtz, Holly. "Columbine Bully Talk Persists: Some Parents Accuse Principal of Wearing Rose-Colored Glasses." *Denver Rocky Mountain News*, August 26, 2000; http://denver.rockymountainnews.com/shooting/0826colu3.shtml.

Larkin, Ralph. *Comprehending Columbine*. Philadelphia: Temple University Press, 2007.

Leppek, Chris. "Dylan Klebold Led Life of Religious Contradictions." *Intermountain Jewish News*, April 30, 1999; www.jewishsf.com/content/2-0-/module/displaystory/story_id/11140/format/html/edition_id/213/displaystory.html.

Lindsay, Sue, and Karen Abbott. "Gun Seller Gets 6 Years in Prison." *Denver Rocky Mountain News*, November 13, 1999; www.denver.rockymountainnews.com/shooting/1113mane1.shtml.

Luzadder, Dan, and Kevin Vaughan. "Amassing the Facts: Bonded by Tragedy, Officers Probe Far, Wide for Answers." *Denver Rocky Mountain News*, December 13, 1999; http://denver.rockymountainnews.com/shooting/1213col1.shtml.

Pooley, Eric. "Portrait of a Deadly Bond," *Time Magazine*, May 10, 1999; www.time.com/printout/0,8816,990917,00.html.

Prendergast, Alan. "Back to School: The Bullet in the Backpack and Other Columbine Mysteries." *Westword*, October 25, 2001; www.westword.com/2001-10-25/news/back-to-school/.

Prendergast, Alan. "Doom Rules: Much of What We Think We Know about Columbine Is Wrong." *Westword*, August 5, 1999; www.westword.com/ issues/1999-08-05/feature2_full.html.

Prendergast, Alan. "Hiding in Plain Sight: Are Columbine's Remaining Secrets Too Dangerous for the Public to Know—or Too Embarrassing for Officials to Reveal?" *Westword*, April 13, 2006; www.westword.com/2006-04-13/news/ hiding-in-plain-sight/.

Prendergast, Alan. "I'm Full of Hate and I Love It." *Westword*, December 6, 2001; www.westword.com/issues/2001-12-06/news/news_print.html.

Prendergast, Alan. "The Missing Motive: Investigators Glossed over the Important Question: Why?" *Westword*, July 13, 2000; www.westword.com/2000-07-13/ news/the-missing-motive/.

Russakoff, Dale, Amy Goldstein, and Joel Achenbach. "In Littleton, Neighbors Ponder What Went Wrong." *Washington Post*, May 2, 1999; www.washingtonpost.com/ wp-srv/national/longterm/juvmurders/stories/families050299.htm.

Vaughan, Kevin, and Lynn Bartels. "Brutal Klebold Emerges in Accounts." *Denver Rocky Mountain News*, June 6, 1999; http://denver.rockymountainnews.com/ shooting/0606dyll.shtml.

Wilgoren, Jodi, and Dirk Johnson. "Sketch of 2 Killers: Contradictions and Confusion." *New York Times*, April 23, 1999; www.rickross.com/reference/ shootings/shootings7.html.

Wilkinson, Peter. "Humiliation and Revenge: The Story of Reb and VoDkA," *Rolling Stone*, June 10, 1999, p. 49.

http://Columbine.free2host.net/quotes.html.

www.acolumbinesite.com/.

Mitchell Johnson

See Andrew Golden.

Kip Kinkel

"Accused Oregon School Shooter Shows No Emotion in Court." CNN, May 22, 1998; www.cnn.com/US/9805/22/oregon.shooting.pm/.

Bernstein, Maxine. "Kipland P. Kinkel: A Clear Path toward Destruction." *The Oregonian*, August 30, 1998, p. A01. Accessed through http://nl.newsbank.com.

Bernstein, Maxine, Dana Tims, and J. Todd Foster. "Home Filled with Dark Discoveries." *The Oregonian*, May 24, 1998, p. A01. Accessed through http:// nl.newsbank.com.

King, Patricia, and Andrew Murr. "A Son Who Spun Out of Control: An Oregon Teen Is Charged with Killing His Parents and His Classmates." *Newsweek*, June 1, 1998, pp. 32–33.

Lieberman, Joseph. *The Shooting Game: The Making of School Shooters*. Santa Ana, CA: Seven Locks Press, 2006.

Swanson, Elisa. "'Killers Start Sad and Crazy': Mental Illness and the Betrayal of Kipland Kinkel." *Oregon Law Review* 79, no. 4 (2000): 1081–1120. www.pbs.org/wgbh/pages/frontline/shows/kinkel/.

Dylan Klebold

See Eric Harris.

Evan Ramsey

Clarke, Jim. "Alaska Boy Warned He'd Kill Principal, Student." Associated Press, February 21, 1997. Accessed through www.lexisnexis.com.

Clarke, Jim. "Teen Gunman Opens Fire in School, Killing Principal, Student." Associated Press, February 20, 1997. Accessed through www.lexisnexis.com.

Dedman, Bill. "Deadly Lessons: School Shooters Tell Why." *Chicago Sun-Times*, October 15, 2000, p. 1.

Fainaru, Steve. "Killing in the Classroom: Alaska School Murders: A Window on Teen Rage." *Boston Globe*, October 18, 1998; www.boston.com/bostonglobe/.

Fainaru, Steve. "Killing in the Classroom: Many Struggle to Put Their World Together." *Boston Globe*, October 20, 1998; www.boston.com/bostonglobe/.

Fainaru, Steve. "Killing in the Classroom: A Tragedy was Preceded by Many Overlooked Signals." *Boston Globe*, October 19, 1998; www.boston.com/bostonglobe/.

Hanrahan, Jenifer. "No Way Out." *San Diego Union-Tribune*, May 14, 2001; www.signonsandiego.com/.

Marin, Carol. "Portrait of High School Killer." *60 Minutes* (CBS News Transcript), March 6, 2001; www.cbsnews.com/stories/1999/04/27/broadcasts/main44660.shtml?source=search_story.

Ramsey v. State (10/11/2002) ap-1832. Court of Appeals No. A-7295. Available at www.touchngo.com/ap/html/ap-1832.htm.

"Rage: A Look at a Teen Killer." *CBS News.* March 7, 2001; www.cbsnews.com/stories/1999/08/17/60II/main58625.shtml.

Toomey, Sheila. "Atwood Dead at Age 89: *Times* Publisher, Statehood Champion Left Lasting Mark." *Anchorage Daily News*, January 11, 1997.

Toomey, Sheila. "Brothers Testify to Hard Life, Then Ramsey Defense Rests." *Anchorage Daily News*, February 3, 1998, p. A1. Accessed through http://nl.newsbank.com.

Jeffrey Weise

Benson, Lorna. "Jeff Weise's Enigmatic Internet Persona." *Minnesota Public Radio*, March 25, 2005; http://news.minnesota.publicradio.org/features/2005/03/25_bensonl_weise3/.

Benson, Lorna. "Web Postings Hold Clues to Weise's Actions." Minnesota Public Radio, March 24, 2005; http://news.minnesota.publicradio.org/features/2005/03/24_ap_moreweise/.

Chanen, David, Pam Louwagie, Richard Meryhew, and Bob Von Sternberg. "Computer Clues Linked Jourdain, Weise." *Minneapolis-St. Paul StarTribune*, March 29, 2005; www.rlnn.com/ArtMar05/ComputerCluesLinkedJourdain.html.

Connolly, Ceci, and Dana Hedgpeth. "Shooter Described as Deeply Disturbed." *Washington Post*, March 24, 2005; www.washingtonpost.com/wp-dyn/articles/A61483-2005Mar23.html.

Davey, Monica. "Behind the Why of a Rampage, Loner with a Taste for Nazism." *New York Times*, March 23, 2005; www.nytimes.com/.

Davey, Monica. "Tribe Buries 3 on a Long Road to Healing." *New York Times*, March 27, 2005, Section 1, p. 16. Accessed through www.lexisnexis.com.

Davey, Monica, and Jodi Wilgoren. "'Clues All There' of Killing to Come." *San Diego Union-Tribune*, March 24, 2005; www.signonsandiego.com/uniontrib/20050324/news_1n24shooting.html.

Estrada, Heron Marquez, Ron Nixon, and John Stefany. "An Internet Trail of a Boy's Death Wish." *Minneapolis-St. Paul StarTribune*, March 23, 2005; www.startribune.com/local/11574851.html.

Gregory, Ted. "Friend Says Shooter had Threatened Violence at School Before." *Chicago Tribune*, March 23, 2005; www.chicagotribune.com/.

Gunderson, Dan. "Who Was Jeff Weise?" Minnesota Public Radio, March 23, 2005; http://newsminnesota.publicradio.org/features/2005/03/22_ap_redlakesuspect/.

Haga, Chuck, and Terry Collins. "Did Friendship Spiral into Conspiracy?" *Minneapolis-St. Paul StarTribune*, November 19, 2005; www.startribune.com/156/v-print/story/44676.html.

Haga, Chuck, Howie Padilla, and Richard Meryhew. "Jeff Weise: A Mystery in a Life Full of Hardship." *Minneapolis-St. Paul StarTribune*, March 23, 2005; www.rlnn.com/ArtMar05/JeffWeiseMystFullHardship.html.

Hanners, Dave. "Web Postings Show Many Sides to Weise." *Duluth News-Tribune*, March 26, 2005, p. 1A. Accessed through http://nl.newsbank.com.

Hanners, Dave. "Weise's Kin Cite Reasons for Rage." *St. Paul Pioneer Press*, April 29, 2005, p. A1. Accessed through http://nl.newsbank.com.

Harden, Blaine, and Dana Hedgpeth. "Red Lake Shooter's Bleak Portrait of Reservation Life Was Accurate." *Pittsburgh Post-Gazette*, March 25, 2005; www.post-gazette.com/pg/05084/477380-84.stm.

Louwagie, Pam, and Chuck Haga. "Jourdain Plea Deal Avoids Trial." *Minneapolis-St. Paul StarTribune*, November 29, 2005; www.startribune.com/local/11575931.html.

Maag, Chris. "The Devil in Red Lake." *Time Magazine*, April 4, 2005, p. 35.

Miron, Molly. "Program Aims to Cut Beltrami County's High Youth Suicide Rate." *Bemidji* (MN) *Pioneer*, September 20, 2007; www.bemidjipioneer.com/.

Miron, Molly. "Summit at Red Lake Addresses Drugs, Gang Issues." *Bemidji* (MN) *Pioneer*, February 15, 2008; www.bemidjipioneer.com/.

Ragsdale, Jim. "39 Knew of Red Lake Killer's Plan." *St. Paul Pioneer Press*, January 31, 2006, p. A1. Accessed through http://nl.newsbank.com.

Rave, Jodi. "Family Still Struggling to Understand Teenager's Rampage in Minnesota." *Missoulian* (Missoula, MT), July 10, 2005; www.missoulian.com/articles/2005/07/11/ jodirave/rave40.prt.

Rave, Jodi. "Portrait Emerges of Youth Who Did Not Seem Violent." *Lincoln* (NE) *JournalStar*, August 5, 2005; www.journalstar.com/.

Ruckdaschel, Michelle. "State and Local Suicide Data Reviewed During Meeting." *Bemidji* (MN) *Pioneer*, December 20, 2007; www.bemidjipioneer.com/.

Walker, Dalton. "For Shooter's Family, It Began as a Typical Day." *Duluth News Tribune*, March 26, 2005. Accessed through http://nl.newsbank.com.

"Second Victim Known as More than Footnote." *St. Paul Pioneer Press*. March 21, 2006; www.twincities.com/mld/pioneerpress/.

Sanchez, Rene, and Chuck Haga. "A Week Soaked in Tears: 'Planning. Waiting. Hating,' He Wrote." *Minneapolis-St. Paul StarTribune*, March 26, 2005; www.startribune.com/nation/11615211.html.

"Poverty Compounds Tough Reservation Life for Indian Youth." *USA Today*, March 27, 2005; www.usatoday.com/news/nation/2005-03-27-reservation-life_x.htm.

Zenere, Frank J. III. "Tragedy at Red Lake: Epilogue," *Communique* 34, no. 1 (2005); www.nasponline.org/publications/cq/cq341redlake.aspx.

http://cryptome.quintessenz.org/mirror/jeff-weise.htm.

http://cryptome.sabotage.org/jeff-weise2.htm.

http://profiles.yahoo.com/verlassen4_20.

http://weise.livejournal.com/.

http://weise.livejournal.com/profile.

www.abovetopsecret.com/forum/thread49741/pg.

www.abovetopsecret.com/forum/viewthread.php?tid=95648.

www.thesmokinggun.com/archive/032405lweisel.html.

Andrew Wurst

DeJong, William, Joel C. Epstein, and Thomas E. Hart. "Bad Things Happen in Good Communities: The Rampage Shooting in Edinboro, Pennsylvania, and Its Aftermath." In National Research Council, ed., *Deadly Lessons: Understanding Lethal School Violence*, pp. 70-100. Washington, DC: National Academies Press, 2003.

Hays, Kristen. "Teacher Killed at School Dance: 14-Year-Old Student Charged." Associated Press, April 25, 1998.

Palattella, Ed. "14-Year-Old Appears Bored during Hearing." *Erie Times-News*, May 22, 1998; www.goerie.com/.

Palattella, Ed. "Friend: Suspect Threatened to Go to the Dance 'And Kill Some People'," *Erie Times-News*, April 26, 1998; www.goerie.com/.

Palattella, Ed. "Next Big Issue in Wurst Case: His Mental State." *Erie Times-News*, May 24, 1998; www.goerie.com/.

Palattella, Ed. "A Portrait of Conflict." *Erie Times-News*, March 7, 1999; www.goerie.com/.

Palattella, Ed. "Reports Give Insight into Wurst's Mind." *Erie Times-News*, January 13, 1999; www.goerie.com/.

Palattella, Ed. "Testimony: Wurst Is Psychotic." *Erie Times-News*, March 10, 1999; www.goerie.com/.

Palattella, Ed, and Tim Hahn. "Students Further Implicate Wurst." *Erie Times-News*, May 22, 1998; www.goerie.com/.

Silver, Jonathan. "As Long as a Month Ago, There Were Signs." *Pittsburgh Post-Gazette*, April 26, 1998. Accessed through http://nl.newsbank.com.

"This Is the Shooter's Mother." *Trenton Times*. April 2, 2000. Accessed through http://nl.newsbank.com.

"Wurst: None of This Is Real." *Erie Times-News*. September 25, 1998; www.goerie.com/.

General References

American Psychiatric Association. *Diagnostic and Statistical Manual of Mental Disorders, Fourth Edition, Text Revision*. Arlington, VA: American Psychiatric Association, 2000.

Aronson, Elliot. *Nobody Left to Hate: Teaching Compassion After Columbine*. New York: Henry Holt and Co., 2001.

Beck, Aaron. *Prisoners of Hate: The Cognitive Basis of Anger, Hostility, and Violence*. New York: HarperCollins, 2000.

Blaney, Paul H. "Paranoid Conditions." In Theodore Millon, Paul H. Blaney, and Roger D. Davis, eds., *Oxford Textbook of Psychopathology*, pp. 339–361. New York: Oxford University Press, 1999.

Bugliosi, Vincent, and Curt Gentry. *Helter Skelter: The True Story of the Manson Murders*. New York: W. W. Norton and Company, 1994.

Caplan, Lincoln. *The Insanity Defense and the Trial of John W. Hinckley, Jr*. New York: Dell, 1987.

Cleckley, Hervey. *The Mask of Sanity: An Attempt to Clarify Some Issues About the So-Called Psychopathic Personality (fifth edition)*. St Louis: Mosby, 1976.

Cobb, Chris, and Bob Avery. *Rape of a Normal Mind*. Markham, Ont.: PaperJacks, 1977.

Coleman, Loren. *The Copycat Effect: How the Media and Popular Culture Trigger the Mayhem in Tomorrow's Headlines*. New York: Simon & Schuster, 2004.

Cornell, Dewey. *School Violence: Fears Versus Facts*. Mahway, NJ: Lawrence Erlbaum Associates, 2006.

Cornell, Dewey, and Peter Sheras. *Guidelines for Responding to Student Threats of Violence*. New York: Sopris West, 2006.

Critical Incident Response Group. *The School Shooter: A Threat Assessment Perspective*. Quantico, VA: National Center for the Analysis of Violent Crime, FBI Academy, 2000. Available at www.fbi.gov/filelink.html?file=/publications/school/school2.pdf.

Douglas, John, and Mark Olshaker. *The Anatomy of Motive: The FBI's Legendary Mindhunter Explores the Key to Understanding and Catching Violent Criminals*. New York: Pocket Books, 1999.

Douglas, John, and Mark Olshaker. *Mindhunter: Inside the FBI's Elite Serial Crime Unit*. New York: Scribner, 1995.

Ezekiel, Raphael. *The Racist Mind: Portraits of American Neo-Nazis and Klansmen*. New York: Viking, 1995.

Fein, Robert A., Bryan Vossekuil, William S. Pollack, Randy Borum, William Modzeleski, and Marissa Reddy. *Threat Assessment in Schools: A Guide to Managing Threatening Situations and to Creating Safe School Climates*. U.S. Department of Education, Office of Elementary and Secondary Education, Safe and Drug-Free Schools Program, and U.S. Secret Service. Washington, DC: National Threat Assessment, 2002. Available at www.ustreas.gov/usss/ntac.shtml.

Fromm, Erich. *The Anatomy of Human Destructiveness*. New York: Holt, Rinehart and Winston, 1973.

Gaura, Maria Alicia, Matthew B. Stannard, and Stacy Fin. "De Anza College Bloodbath Foiled—Photo Clerk Calls Cops." *San Francisco Chronicle*, January 31, 2001; www.sfgate.com.

Grossman, Dave. *On Killing: The Psychological Cost of Learning to Kill in War and Society*. New York: Little, Brown and Company, 1996.

Hare, Robert. *Without Conscience: The Disturbing World of the Psychopaths among Us*. New York: Guilford Press, 1999.

Hare, Robert, David J. Cooke, and Stephen D. Hart. "Psychopathy and Sadistic Personality Disorder." In Theodore Millon, Paul H. Blaney, and Roger D. Davis, eds., *Oxford Textbook of Psychopathology*, pp. 555-584. New York: Oxford University Press, 1999.

"Ill. Student Accused of Terrorist Threat." Yahoo News, July 25, 2007; http://news.yahoo.com/.

Leary, Mark R., Robin M. Kowalski, Laura Smith, and Stephen Phillips. "Teasing, Rejection, and Violence: Case Studies of the School Shootings." *Aggressive Behavior* 29 (2003): 202-214.

Meloy, J. Reid. *The Psychopathic Mind: Origins, Dynamics, and Treatment*. Northvale, NJ: Jason Aronson, 1988.

Meloy, J. Reid, Anthony G. Hempel, Kris Mohandie, Andrew A. Shiva, and B. Thomas Gray. "Offender and Offense Characteristics of a Nonrandom Sample of Adolescent Mass Murderers." *Journal of the American Academy of Child and Adolescent Psychiatry* 40, no. 6 (June 2001): 719–728.

Menninger, Karl. *Man against Himself.* San Diego: Harcourt Brace Jovanovich, 1966.

Millon, Theodore, and Roger Davis. "Ten Subtypes of Psychopathy." In *Psychopathy: Antisocial, Criminal, and Violent Behavior,* edited by Theodore Millon, Erik Simonsen, Morten Birket-Smith, and Roger D. Davis, pp. 161–170. New York: Guilford Press, 1998.

Millon, Theodore, Roger D. Davis, Carrie M. Millon, Andrew Wenger, Maria H. Van Zullen, Marketa Fuchs, and Renee B. Millon. *Disorders of Personality: DSM-IV and Beyond.* New York: John Wiley & Sons, 1996.

Morgan, George Allen. *What Nietzsche Means.* New York: Harper & Row, 1965.

Mulvey, Edward P., and Elizabeth Cauffman. "The Inherent Limits of Predicting School Violence." *American Psychologist* 56, no. 10 (October 2001): 797–802.

National Research Council Institute of Medicine. *Deadly Lessons: Understanding Lethal School Violence.* Washington, DC: Author, 2003.

Newman, Katherine. *Rampage: The Social Roots of School Shootings,* New York: Basic Books, 2004.

Reddy, Marisa, Randy Borum, John Berglund, Bryan Vossekuil, Robert Fein, and William Modzeleski. "Evaluating Risk for Targeted Violence in Schools: Comparing Risk Assessment, Threat Assessment, and Other Approaches." *Psychology in the Schools* 38, no. 2 (2001): 157–172.

Ronningstam, Elsa. "Narcissistic Personality Disorder." In Theodore Millon, Paul H. Blaney, and Roger D. Davis, eds., *Oxford Textbook of Psychopathology,* pp. 674–693. New York: Oxford University Press, 1999.

Sanders, Ed. *The Family.* New York: Avalon, 2002.

Schoetz, David. "Samaritan Helps Foil Columbine-Style Shooting." ABC News, July 13, 2007; http://abcnews.go.com/print?id=3374965.

Shapiro, David. *Autonomy and Rigid Character.* New York: HarperCollins, 1981.

Shapiro, David. *Neurotic Styles.* New York: Harper & Row, 1965.

Twemlow, Stuart W., Peter Fonagy, Frank C. Sacco, Mary Ellen O'Toole, and Eric Vernberg. "Premeditated Mass Shootings in Schools: Threat Assessment." *Journal of the American Academy of Child and Adolescent Psychiatry* 41, no. 4 (April 2002): 475–477.

Verlinden, Stephanie, Michel Hersen, and Jay Thomas. "Risk Factors in School Shootings." *Clinical Psychology Review* 20, no. 1 (2000): 3–56.

Vossekuil, Bryan, Robert A. Fein, Marisa Reddy, Randy Borum, and William Modzeleski. *The Final Report and Findings of the Safe School Initiative: Implications for the Prevention of School Attacks in the United States.* U.S. Department of Education, Office of Elementary and Secondary Education,

Safe and Drug-Free Schools Program, and U.S. Secret Service. Washington, DC: National Threat Assessment Center, 2002. Available at www.ustreas.gov/usss/ntac.shtml.

Waite, Robert G. L. *The Psychopathic God: Adolf Hitler.* New York: Basic Books, 1977.

Index